MAKING AN IMPACT ON SCHOOL BULLYING

Exploring international and intercultural perspectives, *Making an Impact on School Bullying* presents a much-needed insight into the serious problem of bullying in schools. As the effect of bullying on victims can be devastating, and bystanders and even perpetrators are often also negatively affected by the experience, finding successful solutions to the problem of bullying is crucial for improving school life around the world.

This invaluable book looks at a range of practical interventions that have addressed the problem of school bullying. Peter Smith presents a curated collection of seven examples of successful anti-bullying procedures from around the world – including the US, Europe, and Asia – and an exploration of cyberbullying. Each chapter examines the context in which the interventions took place, how theoretical knowledge transferred into practice, and the impact and legacy of the work. Covering the most important and widely-used strategies to combat bullying, the book provides readers with a roadmap to developing practical and impactful interventions.

Ideal reading for students and researchers of education and developmental psychology, *Making an Impact on School Bullying* is also useful for school counsellors and education authorities.

Peter K. Smith is Emeritus Professor of Psychology at the Unit for School and Family Studies, Goldsmiths, University of London, UK. In 2015 he was awarded the William Thierry Preyer Award for Excellence in Research on Human Development from the European Association of Developmental Psychology.

ROUTLEDGE PSYCHOLOGICAL IMPACTS

Series Editor: Graham Davey

Routledge Psychological Impacts is a series of books illustrating how psychological research can make meaningful contributions to social policy. Each book in the series covers a specific topic, showcasing a range of research projects that have either made a direct impact on policy, or brought about a wider awareness of the issues.

Chapters in the books describe the context of specific research projects, discuss the methodological and practical challenges faced by the researchers, and describe how the results are interpreted and communicated before outlining the impact and legacy of the research. Within each chapter, contributors discuss what lessons they learnt in the process, as well as offering advice to the research community about engaging with policy issues.

With the understanding of human behaviour as one of the main purposes of psychological science, psychological research has a great deal to contribute when it comes to finding solutions for our important social problems. This series aims to describe how psychologists are making a difference.

Making an Impact on School Bullying
Edited by Peter K. Smith

For more information about this series, please visit: https://www.routledge.com/Routledge-Pschological-Impacts/book-series/IMPACTS

MAKING AN IMPACT ON SCHOOL BULLYING

Interventions and Recommendations

Edited by Peter K. Smith

Routledge
Taylor & Francis Group

LONDON AND NEW YORK

First published 2019
by Routledge
2 Park Square, Milton Park, Abingdon, Oxon OX14 4RN

and by Routledge
52 Vanderbilt Avenue, New York, NY 10017

Routledge is an imprint of the Taylor & Francis Group, an informa business

First edition published 2019

British Library Cataloguing in Publication Data
A catalogue record for this book is available from the British Library

Library of Congress Cataloging-in-Publication Data
Names: Smith, Peter K., editor.
Title: Making an impact on school bullying : interventions and
recommendations / edited by Peter K. Smith.
Description: Abingdon, Oxon ; New York, NY : Routledge, 2019. |
Series: Routledge psychological impacts | Includes bibliographical
references and index.
Identifiers: LCCN 2019010332 (print) | LCCN 2019014037 (ebook) |
ISBN 9781351201957 (eBook) | ISBN 9780815385295 (hardback) |
ISBN 9780815385301 (pbk.)
Subjects: LCSH: Bullying in schools–Prevention. | School discipline. |
School psychology.
Classification: LCC LB3013.3 (ebook) | LCC LB3013.3 .M247 2019
(print) | DDC 371.5/8–dc23
LC record available at https://lccn.loc.gov/2019010332

ISBN: 978-0-8153-8529-5 (hbk)
ISBN: 978-0-8153-8530-1 (pbk)
ISBN: 978-1-351-20195-7 (ebk)

Typeset in Bembo
by Taylor & Francis Books

CONTENTS

ILLUSTRATIONS

Figures

Tables

CONTRIBUTORS

Amy Barnes is Research Support Officer at the Telethon Kids Institute, University of Western Australia, Perth, Australia.

Marilyn Campbell is Professor at the School of Early Childhood and Inclusive Education, Faculty of Education, Queensland University of Technology, Australia.

Patricia Cardoso is Lecturer in Public Health, School of Medical and Health Sciences, Edith Cowan University, Perth, Australia.

Juli Coffin is Ellison Professor of Aboriginal Health and Wellbeing, Telethon Kimberley, Telethon Kids Institute, Perth, Australia.

Donna Cross is Professor at the University of Western Australia, and Head, Health Promotion and Education, Telethon Kids Institute, Perth, Australia.

Erin Erceg is Honorary Research Associate at Telethon Kids Institute, University of Western Australia, Perth, Australia.

Dorothy L. Espelage is Professor at the Department of Psychology, University of Florida, Gainesville, Florida, USA.

Sanna Herkama is a Senior Researcher at the Department of Psychology, University of Turku, Turku, Finland.

Jun Sung Hong is Associate Professor, Wayne State University, School of Social Work, Detroit, Michigan, USA, and Adjunct Assistant Professor, Sungkyunkwan University, Department of Social Welfare, Seoul, South Korea.

Mari Kontio is a Senior Researcher at the Department of Psychology, University of Turku, Turku, Finland.

Jeoung Min Lee is a Doctoral Candidate at the School of Social Work, Wayne State University, Detroit, Michigan, USA.

Leanne Lester is Associate Professor, Health Promotion Evaluation Unit, University of Western Australia, Perth, Australia.

Susan P. Limber is Dan Olweus Professor at the Institute on Family & Neighborhood Life, and in the Department of Psychology, Clemson University, Clemson, South Carolina, USA.

Ersilia Menesini is Full Professor at the Department of Education, Languages, Intercultures, Literatures and Psychology, University of Florence, Florence, Italy.

Annalaura Nocentini is Associate Professor at the Department of Education, Languages, Intercultures, Literatures and Psychology, University of Florence, Florence, Italy.

Dan Olweus is Research Professor of Psychology, Research Center for Health Promotion, University of Bergen, Bergen, Norway.

Benedetta E. Palladino is a Post-Doctoral Researcher at the Department of Education, Languages, Intercultures, Literatures and Psychology, University of Florence, Florence, Italy.

Natasha Pearce is Senior Research Fellow at the Telethon Kids Institute, University of Western Australia, Perth, Australia.

Kevin Runions is a Research Psychologist with Child & Adolescent Mental Health Services, Department of Health of Western Australia, and Honorary Research Fellow in Health Promotion and Education, Telethon Kids Institute, Perth, Australia.

Miia Sainio is a Senior Researcher at the Department of Psychology, University of Turku, Turku, Finland.

Christina Salmivalli is Professor at the Department of Psychology, University of Turku, Turku, Finland.

Peter K. Smith is Emeritus Professor of Psychology at the Unit for School and Family Studies, Department of Psychology, Goldsmiths, University of London, UK.

Christiane Spiel is Professor and Vice-Head of the Department of Applied Psychology: Work, Education, Economy, Faculty of Psychology, University of Vienna, Vienna, Austria.

Dagmar Strohmeier is Professor at the School of Medical Engineering and Applied Social Sciences at the University of Applied Sciences Upper Austria, Linz, Austria.

Yuichi Toda is Professor at Osaka Kyoiku University (Osaka University of Education), Osaka, Japan.

Albert Valido is Projects Coordinator at the Department of Psychology, College of Liberal Arts and Sciences, University of Florida, Gainesville, Florida, USA.

Valentina Zambuto is a Post-Doctoral Researcher at the Department of Education, Languages, Intercultures, Literatures and Psychology, University of Florence, Florence, Italy.

SERIES EDITOR FOREWORD: ROUTLEDGE PSYCHOLOGICAL IMPACTS. IMPACT ON BULLYING

Graham Davey

Routledge Psychological Impacts is a series of books illustrating how psychological research can make meaningful contributions to social policy. Each book in the series covers a specific topic, showcasing a range of research projects that have either made a direct impact on policy or brought about a wider awareness of the issues.

Chapters in the books describe the context of specific research projects, discuss the methodological and practical challenges faced by the researchers, and describe how the results are interpreted and communicated before outlining the impact and legacy of the research. Within each chapter, contributors discuss what lessons they learnt in the process, as well as offering advice to the research community about engaging with policy issues.

Peter Smith's excellent edited volume *Making an Impact on School Bullying* kicks off the series with a collection of ten chapters on the development of anti-bullying programmes throughout the world. Bullying is a topic that has been researched now for over 30 years and has generated considerable research on the nature, types, causes, and consequences of bullying. It represents a significant social problem worldwide, with an unacceptably high level of prevalence, and significant and often life-threatening negative outcomes – not only for victims but also for perpetrators and bystanders (Chapter 1). During these past 30 years, psychologists of many persuasions have contributed to our understanding of the phenomenon of bullying, and have developed many effective programmes for combating and managing bullying at the level of the individual, the class, the school, and even at the level of society itself, and many of these important and effective programmes are described in the chapters in this volume.

What is exciting about this particular book is its international coverage of anti-bullying programmes from around the world. Chapters describe the development, implementation, and evaluation of programmes from Norway, Finland, Austria, the USA, Australia, Japan, and Italy, and they each in turn analyse and tease apart the details of these programmes that are particularly effective from those that are less effective. At a time when meta-analyses suggest that effective anti-bullying programmes reduce the prevalence of bullying by around 20%, there is still much to be learnt to increase the effectiveness of these programmes. The chapters in this book provide some interesting and candid views on what lessons have been learnt by our contributors.

With the understanding of human behaviour as one of the main purposes of psychological science, psychological research has a great deal to contribute when it comes to finding solutions for our important social problems. This book and this series in general aim to describe how psychologists are making a difference.

Graham Davey
Routledge Psychological Impacts Series Editor
February 2019

1

INTRODUCTION

Peter K. Smith

Bullying in school certainly has a long history in terms of occurrence, but a relatively short history of research. It has been recognized as an issue since the nineteenth century, as for example in *Tom Brown's Schooldays* (Hughes, 1857) in England. But it has only really been studied and better understood since the 1970s. This chapter gives a background to the nature of school bullying, and its causes and consequences. It then surveys the kinds of interventions made to reduce school bullying, and some of the main issues thrown up by these, as a prelude to the eight chapters on specific programmes or topics which follow. A final concluding chapter examines some of the themes coming from these various intervention efforts, and makes some recommendations for future work.

What is bullying?

Bullying is one form of aggressive behaviour. As such, it is taken as intentionally done to hurt another person. The standard definition of bullying, especially in the school context, comes from the work of Dan Olweus, and is discussed by him in Chapter 2. As he makes clear, the distinctive features of bullying are that it is repetitive, and that there is a power imbalance such that it is difficult for the victim to defend himself or herself.

These criteria are widely accepted, but there remain some issues. The definition agreed by the US Centers for Disease Control and Prevention (Gladden et al., 2014; and see Chapter 5) is:

> Bullying is any unwanted aggressive behaviour(s) by another youth or group of youths who are not siblings or current dating partners that involves an observed or perceived power imbalance and is repeated multiple times or is highly likely to be repeated.

This is close to the Olweus criteria, but does limit the concept to youth, and would exclude sibling bullying or dating violence. It would exclude workplace bullying, prison bullying, family abuse, teacher-pupil bullying, and pupil-teacher bullying – all of which have been areas of study! In fact an edited collection by Monks and Coyne (2011), called *Bullying in Different Contexts*, looked at exactly these different kinds of behaviours under the common framework of bullying. A succinct definition that would cover these different contexts is that bullying is the 'systematic abuse of power' (Smith & Sharp, 1994).

Another challenge to the classic definition of bullying has come with online or cyberbullying. This issue is discussed by Campbell in Chapter 9. The most common issue here has concerned that of repetition, as just one aggressive act by a perpetrator could be repeated (passed on, commented on negatively) by many others – so does this single act by the perpetrator count as bullying? Here, the phrase 'is highly likely to be repeated' from Gladden et al. (2014), above, may be helpful, as someone acting in this way – for example, posting a very negative comment on a social network site – can reasonably expect that it will be seen and commented on. As regards imbalance of power, the anonymity often conferred by online attacks can itself be a power imbalance; and if there is no anonymity, the more standard criteria such as status in the peer group may become relevant.

Even if (depending on definition) bullying can occur in many contexts, the earliest sustained work, and the largest volume of research, has concerned school bullying. This is the topic of this book, and the next section overviews how this research programme has developed.

History of research

Figure 1.1 shows the number of publications on bullying, with the keyword 'bully', from ISI Web of Science, by 5 year periods (Smith, 2016). This would include all kinds of contexts for bullying, but the majority are on school bullying. As can be seen, there was very little research activity up to the late 1970s. There was a moderate amount up to the 1990s, and then an exponential growth in research activity in this century.

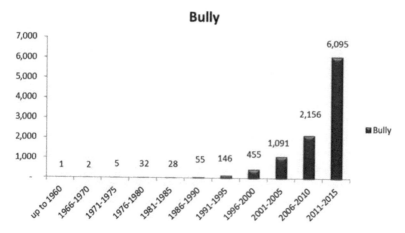

FIGURE 1.1 Number of publications in five-year intervals, up to 2015, from ISI Web of Knowledge searching for the term 'bully'.

The systematic study of bullying in schools in the west started in Scandinavia. The first important publication was Olweus' book *Hackkycklingar och översittare: Forskning om skolmobbning* (1973; expanded version in English translation 1978). Olweus developed a self-report questionnaire (in which pupils could report on their own experiences) to assess bullying. There were also studies in Japan and in South Korea at least from the 1980s (Morita, 1985; Koo, 2007). At that time these research traditions were quite separate.

An important development in the 1990s was a change in researcher's definition of aggression, and hence of bullying. Aggression had previously been thought of as just being physical (e.g. hitting, perhaps damaging belongings) and verbal (e.g. threats, insults). However, researchers in Finland (Björkqvist, Lagerspetz, & Kaukiainen, 1992) and the US (Crick & Grotpeter, 1995) now broadened the concept to include indirect and relational bullying, such as rumour spreading, and social exclusion. This approach became widely accepted.

Another important methodological step during the 1990s was the introduction of participant roles in bullying by Christina Salmivalli and colleagues (Salmivalli et al., 1996). Previously, research had focused on bullies, and victims. The participant role approach divides the bullying role into ringleaders (who initiate and lead the bullying), assistants (who join in) and reinforcers (who laugh or encourage the bullying). Victims can be considered as passive or non-provocative victims, or effectively as bully/victims if they are in both bully and victim roles, someone who annoys others and is in turn attacked (Pikas, 1989). Other roles are defenders (who help the victim in some way), bystanders (who are aware of the bullying but ignore it), and outsiders (who are truly unaware of the bullying).

From the mid-1990s to the mid-2000s, research on traditional or offline bullying became a major international research programme. Researchers from Europe, North America and Japan shared experiences through a UNESCO-supported meeting, and surveys and interventions took place in many countries (Smith et al., 1999).

This century has seen awareness of cyberbullying, using mobile phones and the Internet. Appearing first as text message and email bullying, this has increased and diversified from the mid-2000s (Rivers & Noret, 2010). Since around 2008 the development of smart phones and social networking sites have offered many new tools for cyberbullies. Cyberbullying is considered in some detail in Chapter 9. Compared to traditional bullying, it is much more likely to be perpetrated and experienced outside school; but is still often between class- or school-mates. It is characterized by increased possibilities for anonymity of the perpetrator, a potentially much greater audience for the attacks, and the comparative lack of respite for the victim (Kowalski et al., 2014).

The decade since the mid-2000s has seen a massive increase in publications (Figure 1.1). Many of these describe characteristics of bullying, and many look at predictors of involvement, and effects of this; some of these findings are summarized in the next sections. There have also been more intervention studies; and more use of mixed-method or qualitative studies (Patton et al., 2015; Smith, 2014; Zych et al., 2015). As the number of relevant studies has increased, recent years have seen been more meta-analyses on various topics, including interventions (to be considered later).

Measurement and prevalence of bullying

There are various ways of measuring bullying, but for prevalence rates, self-report questionnaires given to children, usually at school, have been by far the predominant method. The Olweus Bully/Victim Questionnaire was a pioneering exemplar of this approach; it is filled in anonymously, and asks about the frequency with which someone has been bullied, or taken part in bullying others, over a specified time period (often, one school term). There are many other questionnaires available, especially since cyberbullying became common in the last decade.

Such questionnaires are quick and easy to administer, but some researchers question how valid they are given issues of over-sensitivity or denial (in admitting being bullied) or social desirability (in admitting bullying others) (Cornell & Brockenbrough, 2004). Alternatives to self-report questionnaires include peer nominations, widely used on a class basis; teacher nominations, which are used more with younger children; interviews and focus groups; direct observations; and incident reports. Each method has its own advantages and disadvantages, but pupil self-report remains the most feasible for obtaining detailed data on a large scale.

One well-cited source of prevalence data comes from the Health Behaviour in School-aged Children (HBSC) surveys, of about 1,500 pupils each at 11, 13 and 15 years, from around 40 countries, mostly European and North American. Starting in 1993/1994, this data is gathered every four years. The surveys are anonymous self-report, and ask about experiences over the past couple of months. Victim or bully rates are calculated from reporting this happening 'at least two or three times in the past couple of months' or more (ignoring 'it only happened once or twice'). The 2009/2010 HBSC survey (Currie et al., 2012) found rates for bullying others averaged out at 10.3%, and for being bullied at 11.3%. In the most recent 2013/14 survey (Inchley et al., 2016), the corresponding figures were 8.3% and 11.0%.

The prevalence rates reported in different studies vary greatly. Cook et al. (2010a) examined 82 studies published from 1999 to 2006, of which 61 used self-report data. Prevalence rates averaged around 20% for bullies, 23% for victims, and 8% for bully/victims, but with a high variability across studies. These are higher figures than HBSC, probably because bullying that only happened 'once or twice' in a time referent period was often included.

Prevalence data are influenced by many factors: what definition is used (e.g. whether it includes indirect as well as direct forms, and cyberbullying); what frequency is regarded as bullying (e.g. once/twice a term; once a month, once a week or more); and what time span is being asked about (e.g. last month, last term, last year, ever at school). If a short time span (last month, or term) is taken, then the time of giving a questionnaire in the school or calendar year can be important. These issues make it difficult to compare across different studies. It also means that absolute prevalence figures are rather meaningless, when presented on their own. However, they are vital for looking at effectiveness of interventions, where the same methodology will be used for pre-, post- and perhaps follow-up assessments.

Attitudes to bullying and reasons why some children bully others

Although most school pupils say they do not like bullying, a significant minority do say they could join in bullying. These 'pro-bullying' or 'anti-victim' attitudes have been found to increase with age up to around 14 or 15 years, after which they may start to decline (Rigby, 1997). One explanation for this age change comes from the dominance hypothesis (Salmivalli, 2010). This argues that many children who bully do so because of a desire for dominant status in the peer group. Ringleader bullies especially may feel rewarded if assistants and reinforcers support their bullying actions, and if many bystanders remain passive. Concerns about status in the peer group and worries about peer rejection are known to peak during the adolescent years, especially soon after puberty (Ellis et al., 2012). At this mid-adolescent period there may therefore be more motivation to initiate bullying (to exhibit dominance) and to assist or reinforce bullying (to avoid peer rejection or being bullied oneself) (Pouwels, Lansu, & Cillessen, 2018).

Volk et al. (2012) have argued that bullying can be considered as an evolutionary adaptation, in the sense that a perpetrator may get some (at least short-term) benefits from bullying others. Some bullies are popular in the peer group, do not have low self-esteem, and are socially skilled in manipulating others. Several studies have found that bullies, especially ringleader bullies, do well on theory of mind tasks (Smith, 2017); they understand how to hurt a victim effectively and with some peer support, while avoiding adult detection – so-called 'cold cognition'. This may be true of many bullies, but not all; Peeters, Cillessen, and Scholte (2010), in a Dutch sample of 13-year-olds, distinguished three kinds of pupils nominated as bullies by peers: one group was popular and socially intelligent; a second group was relatively popular and with average social intelligence scores; a third group, the smallest numerically, was unpopular and had lower than average scores on social intelligence.

The dominance hypothesis predicts that the likelihood of a child taking part in bullying another will be influenced by peer group norms and expectations about bullying and defending, as well as what support the victim might have. There is considerable evidence supporting this. For example, Kärnä et al. (2010), examining 378 classes from 77 schools in Finland, found that the proportion of defenders in a class reduces risks of victimization, while the proportion of reinforcers increases it. Having high quality friendships is a protective factor against being victimized (Fox & Boulton, 2006). Also, children with high popularity or peer group status can be the most effective defenders (Nickerson et al., 2008; Caravita et al., 2009).

Predictors of involvement

Age differences

Studies of bullying in nursery and infant school classes suggest that the victim role changes frequently, and some researchers therefore prefer to talk of *unjustified aggression* at these younger ages (Monks, Ortega, & Torrado, 2002). It is widely accepted that bullying that is focused on a particular victim emerges clearly by around 7 or 8 years.

Bullying changes in predominant forms, with age. There is a shift away from physical bullying, towards indirect and relational bullying (Rivers & Smith, 1994), and cyberbullying (Kowalski et al., 2014). Bullying peaks in prevalence at around 11 to 14 years (Eslea & Rees, 2001), perhaps a bit later for cyberbullying (Tokunaga, 2010). Increases in bullying have been reported following school transitions, due to the reshuffling of status in peer groups, but the findings are complex (Wang et al., 2016). Bullying prevalence does decline in the later school years, but it still is an issue amongst college students (Cowie & Myers, 2015; Faucher & Jackson, 2019), and there is some continuity to workplace bullying (Smith, Singer, Hoel, & Cooper, 2003).

Gender differences

There are characteristic gender differences, which have been found across many different cultures (Smith, López-Castro, Robinson, & Görzig, 2019). Boys are more numerous in the bully role, but the sexes are more equal in the victim role. Girls are relatively less involved in physical and more involved in relational and cyberbullying, and some studies find girls more involved as cyber victims than boys are, especially on social networking sites (boys may be more involved in bullying on online games). Girls are more often defenders.

Bullying based on disability

A child or young person with a disability can be at considerably higher risk of being bullied. Some characteristics of a disability, such as clumsiness or a stammer or poor hearing, can make someone an easy target for those who enjoy bullying others (Hugh-Jones & Smith, 1999). They may experience some level of negative peer perceptions and social rejection, having fewer friends and lower quality friendships (Mishna, 2003), or lacking some social skills that would help in avoiding or coping with bullying (Van Roekel, Scholte, & Didden, 2009). Studies comparing children with a disability with a well-matched comparison group without a disability, demonstrate this higher risk at a range of ages (RSM McClure Watters, 2011).

Identity-based bullying

Identity-based bullying refers to being victimised on the basis of group rather than individual characteristics: notably, race or ethnicity, faith, gender, and gender identity. In the case of race, and gender, these are often referred to as racial or sexual harassment.

Racist attitudes can be widespread, and in some circumstances ethnic minority children can be at greater risk of being victimized. This does depend considerably on context, however. In Europe, there has been considerable immigration of ethnic and faith minorities this century, and some studies find these children to be at greater risk (Bjereld, Daneback, & Petzold, 2014; Maynard et al., 2016), though depending on aspects such as levels of immigrant concentration (Vitoroulis & Georgiades, 2017). However, in the case of established multicultural communities this is often not the case. For example in England, Tippett, Wolke and Platt (2013) found that in a large sample of 10–15-year-olds, ethnic majority White children were not more involved than other ethnic groups, even controlling for age, gender, parental qualifications, and economic situation. African origin children were more likely to be victims, but Caribbean and Pakistani children were more likely to be bullying perpetrators. Mixed results have also been found in other studies (Vervoort, Scholte & Overbeek, 2010).

Bullying targeted at an individuals' gender is referred to as sexist bullying (based on sexist attitudes) or sexual bullying (based on bullying behaviour that has a specific sexual dimension). Sexual bullying of girls by boys often takes the form of abusive language around a girl's sexual status (Duncan, 1999). Girls also engage in sexual bullying of other girls, for example spreading nasty gossip about a girl's sexual reputation (Jennifer, 2013); girls use of social networking sites now provides a frequent forum for (mainly) girl-to-girl bullying of this kind (Williams, 2013). Boys can also experience sexual harassment, but much of this is likely to reflect on perceived or actual sexual orientation.

Homophobic bullying is directed to lesbian, gay, or bisexual (LGB) people, or those perceived to be LGB, with some studies including transgender persons (LGBT). A meta-analysis of 18 studies (Toomey & Russell, 2013) found the risk of victimization significantly higher for LGBT pupils compared to heterosexual pupils, more so for boys than girls. A large-scale longitudinal study in England (Robinson, Espelage, & Rivers, 2013) confirmed that victimization experiences were higher for LGB young people; they declined with age, but the relative risk compared to heterosexual peers got worse for males but better for females.

Individual and family risk factors for involvement

Cook et al. (2010b) carried out a meta-analysis of 153 independent studies of predictors or correlates of bully, victim, and bully/victim roles. For bullies, significant predictors were showing externalizing behaviours generally – being defiant, disruptive, and aggressive. They also had less empathy; some studies find bullies are lower on affective empathy (sharing the feelings of another) but not on cognitive empathy (recognizing the feelings of another). They generally show high moral disengagement, bypassing the normal kinds of reasoning which hold us back from severely hurting another person (Gini, Pozzoli, & Hymel, 2014). One study found that impulsivity was the most important of a range of personality factors in predicting bullying (Jolliffe & Farrington, 2011).

The Cook et al. (2010b) review found that victims tended to lack social skills, and to be less liked or more rejected in the peer group. These characteristics would make them easier targets for bullies. The children who are bully/victims were generally found to have aspects typical of both bullies and victims, but in addition to score lowest on self-esteem, and on academic performance.

Lereya, Samara and Wolke (2013) reported a meta-analysis of 70 studies on victim and bully/victim roles, related to family factors. Warm and authoritative parenting was a protective factor. Abuse and neglect was a risk factor, very strongly so for bully/victims. Overprotection was another risk factor for being a victim; perhaps because it hinders the development of assertive coping skills. Poor parental support and supervision were strong predictors for being a bully/victim. So far as being a bully is concerned, other studies suggest that poor parental communication with children, inconsistent discipline, and aggression in the home generally (between parents, and siblings) are predictors (Spriggs et al., 2007). A review of 12 studies of sibling bullying found it to be related to parenting quality and behaviour, and to increase the risks of peer bullying at school (Wolke et al., 2015). These findings generally hold for both traditional (offline) and cyber (online) bullying. Other predictors of cyberbullying include involvement in traditional bullying and other antisocial behaviours (Mishna et al., 2012; Läftman et al., 2013); time spent on mobile phones and the Internet (Hinduja & Patchin, 2008; Smith et al., 2008), and more advanced Internet skills (Vandebosch & van Cleemput, 2008, 2009). The role of parents is also significant; good communication with parents is a protective factor (Law et al., 2010), but very restrictive supervision of Internet use can be counter-productive (Sasson & Mesch, 2014).

Parents pass on their genes to their children, as well as providing a rearing environment. In England and Wales the Environmental Risk (E-Risk) Study of over 1,000 twin pairs found a strong genetic influence on children's victimization at 9–10 years (identical or monzygotic twins had more similar victimization experiences than fraternal or dizygotic twins), and also on bullying behaviour (Ball et al., 2008). These genetic factors may operate through factors such as personality disposition, emotion regulation, or social cognition. However, this twin study also showed that maternal and sibling warmth and positive home atmosphere contributed to resilience in coping with victimization, with this being an environmental, not genetic, effect (Bowes et al., 2010).

Class, school, and neighbourhood factors

There can be appreciable differences between classes within a school, on incidence of bullying, victimization, and defending. Much of this is predicted by injunctive norms (what behaviour is commonly expected by other people within the class); and descriptive norms (the perception of what most people in the class actually do). Pozzoli, Gini, and Vieno (2012) examined individual attitudes to bullying, self-reported behaviours in bullying situations, and perceived peer and teacher pressure (what peers and teachers would expect of you), in Italian pupils aged 10 and 13 years from 54 classes. At the classroom level, class pro-victim attitudes, peer injunctive norms, and peer descriptive norms, all predicted defending behaviour.

Saarento, Kärnä, Hodges and Salmivalli (2013) used data from the Finnish KiVa project (Chapter 3) to study individual, classroom, and school effects in 358 classrooms in 74 schools. They found significant classroom effects, related to the extent of anti-bullying attitudes in the class, and injunctive norms (what a pupil thought would be likely to happen to them if they defended a victim). The general perception of home-room teacher's attitude to bullying was a significant predictor of classroom differences, and also contributed significantly to school differences.

School factors contribute further understanding of bully and victim rates. Some studies find their contribution (beyond that of individuals and classes) to be small; when multilevel analyses are done on individual, school, and classroom factors, then classroom variance absorbs much of the non-individual variance, and the school variance is what is finally left over. But the E-Risk study in England and Wales found that school factors were significantly associated with victim risk (Bowes et al., 2009). A study by Muijs (2017) of 35 primary schools in England found that although pupil factors explained nearly 68% of variance in being bullied, school factors explained nearly 20% and classroom factors 13%. A key school factor appeared to be the quality and implementation of anti-bullying policies.

School factors may operate through school climate (how safe and happy pupils feel in school), school policies and anti-bullying strategies. Gendron, Williams and Guerra (2011), in a study of 78 elementary, middle, and high schools in the USA, found that bullying rates were predicted by (poor) school climate, as well as by normative beliefs about bullying. Focusing on homophobic bullying at 27 middle schools in the USA, Birkett, Espelage and Koenig (2009) found that although LGB students tended to feel more depressed and have more suicidal thoughts, this was less so when pupils perceived a positive school climate.

Consequences of involvement in bullying

Many studies suggest negative effects of being victimized (Arseneault, 2018). These effects can be substantial and long-term (Wolke & Lereya, 2015). A major consequence of being victimized is depression. Meta-analyses of many reports from longitudinal studies (Ttofi, Farrington, & Lösel, 2011) showed that even after adjustments for a range of other factors, victims at school were at greater risk of later depression. Data from the E-Risk study (Fisher et al., 2012) found that exposure to frequent bullying in 12-year-old children predicted higher rates of self-harm, even after taking account of prior emotional problems. Victimised twins were more likely to self-harm than their non-victimised co-twin, supporting a direct causal link between peer victimisation and self-harm. Suicide, although rare, can be an outcome to which victim experiences can be a significant contributor (Kim et al., 2009).

Children involved in bullying others are at greater risk of depression as well (Ttofi et al., 2011), but are more significantly at greater risk of later offending (Farrington et al., 2012). Bystanders or witnesses of bullying can also be adversely affected (Rivers et al., 2009).

Individual coping strategies

Pupils adopt a variety of coping strategies when bullied. Studies suggest that the success of these varies, and is age- and gender-dependent, but non-assertive strategies such as crying are less successful than ignoring or seeking help. A study of English pupils aged 13–16 years (Smith et al., 2004) found the five most frequent coping strategies were: talk to someone, ignore it, stick up for yourself, avoid/stay away from bullies, and make more/different friends. Talking to someone appeared the best strategy, as over a two-year period, those who had stopped being victims had more often talked to someone about it (67%) than those who had stayed victims (46%) or become victims (41%).

Another way of assessing effectiveness was used by Frisén, Hasselblad, and Holmqvist (2012). They asked 18-year-old Swedish students who had been bullied during their school career, what had made the bullying stop (if it did); the most frequent replies were support from school personnel, transition to a new school level, and a change of coping strategies.

Although telling teachers about bullying is generally recommended in schools and can often be successful, it does depend on how effectively teachers respond. Also, rates of telling a teacher are less in older pupils, and boys (Hunter & Boyle, 2004). Additional issues arise with cyberbullying. The evidence again is that seeking help or support is likely to be a good strategy. In a longitudinal study, Machmutow et al. (2012) found that over time, support seeking from peers and family was associated with reduced depression, while assertive coping strategies (such as finding and contacting the bully) were associated with increased depression. However at present, many pupils seem to feel unsure about how well teachers will cope with cyberbullying, and such help seeking seems to be directed much more to friends and family than to teachers (Zhou et al., 2013).

School-based intervention/prevention

Systematic anti-bullying interventions started in Norway, following the suicides of three boys in late 1982 due in large part to school bullying. A nationwide anti-bullying campaign was started, and as part of this, Olweus developed a first version of the Olweus Bullying Prevention Program (OBPP). This is described in Chapter 2. Since then, other programmes have been developed, including KiVa in Finland (see Chapter 3), ViSC in Austria (Chapter 4), various programmes in the USA (Chapter 5) and Friendly Schools in Australia (Chapter 6). There have been various initiatives in Japan (Chapter 7), peer support work has been developed in Italy (Chapter 8), and different ways to include tackling cyberbullying have been put forward (Chapter 9).

Programmes and components

Programmes are made up of components. Some interventions use just one or two components. For example, Young (1998) described use of a non-punitive (Support Group) response to bullying incidents, with a high success rate. Nickel et al. (2006) described a brief strategic family therapy intervention to reduce aggressive expression and bullying in teenage girls (with some success). Some other procedures based mainly on one specific method are described in Chapter 7, in Japan.

Programmes such as the OBPP, KiVa, and ViSC are made up of a set of different components. Although the overall programme may be evaluated for effectiveness, it can be difficult to tell how vital or important all the components are. In an attempt to look at this issue across programmes, Ttofi and Farrington (2011) dichotomized components of 44 interventions, and correlated their presence or absence with the amount of change in rates of bullying, and being bullied. For reducing rates of both bullying others and being bullied, components most associated with success were parent training/meetings, disciplinary methods, and cooperative group work; and greater duration and intensity of the programme, both for teachers and children. In addition, bully rates were reduced more in programmes with improved playground supervision, classroom management, teacher training, classroom rules, whole-school policy, and school conferences. Victim rates were reduced more in programmes with more use of videos. Work with peers was associated negatively with victim rates.

However, programmes vary in many aspects, and an association of one component with bully or victim rates may be brought about by a variation in some other feature. In addition, their analysis was limited historically in that the interventions they surveyed covered some 25 years, whereas methods of intervention have been and still are being developed and changed. Two components picked up in a critique by Smith, Cowie and Salmivalli (2012) were the findings on work with peers, and disciplinary methods (see also reply by Ttofi and Farrington, 2012). Much depends on how terms such as 'work with peers' and 'disciplinary methods' are interpreted. A subsequent review of more recent studies by Evans et al. (2014) did not replicate the findings on components reported by Ttofi and Farrington (2011).

A study carried out with 39 Swedish schools by Flygare et al. (2011, 2013) aimed to compare the success of eight anti-bullying programmes. A surprising finding was that all the schools employing an intervention actually used components from more than one programme; and even eight schools selected as non-intervention 'controls' were doing so! Thus the focus of their evaluation changed from comparing programmes, to comparing programme components. They found the most successful components were: training for the majority of staff; having clear procedures for dealing with bullying incidents; having a cooperative anti-bullying team of staff with differing expertise; doing regular follow-up and evaluation of anti-bullying measures; and having pupils participate actively in preventing bullying (not as peer mediators, but 'running activities aimed at creating a good atmosphere'). In addition, some measures were found to work better for girls, some for boys. For girls, monitoring school break times; and for boys, enhancing relationships, having clear rules, and using disciplinary strategies. Finally, some components were identified as having possible negative effects. These included special lessons on bullying (which in this study were found to be often uninteresting and counter-productive), and using pupils as peer mediators (rather than as active participants in anti-bullying activities).

Meta-analyses of programmes

For some years now, there have been enough interventions reported and evaluated in various countries, to allow meta-analyses of their effectiveness. Ttofi and Farrington (2011) analysed 44 school-based intervention programmes; on average, these reduced bullying by around 20–23% and victimization by around 17–20%. An update by Gaffney, Ttofi and Farrington (2019) analysed 100 evaluations, and found reductions in bully perpetration rates of 19–20% and victim rates of 15–16%. Other meta-analyses (Evans, Fraser, & Cotter, 2014; Cantone et al., 2015; Jimenez-Barbero et al., 2016) confirm some degree of success achieved by anti-bullying interventions. Gaffney, Farrington, Espelage and Ttofi (2019) analysed 24 interventions targeting cyberbullying, and found average reductions of 10–15% in cyberbullying perpetration, and about 14% in cyber victimization.

Overall, these meta-analyses show that anti-bullying interventions are usually worthwhile. Some reductions in bullying can be expected, and in some cases these can be substantial. However average reductions of around 15–20% are modest. There is clearly much still to learn about how to make interventions more effective.

Much of the intervention work has been in primary schools. There does appear to be lower success in secondary schools, as discussed by Yeager et al. (2015). This is consistent with the dominance hypothesis for bullying (see above) and possible gains that bullies may obtain in terms of peer status during the adolescent period. From this perspective, Ellis et al. (2012) suggest that interventions against bullying in secondary schools may benefit from more emphasis on providing alternative, prosocial, status-enhancing activities for those likely to be involved in bullying.

Summary

Bullying, especially as it affects young people, at school or in cyberbullying, has been a rapidly growing area of research. It has an appreciable prevalence rate, and is associated with negative outcomes, especially for victims but also for perpetrators and bystanders. Given the imbalance of power present in bullying, there is a moral imperative to intervene on behalf of victims, which would not be so strong in cases of aggression between equals (Greene, 2006).

As the bullying research programme has developed, our increasing knowledge about the nature of bullying has fed into a range of intervention efforts – some based on specific components, some based on a 'set menu' of a combination of components at different levels (e.g. individual, class, school). These have had some, but limited, success. The next eight chapters describe in detail some of the most well-known and successful interventions. They consider what the intervention is, what evaluations have been made, what challenges were encountered, and what lessons have been learnt. A concluding chapter reflects on where we are currently in intervening to reduce bullying, and enhance pupil safety and well-being in schools.

References

Arseneault, L. (2018). Annual Research Review: The persistent and pervasive impact of being bullied in childhood and adolescence: Implications for policy and practice. *Journal of Child Psychology and Psychiatry*, 59, 405–421.

Ball, H. A., Arseneault, L., Taylor, A., Maughan, B., Caspi, A., & Moffitt, T. E. (2008). Genetic and environmental influences on victims, bullies and bully-victims in childhood. *Journal of Child Psychiatry and Psychiatry*, 49, 104–112.

Birkett, M., Espelage, D. L., & Koenig, B. (2009). LGB and questioning students in schools: The moderating effects of homophobic bullying and school climate on negative outcomes. *Journal of Youth and Adolescence*, 38, 989–1000.

Bjereld, Y., Daneback, K., & Petzold, M. (2014). Differences in prevalence of bullying victimization between native and immigrant children in the Nordic countries: A parent-reported serial cross-sectional study. *Child: Care, Health and Development*, 41, 593–599.

Björkqvist, K., Lagerspetz, K. M. J., & Kaukainen, A. (1992). Do girls manipulate and boys fight? Developmental trends in regard to direct and indirect aggression. *Aggressive Behavior*, 18, 117–127.

Bowes, L., Arseneault, L., Maughan, B., Taylor, A., Caspi, A., & Moffitt, T. E. (2009). School, neighborhood, and family factors are associated with children's bullying involvement: A nationally representative longitudinal study. *Journal of the American Academy of Child and Adolescent Psychiatry*, 48, 545–553.

Bowes, L., Maughan, B., Caspi, A., Moffitt, T. E., & Arseneault, L. (2010). Families promote emotional and behavioural resilience to bullying: Evidence of an environmental effect. *Journal of Child Psychology & Psychiatry*, 51, 809–817.

Cantone, E., Piras, A. P., Vellante, M., Preti, A., Danielsdottir, S., D'Ajola, E., Lesinskiene, S., Angermeyer, M. C., Carta, M. G., & Bhugra, D. (2015). Interventions on bullying ands cyberbullying in schools: A systematic review. *Clinical Practice & Epidemiology in Mental Health*, 11 (Suppl 1: M4), 58–76.

Caravita, S., DiBlasio, P., & Salmivalli, C. (2009). Unique and interactive effects of empathy and social status on involvement in bullying. *Social Development*, 18, 140–163.

Cassidy, W., Faucher, C., & Jackson, M. (Eds.) (2019). *Cyberbullying at university in international contexts*. Oxford: Routledge.

Cook, C. R., Williams, K. R., Guerra, N. G., & Kim, T. E. (2010a). Variability in the prevalence of bullying and victimization: A cross-national and methodological analysis. In S. R. Jimerson, S. M. Swearer, & D. L. Espelage (Eds.), *Handbook of bullying in schools: An international perspective* (pp. 347–362). New York & London: Routledge.

Cook, C. R., Williams, K. R., Guerra, N. G., Kim, T. E., & Sadek, S. (2010b). Predictors of bullying and victimization in childhood and adolescence: A meta-analytic investigation. *School Psychology Quarterly*, 25, 65–83.

Cornell, D. G., & Brockenbrough, K. (2004). Identification of bullies and victims: A comparison of methods. *Journal of School Violence*, 3, 63–87.

Cowie, H., & Myers, C-A. (Eds.) (2015). *Bullying among university students: Cross-national perspectives*. London: Routledge.

Crick, N. R., & Grotpeter, J. K. (1995). Relational aggression, gender, and social-psychological adjustment. *Child Development*, 66, 710–722.

Currie, C. *et al.* (Eds.). (2012). *Social Determinants of health and well-being among young people. Health behaviour in school-aged children (HBSC) study: International report from the 2009/23010 survey.* Copenhagen: WHO Regional Office for Europe.

Duncan, N. (1999). *Sexual bullying: Gender conflict and pupil culture in secondary schools.* London: Routledge.

Ellis, B. J., del Guidice, M., Dishion, T. J., Figueredo, A. J., Gray, P., Griskevicius, V., Hawley, P. H., Jacobs, W. J., James, J., Volk, A. A., & Wilson, D. S. (2012). The evolutionary basis of risk taking behavior: Implications for science, policy, and practice. *Developmental Psychology, 48,* 598–623.

Eslea, E., & Rees, J. (2001). At what age are children most likely to be bullied at school? *Aggressive Behavior, 27,* 419–429.

Evans, C. B. R., Fraser, M. W., & Cotter, K. L. (2014). The effectiveness of school-based bullying prevention programs: A systemic review. *Aggression and Violent Behavior, 19,* 532–544.

Farrington, D. P., Lösel, F., Ttofi, M. M., & Theodorakis, N. (2012). *School bullying, depression and offending behaviour later in life: An updated systematic review of longitudinal studies.* Stockholm: Swedish National Council for Crime Prevention.

Fisher, H. L., Moffitt, T. E., Houts, R. M., Belsky, D. W., Arseneault, L., & Caspi, A. (2012). Bullying victimisation and risk of self harm in early adolescence: Longitudinal cohort study. *British Medical Journal, 344,* e2683.

Flygare, E., Frånberg, G-M., Gill, P., Johansson, B., Lindberg, O., Osbeck, C., & Söderström, Å. (2011). *Evaluation of anti-bullying methods.* Report 353, National Agency for Education, Stockholm. www.skolverket.se.

Flygare, E., Gill, P. E., & Johansson, B. (2013). Lessons from a concurrent evaluation of eight antibullying programs used in Sweden. *American Journal of Evaluation, 34,* 170–189.

Fox, C. L., & Boulton, M. J. (2006). Friendship as a moderator of the relationship between social skills problems and peer victimisation. *Aggressive Behavior, 32,* 110–121.

Frisén, A., Hasselblad, T., & Holmqvist, K. (2012). What actually makes bullying stop? Reports from former victims. *Journal of Adolescence, 35,* 981–990.

Gaffney, H., Farrington, D. P., Espelage, D. L., & Ttofi, M. M. (2019). Are cyberbullying intervention and prevention programs effective? A systematic and meta-analytical review. *Aggression and Violent Behavior, 45,* 134–153,

Gaffney, H., Ttofi, M. M., & Farrington, D. P. (2019). Evaluating the effectiveness of school bullying prevention programs: An updated meta-analytical review. *Aggression and Violent Behavior, 45,* 111–133.

Gendron, B. P., Williams, K. R., & Guerra, N. (2011). An analysis of bullying among students within schools: Estimating the effects of individual normative beliefs, self-esteem, and school climate. *Journal of School Violence, 10,* 150–164.

Gini, G., Pozzoli, T., & Hymel, S. (2014). Moral disengagement among children and youth: A meta-analytic review of links to aggressive behavior. *Aggressive Behavior, 40,* 56–68.

Gladden, R. M., Vivolo-Kantor, A. M., Hamburger, M. E., & Lumpkin, C. D. (2014). *Bullying surveillance among youths: Uniform definitions for public health and recommended data elements, version 1.0.* Atlanta, GA; National Center for Injury Prevention and Control, Centers for Disease Control and Prevention and U. S. Department of Education.

Greene, M. B. (2006). Bullying in schools: A plea for a measure of human rights. *Journal of Social Issues*, 62, 63–79.

Hinduja, S., & Patchin, J. W. (2008). Cyberbullying: An exploratory analysis of factors related to offending and victimization. *Deviant Behavior*, 29, 1–29.

Hughes, T. (1857). *Tom Brown's Schooldays.* Cambridge: Macmillan.

Hugh-Jones, S., & Smith, P. K. (1999). Self-reports of short-and long-term effects of bullying on children who stammer. *British Journal of Educational Psychology*, 69, 141–158.

Hunter, S. C., & Boyle, J. M. E. (2004). Appraisal and coping strategy use of victims of school bullying. *British Journal of Educational Psychology*, 74, 83–107.

Inchley, J., Currie, D., Young, T., Samdal, O., Torsheim, T., Augustson, L., Mathison, F., Aleman-Diaz, A., Molcho, M., Weber, M., & Barnekow, V. (Eds.) (2016). *Growing up unequal: Gender and socioeconomic differences in young people's health and well-being: Health behaviour in school-aged children (HBSC) study: International report from the 2013/2014 survey.* Copenhagen: WHO Regional Office for Europe.

Jennifer, D. (2013). Girls and indirect aggression. In I. Rivers, & N. Duncan (Eds.), *Bullying: Experiences and discourses of sexuality and gender* (pp. 47–59). London and New York: Routledge.

Jiménez-Barbero, J. A., Ruiz-Hernández, J. A., Llor-Zaragoza, L., Pérez-Garćia, M., & Llor-Esteban, B. (2016). Effectiveness of anti-bullying school programs: A meta-analysis. *Children and Youth Services Review*, 61, 165–175.

Jolliffe, D., & Farrington, D. P. (2011). Is low empathy related to bullying after controlling for individual and social background variables? *Journal of Adolescence*, 34, 59–71.

Kärnä, A., Voeten, M., Poskiparta, E., & Salmivalli, C. (2010). Vulnerable children in varying classroom contexts: Bystanders' behaviors moderate the effects of risk factors on victimization. *Merrill-Palmer Quarterly*, 56, 261–282.

Kim, Y-S., Leventhal, B., Koh, Y-J., & Boyce, W. T. (2009). Bullying increased suicide risk: Prospective study of Korean adolescents. *Archives Suicide Research*, 13, 15–30.

Koo, H. (2007). A time line of the evolution of school bullying in differing social contexts. *Asia Pacific Education Review*, 8, 107–116.

Kowalski, R. M., Giumetti, G. W., Schroeder, A. N., & Lattanner, M. R. (2014). Bullying in the digital age: A critical review and meta-analysis of cyberbullying research among youth. *Psychological Bulletin*, 140, 1073–1137.

Läftman, S. B., Modin, B., & Östberg, V. (2013). Cyberbullying and subjective health: A larger-scale study of students in Stockholm, Sweden. *Children and Youth Services Review*, 35, 112–119.

Law, D. M., Shapka, J. D., & Olson, B. F. (2010). To control or not to control? Parenting behaviours and adolescent online aggression. *Computers in Human Behavior*, 26, 1651–1656.

Lereya, S. T., Samara, M., & Wolke, D. (2013). Parenting behavior and the risk of becoming a victim and a bully/victim: A meta-analysis study. *Child Abuse & Neglect*, 37, 1091–1108.

Machmutow, K., Perren, S., Sticca, F., & Alsaker, F. D. (2012). Peer victimisation and depressive symptoms: Can specific coping strategies buffer the negative impact of cybervictimisation? *Emotional and Behavioural Difficulties*, 17, 403–420.

Maynard, B. R., Vaughn, M. G., Salas-Wright, C. P., & Vaughn, S. (2016). Bullying victimization among school-aged immigrant youth in the United States. *Journal of Adolescent Health*, 58, 337–344.

Mishna, F. (2003). Learning disabilities and bullying: Double jeopardy. *Journal of Learning Disabilities*, 36, 336–347.

Mishna, F., Khoury-Kassabri, M., Gadalla, T., & Daciuk, J. (2012). Risk factors for involvement in cyberbullying: Victims, bullies and bully-victims. *Children and Youth Services Review*, 34, 63–70.

Monks, C., & Coyne, I. (Eds.) (2011). *Bullying in different contexts*. Cambridge: Cambridge University Press.

Monks, C. P., Ortega, R., & Torrado, E. (2002). Unjustified aggression in a Spanish pre-school. *Aggressive Behavior*, 28, 458–476.

Morita, Y. (1985). *Ijime shuudan no kouzo ni kansuru shakaigakuteki kenkyu* [Sociological study on the structure of bullying group]. Osaka: Department of Sociology, Osaka City University.

Muijs, D. (2017). Can schools reduce bullying? The relationship between school characteristics and the prevalence of bullying behaviours. *British Journal of Educational Psychology*, 87(2), 255–272. doi:10.1111/bjep.121488.

Nickel, M., Luley, J., Krawczyk, J., Nickel, C., Wildermann, C., Lahmann, C., Muehlbacher, M., Forthuber, P., Kettler, C., Leiberich, P., Tritt, K., Mitterlehner, F., Kaplan, P., Gil, F. P., Rother, W., & Loew, T. (2006). Bullying girls – changes after brief strategic family therapy: A randomized, prospective, controlled trial with one-year follow-up. *Psychotherapy and Psychosomatics*, 75, 47–55.

Nickerson, A. B., Mele, D., & Princiotta, D. (2008). Attachment and empathy as predictors of roles as defenders or outsiders in bullying interactions. *Journal of School Psychology*, 46, 687–703.

Olweus, D. (1973/1978). *Hackkycklingar och översittare: Forskning om Skolmobbning*. Stockholm, Sweden: Almqvist & Wiksell (expanded version in English translation, *Aggression in Schools: Bullies and Whipping Boys*. Washington DC: Hemisphere).

Patton, D. U., Hong, J. S., Patel, S., & Kral, M. J. (2015). A systematic review of research strategies used in qualitatiove studies on school bullying and victimization. *Trauma, Violence & Abuse*, 1–14.

Peeters, M., Cillessen, A. H. N., & Scholte, R. H. J. (2010). Clueless or powerful? Identifying subtypes of bullies in adolescence. *Journal of Youth and Adolescence*, 39, 1041–1052.

Pikas, A. (1989). A pure concept of mobbing gives the best results for treatment. *School Psychology International*, 10, 95–104.

Pouwels, J. L., Lansu, T. A. M., & Cillessen, A. H. N. (2018). A developmental perspective on popularity and the group process of bullying. *Aggression and Violent Behavior*, 43, 64–70.

Pozzoli, T., Gini, G., & Vieno, A. (2012). The role of individual correlates and class norms in defending and passive bystanding behavior in bullying: A multilevel analysis. *Child Development*, 83, 1917–1931.

Rigby, K. (1997). Attitudes and beliefs about bullying among Australian school children. *Irish Journal of Psychology*, 18, 202–220.

Rivers, I., & Noret, N. (2010). 'I h8 u': Findings from a five-year study of text and email bullying. *British Educational Research Journal*, 36, 643–671.

Rivers, I., & Smith, P. K. (1994). Types of bullying behaviour and their correlates. *Aggressive Behavior*, 20, 359–368.

Rivers, I., Poteat, V. P., Noret, N., & Ashurst, N. (2009). Observing bullying at school: The mental health implications of witness status. *School Psychology Quarterly*, 24, 211–223.

Robinson, J. P., Espelage, D. L., & Rivers, I. (2013). Developmental trends in peer victimization and emotional distress in LGB and heterosexual youth. *Pediatrics*, 131, 423–430.

RSM McClure Watters (2011). *The Nature and Extent of Pupil Bullying in Schools in the North of Ireland*, Volume 56. Bangor, UK: Department of Education for Northern Ireland.

Saarento, S., Kärnä, A., Hodges, E. V. E., & Salmivalli, C. (2013). Student-, classroom-, and school-level risk factors for victimization. *Journal of School Psychology*, 51, 421–434.

Salmivalli, C. (2010). Bullying and the peer group: A review. *Aggression and Violent Behavior*, 15, 112–120.

Salmivalli, C., Lagerspetz, K., Björkqvist, K., Österman, K., & Kaukiainen, A. (1996). Bullying as a group process: Participant roles and their relations to social status within the group. *Aggressive Behavior*, 22, 1–15.

Sasson, H., & Mesch, G. (2014). Parental mediation, peer norms and risky online behavior. *Computers in Human Behavior*, 33, 32–38.

Smith, P. K. (2014). *Understanding school bullying: Its nature & prevention strategies*. London: Sage Publications.

Smith, P. K. (2016). Bullying: Definition, types, causes, consequences and intervention. *Social and Personality Psychology Compass*, 10/9, 519–532.

Smith, P. K. (2017). Bullying and theory of mind: A review. *Current Psychiatry Reviews*, 13, 90–95.

Smith, P. K., & Sharp, S. (Eds.) (1994). *School bullying: Insights and perspectives*. London: Routledge.

Smith, P. K., López-Castro, L., Robinson, S., & Görzig, A. (2019). Consistency of gender differences in bullying in different cross-cultural surveys. *Aggression and Violent Behavior*, 45, 33–40.

Smith, P. K., Mahdavi, J., Carvalho, M., Fisher, S., Russell, S., & Tippett, N. (2008). Cyberbullying, its forms and impact in secondary school pupils. *Journal of Child Psychology and Psychiatry*, 49, 376–385.

Smith, P. K., Morita, Y., Junger-Tas, J., Olweus, D., Catalano, R., & Slee, P. (Eds.) (1999). *The Nature of School Bullying: A Cross-national Perspective*. London and New York: Routledge.

Smith, P. K., Singer, M., Hoel, H., & Cooper, C. L. (2003). Victimisation in the school and the workplace: Are there any links? *British Journal of Psychology*, 94, 175–188.

Smith, P. K., Salmivalli, C. & Cowie, H. (2012). Effectiveness of school-based programs to reduce bullying: A commentary. *Journal of Experimental Criminology*, 8, 433–441.

Smith, P. K., Talamelli, L., Cowie, H., Naylor, P., & Chauhan, P. (2004). Profiles of non-victims, escaped victims, continuing victims and new victims of school bullying. *British Journal of Educational Psychology*, 74, 565–581.

Spriggs, A. L., Iannotti, R. J., Nansel, T. R., & Haynie, D. L. (2007). Adolescent bullying involvement and perceived family, peer and school relations: Commonalities and differences across race/ethnicity. *Journal of Adolescent Health*, 41, 283–293.

Tippett, N., Wolke, D., & Platt, L. (2013). Ethnicity and bullying involvement in a national UK youth sample. *Journal of Adolescence*, 36, 639–649.

Tokunaga, R. S. (2010). Following you home from school: A critical review and synthesis of research on cyberbullying victimization. *Computers in Human Behavior*, 26, 277–287.

Toomey, R. B., & Russell, S. T. (2013). The role of sexual orientation in school-based victimization: A meta-analysis. *Youth & Society*, 45, 500–522.

Ttofi, M. M., & Farrington, D. P. (2011). Effectiveness of school-based programs to reduce bullying: A systematic and meta-analytic review. *Journal of Experimental Criminology*, 7, 27–56.

Ttofi, M. M., & Farrington, D. P. (2012). Bullying prevention programs: The importance of peer intervention, disciplinary methods and age variations. *Journal of Experimental Criminology*, 8, 443–462.

Ttofi, M. M., Farrington, D. P., & Lösel, F. (2011). Do the victims of school bullies tend to become depressed later in life? A systematic review and meta-analysis of longitudinal studies. *Journal of Aggression, Conflict and Peace Research*, 3, 63–73.

Van Roekel, E., Scholte, R. H. J., & Didden, R. (2009). Bullying among adolescents with autism spectrum disorders: Prevalence and perception. *Journal of Autism and Developmental Disorders*, 40, 63–73.

Vandebosch, H., & van Cleemput, K. (2008). Defining cyberbullying: A qualitative research into the perceptions of youngsters. *CyberPsychology & Behavior*, 11, 499–503.

Vandebosch, H., & van Cleemput, K. (2009). Cyberbullying among youngsters: Profiles of bullies and victims. *New Media & Society*, 11, 1349–1371.

Vervoort, M. H. M., Scholte, R. H. J., & Overbeek, G. (2010). Bullying and victimization among adolescents: The role of ethnicity and ethnic composition of school class. *Journal of Youth and Adolescence*, 39, 1–11.

Vitoroulis, I., & Georgiades, K. (2017). Bullying among immigrant and non-immigrant early adolescents: School- and student-level effects. *Journal of Adolescence*, 61, 141–151.

Volk, A. A., Camilleri, J. A., Dane, A. V., & Marini, Z. A. (2012). Is adolescent bullying an evolutionary adaptation? *Aggressive Behavior*, 38, 222–238.

Wang, W., Brittain, H., McDougall, P., & Vaillancourt, T. (2016). Bullying and school transition: Context or development? *Child Abuse & Neglect*, 51, 237–248.

Williams, S. (2013). Sexual bullying in one local authority. In I. Rivers, & N. Duncan (Eds.), *Bullying: Experiences and discourses of sexuality and gender* (pp. 60–74). London and New York: Routledge.

Wolke, D., & Lereya, S. T. (2015). Long-term effects of bullying. *Archives of Disease in Childhood*, 100, 879–885.

Wolke, D., Tippett, N., & Dantchev, S. (2015). Bullying in the family: Sibling bullying. *The Lancet Psychiatry*, 2, 917–929.

Yeager, D. S., Fong, C. J., Lee, H. Y., & Espelage, D. L. (2015). Declines in efficacy of anti-bullying programs among older adolescents: Theory and a three-level meta-analysis. *Journal of Applied Developmental Psychology*, 37, 36–51.

Young, S. (1998). The Support Group approach to bullying in schools. *Educational Psychology in Practice*, 14, 32–39.

Zhou, Z., Tang, H., Tian, Y., Wei, H., Zhang, F., & Morrison, C. M. (2013). Cyberbullying and its risk factors among Chinese high school students. *School Psychology International*, 34, 630–647.

Zych, I., Ortega-Ruiz, R., & del Rey, R. (2015). Scientific research on bullying and cyberbullying: Where have we been and where are we going. *Aggression and Violent Behavior*, 23, 1–21.

2

THE OLWEUS BULLYING PREVENTION PROGRAM (OBPP)

New evaluations and current status

Dan Olweus and Susan P. Limber

In writing this chapter about the Olweus Bullying Prevention Program (OBPP), we felt that it was necessary to consider several methodological and conceptual issues before describing the effects of the program. We are convinced that careful consideration and detailed discussion of such issues are of critical importance for an adequate evaluation of our own conclusions, and indeed, for progress of the whole field of anti-bullying research. Accordingly, we devote a good deal of space to the theme of establishing bullying as a scientific concept and to selected issues of design and analysis and pay less attention to the research design and effect sizes. Relevant information about such issues is easily available in other publications (e.g. Olweus, 1991, 2005; Olweus & Limber, 2010a; Limber, Olweus, Wang, Masiello, & Breivik, 2018; Solberg & Olweus, 2003).

Bullying as a scientific concept

A strong societal interest in the phenomenon of peer harassment began in Sweden in the late 1960s and early 1970s under the designation *mobbning* (Heinemann, 1969, 1972, 1974). Since there were no empirical data to answer the many questions involved in the public discussions, Olweus began a large-scale research project in 1970 comprising some 1,000 boys from Greater Stockholm (Olweus, 1974). This research has later been generally acknowledged as the first scientific study of bullying in the world.

Although Olweus developed a conceptual framework to guide empirical research and analyses in his first project, he did not provide a precise definition of the phenomenon. However, the need for a clear and circumscribed definition became urgent in connection with a government-initiated campaign against bullying in Norway in 1983 (Olweus 1983, 1993; Olweus & Roland, 1983). Specifically, an important part of this campaign was nationwide registration of bullying problems by means of a student questionnaire that Olweus was commissioned to develop (Olweus, 1983). The basic view of bullying underlying the construction of the questionnaire was the following:

> A student is being bullied or victimized when he or she is exposed, repeatedly and over time, to negative (presumably unpleasant or hurtful) actions on the part of one or more other students. It was further specified that in bullying there is a certain imbalance of power or strength in favor of the perpetrator(s); the student who is exposed to negative actions has difficulty defending himself or herself.

Present in this definition were the three criteria of bullying, which were later discussed in detail in the book *Bullying as School: What We Know and What We Can Do* (for further details, see Olweus 1993, 2013): Bullying is negative behaviour that: is (a) *intentional* (perpetrators know/understand that their behaviour is unpleasant or hurtful to the target); (b) usually *repetitive*; and c) involves some degree of *power imbalance* between the targeted individual and the perpetrator(s) in favour of the latter. The repetitive nature of the phenomenon also connotes the existence of a kind of (unwanted) *relationship*, implying that the targeted individual typically has at least some superficial knowledge of his or her perpetrator(s).

It may be of interest to note that when the U.S. Centers for Disease Control and Prevention (CDC) and the U.S. Department of Education were tasked to develop a 'uniform definition of bullying', they landed on a definition that is essentially the definition that Olweus developed some 30 years earlier (Gladden, Vivolo-Kantor, Hamburger, & Lumpkin, 2014). Olweus was also credited for the origin of the uniform definition (Gladden et al., 2014, p. 7). In addition, in the context of the nationwide campaign, a first version of a measurement instrument (Questionnaire; Olweus, 1983, 1991) was developed which later became refined and expanded into a revised version, the Olweus Bullying Questionnaire (OBQ; Olweus, 1996).

The combination of a definition with approximate boundaries (inclusion/ exclusion criteria; content validity) and an instrument for the measurement of the phenomenon is a good and necessary start for the development of *bullying as a scientific concept.* But to make it a useful and attractive concept, it is critically important to document the *construct validity* of the phenomenon and the measurement instrument (or other instruments). To do so is a gradual process, often over many years, aimed at showing that the concept as measured or used actually captures what it is intended to capture.

Convergent validity

In this process, the concepts of convergent and discriminant validity are essential (Campbell & Fiske, 1959). The degree of correlation between measures of a particular trait/characteristic/variable measured with different methods is a common way of assessing *convergent validity.* With regard to the OBQ, such data have been provided by the KiVa research project, which has used both the OBQ and peer ratings about physical, verbal, and indirect bullying victimization and perpetration in several large-scale studies (e.g. Kärnä et al. 2011). The correlations between the global (OBQ) item and the (OBQ) scale (nine items) of being bullied versus similar peer ratings of bullying victimization were 0.39 and 0.40, respectively. Corresponding correlations for the global bullying others item and the scale of bullying others (nine items) with the relevant peer ratings were 0.36 and 0.34 (C. Salmivalli, personal communication, Olweus, 2013). With correction for unreliability (attenuation correction), these convergent validity correlations, based on almost 20,000 students, would be even higher (Guilford, 1956). The results must be considered quite satisfactory, given the fact that a good deal of bullying is of a subtle and somewhat secretive nature, which may be difficult for peers to observe (also see Olweus, 2010, 2013). These correlations are clearly higher than the average association between self-reports and peer data described in a well-known meta-analysis of cross-informant reports on child behaviour problems ($r = 0.26$; Achenbach et al. 1987), for example.

Discriminant validity

Discriminant validity concerns documentation that presumably/theoretically distinct traits, characteristics, or variables measured with a particular method do not correlate too strongly. Concepts or measurement instruments can thus be invalidated by too high correlations with other concepts/instruments from which they were intended to differ. In the Solberg and Olweus article (2003), the global being bullied variable was correlated with two measures of externalizing problems (aggression and antisocial behaviour) which were clearly correlated with the global bullying others variable, as expected. Similarly, the global bullying others variable was correlated with three measures of internalizing problems (social disintegration, poor self-esteem, and depression), which were clearly associated with the global being bullied variable, again as expected. All of these cross-over correlations were basically zero, which was thus a good indication of discriminant validity and thereby also of construct validity.

Sensitivity to change

A third criterion of good construct validity is that the measured variables are sensitive to change and can adequately reflect real differences between groups or across time points. A well-constructed questionnaire measures salient and often quite painful subjective experiences of being bullied, and if clear changes in the levels of bullying occur at school, this is likely to be quickly registered by the targeted student. Similarly, students who bully others will tend to note if their behaviour is questioned, blocked or confronted by teachers or peers, and maybe reported to parents. Accordingly, it is natural to expect that self-reports will be able to reflect real differences between groups and time points, including real changes due to systematic interventions (Olweus, 2010, 2013).

Reliability

A final consideration concerns reliability. There are different forms of reliability (Nunnally & Bernstein, 1994) and, with regard to internal consistency reliability, a number of independent researchers have reported quite high (Cronbach's) alpha coefficients, usually in the .80s – .90s, for the scales of being bullied or bullying others. These scales consist of 9–10 items about verbal, physical, indirect (and cyber) bullying (Olweus, 1996, 2013; Breivik & Olweus, 2015). In our evaluation research, we have often also used the global single items of being bullied and bullying others. On this point, it is important to realize that programme/intervention effects are usually based on higher-level aggregated units such as schools or classrooms (percentage of bullied students per school, for example) and these aggregate reliabilities are usually quite high, again in the .80s or .90s (see e.g. Limber, Olweus, Wang,

Masiello, & Breivik, 2018; Snijders & Bosker, 2012, p. 26). Such aggregated single-item variables can thus differentiate the relevant higher-level units with excellent reliability in contrast to what is, or has been, commonly believed.

Two conclusions

Taken together, the above results and considerations substantiate the following *two conclusions*. First, our own definition and results, combined with those of many other researchers using a similar approach, do suggest that bullying has gradually become a meaningful scientific concept with considerable construct validity. Second, with regard to measurement, we have come to the conclusion that a well-constructed, validated self-report instrument such as the OBQ is the best method for the measurement of bullying problems for most purposes. At the same time, it must be recognized that some children who bully other students, will likely choose not to respond completely honestly on the relevant items, which may lead to some underreporting. Also, although there is still some controversy as to whether and how the usual three criteria of bullying (above) can be applied when electronic ways of communication are used, we have tentatively concluded that it is natural to regard such communications as a form of bullying, in line with verbal, physical, and indirect/relational forms bullying (Olweus, 2017; Olweus & Limber, 2018; Smith, del Barrio, & Tokunaga, 2012).

Initial evaluation of the OBPP

The OBPP was first implemented and evaluated in the First Bergen Project against Bullying, a longitudinal study that followed approximately 2,500 school children over a period of two and a half years, from 1983 to 1985. Because the project was part of a nationwide campaign against bullying, it was not possible to conduct an experimental study with schools or classes randomly assigned to treatment and control conditions. Instead, an 'extended selection cohorts design' was utilized in which same-aged students from the same schools were compared across three points in time (see below). At Time 1, participants belonged to 112 classes in grades 5–8 (modal ages 11 to 14 years) from 28 elementary and 14 junior high schools in Bergen, Norway.

Results from the evaluation revealed marked and statistically highly significant reductions in self-reports of bully/victim problems (based on the early version of the Olweus Bully/Victim Questionnaire, 1983). Substantial reductions in both the being bullied and the bullying others variables could be registered in both the 83/84 and the 83/85 evaluations (Olweus, 1991, 1993, 1997; Olweus & Alsaker, 1991). Similar results were obtained for two aggregated peer rating variables and teacher ratings of bully/victim problems at the classroom level. A marked 'dosage-response' relationship ($r = .52$, $n = 80$ teachers) was observed, such that those classes in which essential components of the program (classroom rules against bullying, use of role playing, and classroom meetings) had been implemented more fully, experienced greater reductions in bullying problems (Olweus & Alsaker, 1991; Olweus & Kallestad, 2010). Finally, the study also documented significant reductions in self-reports of general antisocial behaviour, including vandalism, theft, and truancy, and improvements in aspects of the 'social climate' of the class: improvements in students' self-reports of satisfaction with school life, improved order and discipline, more positive social relationships, and a more positive attitude toward school work and the school in general.

Prior to 2001, three additional evaluations (with positive results) of the OBPP were conducted in Norway. They have been briefly described in another context (Olweus & Limber, 2010a) and will not be discussed further in this chapter. Here we will focus on evaluations in Norway that were conducted after 2001 and some evaluations in the US. In addition, we will report on a quite recent study that has examined the long-term school-level effects of the OBPP. Before presenting results of these studies, we briefly discuss some general methodological considerations that apply to most of the reported studies.

A brief note about methodology

In all of these evaluations, we used the 'extended age cohort design' as developed by Olweus (Olweus, 2005; Olweus & Limber, 2010a; Shadish, Cook, & Campbell, 2002). In this design, same-aged students from the same schools are compared across periods in time. The schools thus serve as their own controls and in this way, the problem with initial differences between the groups to be compared can be largely reduced or avoided. In other words, the 'pretest' (T0) values for the individual schools can be considered good answers to the critical counterfactual question in all evaluation research: *How do we obtain reasonable estimates of what the result would have been, if the intervention subjects had not been exposed to the intervention* (e.g. Cook, Shadish, & Wong, 2008)? As has been repeatedly documented, attempts to statistically correct for preexisting initial differences in common quasi-experimental designs (with non-equivalent control and intervention groups) are fraught with great difficulties (see e.g. Judd & Kenny, 1981; Shadish et al., 2002; Weisberg, 1979). This design can thus be regarded as a strong quasi-experimental design (see Olweus, 2005; Olweus & Limber, 2010a; Limber et al., 2018, for more details.)

The Olweus Bullying Prevention Program

The Olweus Bullying Prevention Program (Olweus, 1991, 1993, Olweus & Limber, 2010a, 2010b), which is the oldest and most researched school-based bullying prevention program (National Academies of Sciences, Engineering, and Medicine [National Academies], 2016), was first developed and evaluated by Olweus in Norway in the mid-1980s (above). Initially designed for students in elementary, middle, and junior high school grades, the goals of the OBPP are to reduce bullying among children and youth, prevent new bullying problems, and more generally, achieve better relations among peers at school (Olweus, 1993; Olweus & Limber, 2010a). To achieve these goals, school personnel focus on restructuring the school environment to reduce opportunities and rewards for bullying and on building a sense of community. The OBPP is based on four key principles, which were derived from research on aggression (Olweus, 1993). Adults within a school environment should: (a) show warmth and positive interest in students; (b) set limits to unacceptable behaviour; (c) use consistent positive consequences to reinforce positive behaviour, and consistent, non-hostile consequences when rules are broken; and (d) act as positive role models for appropriate behaviour (Olweus, 1993; Olweus & Limber, 2007; Olweus et al., 2007).

These principles are translated into a number of school-wide interventions, classroom-level interventions, individual interventions, and (in particular in the US) community-level interventions designed to ensure community support of the school's efforts. For a more detailed description of programme elements and resources to support programme implementation, see Limber & Olweus, 2017; Limber et al., 2018; Olweus, 2012; Olweus & Limber, 2007; Olweus et al., 2007; Olweus & Limber, 2010a). School staff are supported in their implementation by a manual/manuals for teachers and training and ongoing consultation are provided by certified OBPP trainers/instructors/consultants, who help schools address challenges and maintain fidelity to the model.

From the start, it has been the programme developer's conviction that *successful outcomes will require both a research-based, well-organized programme and a good implementation model* that will be able to transfer the knowledge embodied in the programme to the schools' staff, their students, and parents. In addition, it is important *not* to regard OBPP as *a 'program' in a narrow sense* but rather as a coordinated collection of research-based components that form a unified whole-school approach to bullying. In our view, most of these components should be in place in all schools that want to create a safe and productive learning environment for their students.

A new national initiative against bullying in Norway

In late 2000, the Department of Education and Research (UFD) and the Department of Children and Family Affairs (BFD) decided that the OBPP was to be offered on a large-scale basis to Norwegian comprehensive schools over a period of years. Between 2001 and 2008, the programme was implemented in more than 500 schools and more than 125 OBPP instructors received thorough training in use of the programme. From an evaluation perspective, the new national initiative provided a unique opportunity to examine the effects of the OBPP on large samples of students and schools under ordinary conditions (i.e. without special efforts in terms of staff input or other resources) in the context of large-scale dissemination (Flay et al., 2005).

Our evaluations have been mainly focused on elementary schools in the first six cohorts of schools that started with the programme (made the baseline survey) at half-year intervals from the fall of 2001 to the spring of 2004. Here we will present evaluation results for 'pure elementary schools' (grades 4–7, with modal ages 9/10–12/13 years). There were 225 pure elementary schools (with grades 1–7 only) distributed across the six cohorts.

All of these 225 schools had performed both the baseline survey (T0) and the follow-up surveys one year later (T1),which we regard as an indicator or marker variable signalling that such schools had continued to follow the programme's principles and routines, at least to a certain extent, throughout the implementation period.

We have previously reported in some detail on the results from the first three cohorts of schools (Olweus & Limber, 2010a, 2010b), but here we will present the results for all six cohorts of pure elementary schools. The six cohorts consisted of 38, 34, 41, 81, 10, and 21 different schools (a total of 225 schools), and the total number of students in these six cohorts were 27,139 at base line and 26,947 at one-year follow-up.

The main results for the six separate evaluations are presented in Figure 2.1. The numbers on top of each line represent the percentage of bullied students

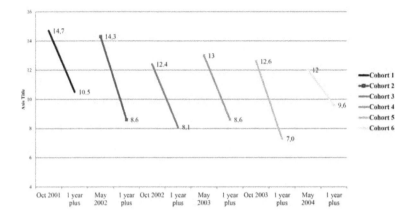

FIGURE 2.1 Percentage students being bullied before (upper figures) and 8 months after (lower figures) implementation of the olweus bullying program (obpp). six cohorts of schools (n= 225 schools and > 50 000 students), grades 4–7 with modal ages 10–13 years.

(two or three times a month or more often) at baseline (T0), 3–4 months before start of implementation of the OBPP. The numbers at the end of each line are the percentages of bullied students in the same schools and grades at follow-up (T1), one year later. To exemplify, among the approximately 6,000 students in grades 4–7 from Cohort 1 (farthest to the left in Figure 2.1) 14.7% reported having been bullied 2–3 times per month or more often at baseline. This percentage had then decreased to 10.5% among the approximately 6,000 students in the same grades from the same schools at Time 1. These students, who were in one grade lower and unexposed at T0, had then been exposed to the programme for 8–9 months.

Results for the various cohorts were basically very similar and highly significant (p<.001 in five out of six evaluations and p=.03 in the sixth) and thus represent replications of the positive programme effects (cf. 'The desperate need for replications', Hunter, 2001). The average results for all six cohorts combined amounted to an absolute change of 4.4 percentage points from 13.3% at T0 to 8.9% at T1. This represents a relative change of 33.1%. When data were analysed in multilevel format (a standard two-level model with students nested in schools and programme year, T0 versus T1, as predictor; see Limber et al., 2018), the t-value for programme effect for the key variable, *being bullied*, was a marked 22.71, p<.001. School level Cohen's *d* (with the between-school standard deviation in the denominator; Hedges, 2007) could be estimated at 1.33.

Similar results, with consistent reductions as a function of 8–9 months' of programme intervention were obtained, for the other key variable, *bullying other students*. Again, for five of the six cohorts, the p-value was less than .001 (and p=.02 in the sixth). The average percentage of students who bullied others across cohorts was reduced by an absolute change value of 2.2 percentage points from 5.1% to 2.9%. This corresponds to a relative change of 43.1%. In multi-level analyses of the underlying *bullying others* variable, the programme effect amounted to a t-value of 23.73, p<.001. Cohen's school level *d* was 1.19.

In this context, it is also worth mentioning that the positive programme effects also applied to students exposed to, or involved in, more serious bullying (weekly or more often, not only two or three times a month or more). Another positive programme effect was that students' reports on a two-item scale of well-being/satisfaction with school life showed a clear increase (*t*=15.33, p<.001; Cohen's school-level *d*=.69).

Evaluations in the United States

The effectiveness of OBPP has been evaluated in two relatively large-scale studies in the US. The first took place in the mid-1990s and involved elementary and middle schools in six rural school districts in South Carolina with high percentages of African American students (Limber, Nation, Tracy, Melton, & Flerx, 2004). In addition, Bauer, Lozano, and Rivara (2007) used a nonrandomized controlled design to evaluate the OBPP with seven intervention and three control schools in Washington State (see Olweus & Limber, 2010a for more details). Although results from these US studies were encouraging, it is also clear that the findings were not uniformly positive, providing both positive and some negative outcomes.

Concern about lack of positive effects of anti-bullying programmes in the US is also echoed in a recent review of evaluations of bullying prevention programmes (Evans, Fraser, & Cotter, 2014), which was completed after the Ttofi and Farrington meta-analysis (2009, 2011) In spite of some limitations of the studies included, it is worth noting that six of the eight studies examining bullying victimization with non-significant results were conducted in the US, as were six of the ten non-significant studies examining bullying perpetration. Several US researchers have expressed doubt about the usefulness and likely success of bullying prevention efforts in general, and in particular of programmes implemented in the US which had been developed outside the US (e.g. Cohen, Espelage, Twemlow, Berkowitz, & Comer, 2015; Espelage, King, & Colbert, 2018; Hong & Espelage, 2012).

In view of these concerns, there was obviously a marked need for a new large-scale study of the OBPP in the US, in which the programme had been systematically implemented over a period of at least two years and data from a sample of appropriate size had been adequately analysed with multilevel techniques taking clustering effects into account. The results of such a study has recently been published (Limber et al., 2018), and here we provide a brief summary of the main findings.

Using the extended age-cohort design, two major sets of analyses were conducted, one based on 210 schools followed over two years (Study 1; n= 70,998 at baseline) and the other following a subsample of 95 schools over three years (Study 2; n= 31,675 at baseline). Schools were located in 49 counties in central and western Pennsylvania. The Mplus 7.0 programme was used to analyse the data which had a multilevel structure, with students nested in schools, and programme effects based on highly reliable school-aggregated outcome variables.

For almost all grades, there were clear reductions in the two key dimensions: being bullied and bullying other students. Results were generally consistent for both global questions and scale scores. Average absolute change amounted to approximately 3%, implying, conservatively, that almost 2,000 students had escaped being bullied in the two-year study (and, very likely, more). A similar number of students had stopped bullying others. The majority of analyses indicated roughly similar programme effects for boys and girls and there were some indications of slightly weaker effects in higher grades. School-level Cohen's d's were large, often greater than 1.00, or fairly large.

The longitudinal analyses over three years also documented increases in students' expressions of empathy with bullied peers, marked decreases in their willingness to join in bullying, and perceptions that their primary teacher had increased his or her efforts to address bullying. Overall, effects were stronger the longer the programme had been in place. More generally, these and other reported results can also be seen as confirming evidence that the programme had achieved positive changes with regard to bullying in these schools and that the changes had been marked enough for the students to perceive them.

Given a lack of positive programme effects for Black students in an earlier study (Bauer et al., 2007), we were interested in examining the results for this group of students. Unfortunately, a substantial number of students (17%) did not respond to the questions about race/ethnic background and, due to the relatively small number of Black students in the samples, analyses had to be restricted to two grade groupings, grades 3–5 and grades 6–8. Results for these Black students were generally similar to the results for

White students but because of lack of statistical power, only one out of four analyses reached significance in the two-year study. These and other issues including programme effects on different forms of bullying (direct verbal, direct physical, indirect/relational and cyber forms) are being revisited in a subsequent article (Olweus, Limber, & Breivik, 2019).

In summary, using a very large sample and a strong quasi-experimental design, our analyses provided substantial support for the effectiveness of the OBPP with US students in elementary, middle, and early high school grades. The findings documented that a programme developed in Norway (with some adaptations to cultural and educational conditions) can be quite effective in reducing bullying among students in the US Although an absolute reduction by 2–4% may superficially not look very impressive, it means in practice that a considerable number of children and youth in the project have escaped bullying, have experienced an improved school situation, and, in many cases, have been provided a platform for a positive turning point in their lives. With these results, the vocal calls for completely new approaches to bullying prevention (Cohen et al., 2015; Espelage, King, & Colbert, 2018; Hong & Espelage, 2012) may seem a bit premature. See Limber et al. (2018) and Olweus et al. (2018) for more detailed information about the study.

Long-term effects

A first natural criterion of the usefulness of a particular anti-bullying (or other) programme is that it can be convincingly documented using a strong research design (usually, randomized control or strong quasi-experimental design) that it has positive programme effects on the targeted units within a reasonable time period. The time it takes to fully implement a programme can vary, but with regard to the OBPP, we expect that, with adequate implementation, it will usually be possible to register such 'short-term' effects within one to two years after programme start. Although it is fundamentally important to document short-term effects of an anti-bullying programme, it is obvious that the value and practical usefulness of such a programme will markedly increase if longer-term effects can be established. To the best of our knowledge, very little, if any, research on anti-bullying programmes has focused on long-term effects to date. To examine such effects was a major aim of our recent study (Olweus, Solberg, & Breivik, 2018). Here we provide a summary of our main results and conclusions.

The study compared the long-term development of two groups of pure elementary schools (with students in grades 1–7) that implemented the OBPP in 2001–2005. We designated one group of 70 schools as 'A-schools with continued use' (of the OBQ) and the other group of 102 schools as 'B-schools without continued use' (of the OBQ). These two groups of schools all belonged to the six cohorts of schools whose short-term programme results were shown in Figure 2.1.

The OBQ surveys serve both as a research instrument and as an active component of the programme, which help the school leadership and staff, parents, and to some extent the students, to get a reasonably realistic picture of the bullying situation at their school. All of this is likely to raise awareness and engagement and can help give a clear direction to the school's anti-bullying efforts.

Although use of the OBQ is a key component of the programme, we did not expect that administration of it would in itself have an effect on the level of bullying problems in a school. We assumed, however, that regular use of the OBQ in the follow-up period could be seen as an indicator or marker variable signalling that such schools had continued to follow the programme's principles and routines, at least to some extent. In contrast, schools that had not used the OBQ in that period were assumed to have followed the programme to a clearly lesser extent, or perhaps not at all.

The selected follow-up period was the four years, from 2007 to 2010, representing two to eight years after original implementation. And most important, the key outcome variable – percentage of bullied students – was measured for both groups of schools with a completely independent data source, the annual National Pupil Survey which typically collects student responses from 80 to 90% of all schools in Norway.

The statistical analyses of the National Pupil Survey documented that the 70 elementary schools (A-schools) with continued and repeated use of the OBQ in the four-year follow-up period of 2007–2010, two to eight years after original implementation of the OBPP, had a clearly more favourable long-term development with regard to the percentage of students who had been bullied, compared to the 102 B-schools that had not conducted any OBQ surveys in the same period. The odds of being bullied for students in A-schools with continued use (average of 7.1% bullied students) were approximately 25% lower (p<.001) than for students in the B-schools (average 9.2%). This result was in line with our first key prediction. The prevalence values (percentage of bullied students) in A-schools were also clearly lower than the national average in the National Pupil Survey, 7.1%

versus 9.6% (p<.001). The odds of being bullied for students in an average elementary school ('non-Olweus school') were 40% higher than for students in an A-school. These results confirmed our second key prediction. At the same time, the B-schools without continued use had levels of being bullied problems that were fairly close to the national average. All of these results clearly strengthen the construct validity of our conclusions and the project as a whole (Shadish, Cook, & Campbell, 2002).

The reported results are of considerable interest also from a purely descriptive point of view, given the fact that the national average of being bullied problems in Norway has remained basically unchanged over a period of approximately 10 years (disregarding a couple of years with clearly biased measurement, in 2012–2014) A substantial proportion of schools that had implemented the OBPP, had thus systematically lower levels of being bullied problems over several years, up to eight years after original implementation.

It is important to note that the reduced levels of being bullied in the A-schools remained largely unchanged throughout the whole four-year follow-up period from 2007 to 2010. This suggests that the A-schools had learned some important lessons and most likely had changed their 'school culture' for the better with regard to awareness, preparedness, and competence in handling and preventing bullying. This form of school development or 'organizational learning' (Schechter & Mowafaq, 2013) has major consequences in that completely new groups of students will benefit from an improved school environment in A-schools, with a significantly lower risk of being exposed to bullying.

Some common challenges in implementation

Although a comprehensive whole-school anti-bullying programme such as the OBPP obviously holds much promise for reducing bullying within a school environment, educators seeking to get the programme implemented in an individual school or a school district face some common challenges. Limber and Olweus (2017) discussed several such issues in some detail in a recent chapter. Here, we summarize a few main points from this chapter and make additional observations.

Resistance and scepticism on the part of administrators and staff

Although public attention to the issue of bullying problems in school has grown significantly over the years, it is by no means uncommon to find administrators, staff, and parents at any given school who think that bullying among students is not a concern. Some adults underestimate the frequency of bullying, while others acknowledge its existence but seriously misjudge the social, emotional, and academic consequences and costs of bullying and the ability of children and youth to effectively address it without adult support. In Norway, a good many schools have been provided an alibi for doing nothing/not engaging themselves by a small group of 'pundits' who have been given much space in the media to express doubts about the effectiveness of programmes such as the OBPP, completely disregarding the research evidence and international meta-analytic evaluations (such as Ttofi & Farrington, 2009, 2011) and several national, thorough evaluations (such as Eriksen, Hegna, Bakken, & Lyng, 2014). This has clearly contributed to a decreased interest in using research-based programmes and strategies in Norwegian schools.

Focus on simple or short-term approaches

With an increased focus on bullying problems and legal requirements to develop anti-bullying policies, many administrators/school leaders feel both a desire to address bullying and a pressure to do so in a manner that will take as little time as possible from instruction. Often this translates into school leadership and their staff adopting a short-term or piecemeal approach to bullying prevention. Bullying may be the topic of a staff in-service training, a Parent-Teacher Association/Organization meeting, a school-wide assembly, or lessons taught by individual teachers. Although each of these efforts may represent important initial steps in adoption of a comprehensive, research-based long-term-strategy, they likely will do little to significantly reduce bullying problems on their own. Efforts to educate school leaders and staff about effective (and ineffective) prevention efforts are critical.

Lack of preparedness of school staff to implement and sustain a comprehensive effort

Even where awareness and commitment exist to implement a comprehensive effort to address bullying, school administrators and staff may find themselves unready to do so if needed preparations are not taken. Molnar-Main and Cecil (2014) identified three categories of variables related to the readiness of a school to implement comprehensive prevention initiatives: (a) organizational capacity, which includes resources, structures, and organizational practices of the school; (b) implementer characteristics, which include buy-in, commitment, and self-efficacy of faculty and staff; and (c) leadership factors, which include such variables as leadership stability, an ethos of shared leadership and a commitment to ongoing improvement, encouragement of parental engagement, and a clear understanding on the part of school leaders of the programme requirements.

Issues related to schools' organizational capacity – particularly those related to limited time and financial resources – have proven particularly challenging for some schools. In the US context, for example, increased time pressures on educators in recent years have reduced the hours available for staff development in bullying prevention in many schools. Moreover, funding for bullying prevention effort is quite limited in many areas. For example, the last decade has seen significant decreases in federal support for initiatives dedicated to school safety and student supports in the US (Harper, 2017). Although comprehensive bullying prevention efforts need not require significant time or financial resources, they certainly exceed the demands of most short-term approaches.

To help school personnel determine their readiness to implement the OBPP within US schools, OBPP authors developed a readiness checklist, which assesses aspects of all three categories of variables. Systematic use of this checklist will help schools making more realistic decisions about the timing of possible implementation of the OBPP, and also, very likely, contribute to more successful outcomes over time.

Implementation with fidelity

Another challenge experienced in the dissemination of the OBPP (as well as many other prevention efforts) relates to implementation of programme components with fidelity (Olweus & Limber, 2010a). In the light of the numerous stressors and competing demands for educators' attention, it is not surprising that some school personnel are inclined to embrace programme elements that appear less demanding to implement and fail to give sufficient attention to those that may require more time, attention, and training (Olweus & Limber, 2010a). An example of one such key programme element is holding classroom meetings to discuss bullying and related social issues. The OBPP recommends holding meetings on a weekly basis throughout the school year. In these meetings ("circle time" with much use of role playing and discussions of four anti-bullying school rules) students can freely express ideas and concerns about bullying and peer relations and learn important social skills. They also enable teachers to keep their fingers on the pulse of students' concerns and learn about the power relations among the students. In addition, such meetings provide time and space for teachers and students to build a sense of caring and community within the classroom.

Olweus (1993; Olweus & Kallestad, 2010) has shown that teachers/ classrooms that held regular classroom meetings had significantly greater reductions of bullying than those that did so to a lesser extent. Moreover, anecdotal reports suggest that OBPP class meetings are a good investment of educators' time. By setting aside 20–30 minutes each week to discuss bullying and peer relations within a classroom, teachers may spend less time dealing with related problems as they arise throughout the school week. To support schools' efforts to implement the OBPP with fidelity, OBPP authors developed several fidelity checklists, which teachers and leaders of OBPP teams complete twice per school year and which are regularly reviewed by OBPP coordinating teams to improve implementation (Olweus et al., 2007).

Administrator turnover

Fidelity of implementation of the OBPP (or any comprehensive educational initiative) may be seriously compromised if there are changes in school leadership or significant attrition of teachers who are committed to the model. Building-level administrators play critical roles in the success of the OBPP, as they model commitment to the importance of bullying prevention and the principles and components of the programme; ensure that the OBPP coordinating team has appropriate membership and support; and help to ensure the necessary time and resources are available to implement the program. In the US, turnover of building-level administrators is an ongoing challenge, as more than one in five schools loses its principal during any given year (Goldring & Taie, 2014). New administrators may not share their predecessor's commitment to bullying prevention, or they may have their own ideas of strategies to address bullying, which may or may not be consistent with the OBPP or best practices. Moreover, their time and attention is likely pulled in many directions as they work to get 'up to speed' on the many initiatives in place in their new school, which may compromise the implementation of the OBPP.

High teacher turnover also poses challenges to the implementation of the OBPP. Within the US, an average of 16% of teachers change schools or leave the profession each year (Goldring, Taie, & Riddles, 2014). Training of new staff in the OBPP is a natural and important role of the coordinating team at each school, but large turnovers of staff within a school likely will weaken implementation, as time is needed to adjust to new school cultures and practices.

External evaluations

The OBPP was represented with 5 out of 44 school-based evaluation studies in the most comprehensive meta-analysis to date conducted by Ttofi and Farrington (2009, 2011). Although the authors concluded that anti-bullying programmes were effective in reducing bullying and/or victimization by a relatively small 17–23% effect, there was great variation in programme effects. Indeed, while the average Odds Ratio for all included studies was 1.36 for bullying perpetration and 1.29 for bullying victimization, the (unweighted) average for evaluations of the OBPP was markedly higher, 1.83 and 1.80, respectively (Ttofi & Farrington, 2011, Table 3, pp. 36–37). They also noted that programmes implemented in Europe were more effective than those implemented in the US. The authors further observed that 'Future interventions could be grounded in the successful Olweus programme' and 'programmes inspired by the work of Dan Olweus worked best' (Ttofi & Farrington, 2011, p. 23).

Summary

Overall, the many large-scale, replicated results reported in this chapter have shown that it is fully possible – despite a good many implementation challenges – to systematically and substantially reduce bully/victim problems in schools not only in one-year evaluations but also in the long term, up to eight years after original implementation, with a programme such as the OBPP. But this presupposes that the schools continue, at least to some extent, to use the programme after original implementation.

References

Achenbach, T. M., McConaughy, S. H., & Howell, C. T. (1987). Child/adolescent behavioral and emotional problems: Implications of cross-informant correlations for situational specificity. *Psychological Bulletin*, 101, 213–232.

Bauer, N. S., Lozano, P., & Rivara, F. P. (2007). The effectiveness of the Olweus Bullying Prevention Program in public middle schools: A controlled trial. *Journal of Adolescent Health*, 40, 266–274.

Breivik, K., & Olweus, D. (2015). An item response theory analysis of the Olweus Bullying scale. *Aggressive Behavior*, 41, 1–13.

Campbell, D., & Fiske, D. W. (1959). Convergent and discriminant validation by the multitrait-multimethod matrix. *Psychological Bulletin*, 56, 81–105.

Cohen, J., Espelage, D. L., Twemlow, S. W., Berkowitz, M. W., & Comer, J. P. (2015). Rethinking effective bully and violence prevention efforts: Promoting healthy school climates, positive youth development, and preventing bully-victim-bystander behavior. *International Journal of Violence and Schools*, 15(1), 2–40.

Cook, T. D., Shadish, W. R., & Wong, V. C. (2008). Three conditions under which experiments and observational studies produce comparable causal estimates: New findings from within-study comparisons. *Journal of Policy Analysis and Management*, 27, 724–750.

Eriksen, I. M., Hegna, K., Bakken, A., & Lyng, S. T. (2014). *Felles fokus. En studie av skolemiljøprogrammer i norsk skole.* NOVA Rapport 15/2014.

Espelage, D. L., King, M. T., & Colbert, C. L. (2018). Emotional intelligence and school-based bullying prevention and intervention. In Kateryna V. Keefer, James D. A. Parker, & Donald Saklofske (Eds.), *Emotional intelligence in education* (pp. 217–242). New York: Springer.

Evans, C. B., Fraser, M. W., & Cotter, K. L. (2014). The effectiveness of school-based bullying prevention programs: A systematic review. *Aggression and Violent Behavior*, 19, 532–544.

Flay, B. R., Biglan, A., Boruch, R. F., Castro, F. G., Gottfredson, D., Kellam, S., Moscicki, E. K., Schinke, S., Valentine, J. C., & Ji, P. (2005). Standards of evidence: Criteria for efficacy, effectiveness and dissemination. *Prevention Science*, 6, 151–175.

Gladden, R. M., Vivolo-Kantor, A. M., Hamburger, M. E., & Lumpkin, C. D. (2014). *Bullying surveillance among youths: Uniform definitions for public health and recommended data elements, version 1.0.* Atlanta, GA: National Center for Injury Prevention and Control, Centers for Disease Control and Prevention and U.S. Department of Education.

Goldring, R., & Taie, S. (2014). *Principal attrition and mobility: Results from the 2012–13 principal follow-up survey, first look. (NCES 2014–064).* U.S. Department of Education. Washington, DC: National Center for Education Statistics.

Goldring, R., Taie, S., & Riddles, M. (2014). *Teacher attrition and mobility: Results from the 2012–13 teacher follow-up survey (NCES 2014–077).* U.S. Department of Education. Washington, DC: National Center for Education Statistics.

Guilford, J. P. (1956). *Fundamental statistics in psychology and education.* New York: McGraw-Hill.

Harper, K. (2017). A new federal budget for safe and healthy schools? Available from: https://www.childtrends.org/new-federal-budget-safe-healthy-schools.

Hedges, L. (2007). Effect sizes in cluster-randomized designs. *Journal of Educational and Behavioral Statistics*, 32, 341–370.

Heinemann, P.-P. (1969). Apartheid. *Liberal debatt*, 22, 3–14.

Heinemann, P. P. (1972). *Mobbning: Gruppvåld blant barn og vuxna* [Mobbing: Group violence among children and adults]. Stockholm: Natur och Kultur.

Hong, J. S. & Espelage, D. L. (2012). A review of research on bullying and peer victimization in school: An ecological system analysis. *Aggression and Violent Behavior*, 17, 312–322.

Hunter, J. E. (2001). The desperate need for replications. *Journal of Consumer Research*, 28, 149–158.

Judd, C. M., & Kenny, D. A. (1981). *Estimating the effects of social interventions.* New York: Cambridge University Press.

Kärnä, A., Voeten, M., Little, T. D., Poskiparta, E., Alanen, E., & Salmivalli, C. (2011). Going to scale: A nonrandomized nationwide trial of the KiVa antibullying program for grades 1–9. *Journal of Consulting and Clinical Psychology*, 79, 796–805.

Kärnä, A., Voeten, M., Little, T. D., Poskiparta, E., Kaljonen, A., & Salmivalli, C. (2011). A large-scale evaluation of the KiVa antibullying program: Grades 4–6. *Child Development*, 82, 311–330.

Limber, S. P., Nation, M., Tracy, A. J., Melton, G. B., & Flerx, V. (2004). Implementation of the Olweus Bullying Prevention programme in the southeastern United States. In P. K. Smith, D. Pepler, & K. Rigby (Eds.), *Bullying in schools: How successful can interventions be?* (pp. 55–79). Cambridge: Cambridge University Press.

Limber, S. P. & Olweus, D. (2017). Lessons learned from scaling-up the Olweus Bullying Prevention Program. In C. Bradshaw (Ed.), *Handbook on bullying prevention: A life course perspective* (pp. 189–199). Washington, DC: National Association of Social Workers Press.

Limber, S. P., Olweus, D., Wang, W., Masiello, M., & Breivik, K. (2018). Evaluation of the Olweus Bullying Prevention Program: A large scale study of U.S. students in grades 3–11. *Journal of School Psychology*, 69, 56–72.

Lindzey, G. (Ed.) (1954). *Handbook of social psychology* (Vol.1). Cambridge, MA: Addison-Wesley.

Molnar-Main, S., & Cecil, H. (2014). Readiness and bullying prevention. In M. G. Masiello, & D. Schroeder (Eds.), *A public health approach to bullying prevention* (pp. 149–172). Washington, DC: American Public Health Association Press.

National Academies of Sciences, Engineering, and Medicine (2016). *Preventing bullying through science, policy, and practice.* Washington, DC: The National Academies Press.

Nunnally, J. C., & Bernstein, I. H. (1994). *Psychometric theory.* New York: McGraw-Hill.

Olweus, D. (1973). *Hackkycklingar och översittare: Forskning om skolmobbning* [Victims and bullies: Research on school bullying]. Stockholm: Almqvist and Wiksell.

Olweus, D. (1974). Personality factors and aggression: With special reference to violence within the peer group. In J. DeWit & W. W. Hartup (Eds.), *Determinants and origins of aggressive behavior* (pp. 535–565). The Hague: Mouton.

Olweus, D. (1978). *Aggression in the schools: Bullies and whipping boys.* Washington, D C: Hemisphere Press (Wiley).

Olweus, D. (1983). *The Olweus Bully/Victim Questionnaire*. Mimeo. Bergen, Norway: Research Center for Health Promotion (HEMIL), University of Bergen.

Olweus, D. (1991). Bully/victim problems among schoolchildren: Basic facts and effects of a school based intervention program. In D. Pepler & K. Rubin (Eds.), *The development and treatment of childhood aggression* (pp. 411–448). Hillsdale, N J: Erlbaum.

Olweus, D. (1993). *Bullying at school: What we know and what we can do*. Oxford: Blackwell Publishers.

Olweus, D. (1996). *The Olweus Bully/Victim Questionnaire. Revised version*. Mimeo. Bergen, Norway: Research Center for Health Promotion (HEMIL), University of Bergen.

Olweus, D. (1997). Bully/victim problems in school: Facts and intervention. *European Journal of Psychology of Education*, 12, 495–510.

Olweus, D. (2005). A useful evaluation design, and effects of the Olweus Bullying Prevention Program. *Psychology, Crime & Law*, 11, 389–402.

Olweus, D. (2010). Understanding and researching bullying: Some critical issues. In S. S. Jimerson, S. M. Swearer, & D. L. Espelage (Eds.), *Handbook of bullying in schools: An international perspective* (pp. 9–33). New York, NY: Routledge.

Olweus, D. (2012). *Olweusprogrammet mot mobbing og antisosial atferd. Personalhandledning* [Olweus program against bullying and antisocial behaviour: Staff guide]. Bergen, Norway: Uni Helse.

Olweus, D. (2013). School bullying: Development and some important challenges. *Annual Review of Clinical Psychology*, 9, 751–780.

Olweus, D. (2017). Cyber bullying: A critical overview. In B. Bushman (Ed.), *Aggression and violence: A social psychological perspective* (pp. 225–240). New York: Routledge.

Olweus, D., & Alsaker, F. D. (1991). Assessing change in a cohort longitudinal study with hierarchical data. In D. Magnusson, L. R. Bergman, G. Rudinger, & B. Törestad (Eds.), *Problems and methods in longitudinal research* (pp. 107–132). New York: Cambridge University Press.

Olweus, D., & Kallestad, J. H. (2010). The Olweus Bullying Prevention Program: Classroom effects at different grade levels. In K. Österman (Ed.), *Direct and indirect aggression* (pp. 115–131). New York: Peter Lang.

Olweus, D., & Limber, S. P. (2007). *Olweus Bullying Prevention Program. Teacher Guide*. Center City, MN: Hazelden.

Olweus, D., & Limber, S. P. (2010a). The Olweus Bullying Prevention Program: Implementation and evaluation over two decades. In S. R. Jimerson, S. M. Swearer, & D. L. Espelage (Eds.), *Handbook of bullying in schools: An international perspective* (pp. 377–401). New York: Routledge.

Olweus, D., & Limber, S. P. (2010b). Bullying in school: Evaluation and dissemination of the Olweus Bullying Prevention Program. *American Journal of Orthopsychiatry*, 80, 124–134.

Olweus, D., & Limber, S. P. (2018). Some problems with cyber bullying research. *Current Opinion in Psychology*, 19, 139–143.

Olweus, D., & Roland, E. (1983). *Mobbing – bakgrunn og tiltak* [Bullying – background and intervention]. Oslo: Kirke- og undervisningsdepartementet.

Olweus, D., Limber, S., & Breivik, K. (2019). Addressing specific forms of bullying: A large-scale evaluation of the Olweus Bullying Prevention Program. *International Journal of Bullying Prevention*, 1, 70–84.

Olweus, D., Limber, S., Flerx, V. C., Mullin, N., Riese, J., & Snyder, M. (2007). *Olweus Bullying Prevention Program: Schoolwide guide*. Center City, MN: Hazelden.

Olweus, D., Solberg, M., & Breivik, K. (2018). Long-term school-level effects of the Olweus Bullying Prevention Program (OBPP). *Scandinavian Journal of Psychology*. doi.org/10.1111/sjop.12486.

Salmivalli, C., Kaukiainen, A., & Voeten, M. (2005). Anti-bullying intervention: Implementation and outcome. *British Journal of Educational Psychology*, 75, 465–487.

Schechter, C., & Mowafaq, Q. (2013). From illusion to reality: Schools as learning organizations. *International Journal of Educational Management*, 27, 505–516.

Shadish, W. R., Cook, T. D., & Campbell, D. T. (2002). *Experimental and quasi-experimental design for generalized causal inference*. Boston: Houghton-Mifflin.

Smith, P. K., del Barrio, C., & Tokunaga, R. (2013). Definitions of bullying and cyberbullying: How useful are the terms? In S. Bauman, J. Walker, & D. Cross (Eds.), *Principles of cyberbullying research: Definitions, measures, and methodology* (pp. 26–40). New York: Routledge.

Snijders, T. A. B., & Bosker, R. J. (2012). *Multilevel analysis* (2nd ed.). London: Sage.

Solberg, M. E., & Olweus, D. (2003). Prevalence estimation of school bullying with the Olweus Bully/Victim Questionnaire. *Aggressive Behavior*, 29, 239–268.

Ttofi, M. M., & Farrington, D. P. (2009). What works in preventing bullying: Effective elements of anti-bullying programmes. *Journal of Aggression, Conflict and Peace Research*, 1, 13–24.

Ttofi, M. M., & Farrington, D. P. (2011). Effectiveness of school-based programs to reduce bullying: A systematic and meta-analytic review. *Journal of Experimental Criminology*, 7, 27–56.

Weisberg, H. I. (1979). Statistical adjustments and uncontrolled studies. *Psychological Bulletin*, 86, 1149–1164.

3

KIVA ANTI-BULLYING PROGRAMME

Miia Sainio, Sanna Herkama, Mari Kontio and Christina Salmivalli

The KiVa programme: background, development, and initial trial period

In this chapter, we introduce the KiVa anti-bullying programme which was developed at the University of Turku, Finland in 2006 with funding from the Finnish Ministry of Education and Culture (at that time, Ministry of Education) and then widely implemented in elementary and middle schools across the country. After describing the background and key elements of KiVa, along with the initial evaluation findings from randomized controlled trials, we focus on the large-scale implementation of the programme in Finnish schools, and especially on the challenge of sustainability.

Background

The first Finnish study on bullying was done at Åbo Akademi, the Swedish-speaking university in Turku in 1982 (Lagerspetz, Björkqvist, Berts, & King, 1982). In their article, the authors referred to the phenomenon as 'group aggression among school children' and 'mobbing', in line with Scandinavian languages. At that time, discussion on school bullying had not yet started in the Finnish society; it started to rise in the late 1980s and early 1990s, probably triggered by a tragic shooting where a 14-year-old boy killed two of his schoolmates in the classroom during a regular lesson. This was the first (less well-known) school shooting in Finland. The boy doing the shooting told that the reason was bullying, which he had suffered from during elementary school years. Bullying became a big concern in societal discussion and it received plenty of media attention. Three books on bullying, written in Norway and Sweden by Roland (1983), Pikas (1987) and Olweus (1986) had now been translated into Finnish, and the first Finnish, practically oriented book written by two special education teachers was published (Harjunkoski & Harjunkoski, 1994). By that time, Professor Kirsti Lagerspetz had moved to the University of Turku, where research on bullying continued.

The initial response to the demands to tackle the problem of bullying in schools was normative regulation. In 1998, the Finnish Basic Education Act (29§) stated that each and every student has a right to a safe school environment. In 2003, education providers were mandated to draw up a plan for safeguarding pupils against violence, bullying, and harassment, execute the plan, and supervise adherence to it and its implementation (Finlex, 2010). At that time, the Olweus Bullying Prevention Program (OBPP) was already implemented in Norway and the positive results had been reported. In Finland, however, such systematic and concrete guidelines were missing. Instead, each and every school had to create their own approach to prevent bullying. The trend data, collected since 1996 by Stakes (National Research and Development Centre for Welfare and Health) and later on by the National Institute for Health and Welfare (School Health Promotion Study) showed no decrease in the prevalence of students being bullied in Finnish middle schools: there was actually a slight increase over the years.

The demand to 'do something' is a good start, but not enough to combat bullying. It takes a lot of resources if every school starts developing their own anti-bullying policy from scratch. Self-invented school policies may also not provide the concrete tools needed to guide prevention and intervention actions in practice. The need for a comprehensive bullying prevention programme was acknowledged and in 2006, the Finnish Ministry of Education made a contract with the University of Turku research group to develop such a programme for schools providing basic education (elementary and middle schools, Grades 1–9). The work was led by the last author, a former student of Lagerspetz and now a Professor of Psychology, together with special researcher, PhD Elisa Poskiparta.

The basis for the KiVa anti-bullying programme had been built in years of research, especially in studies investigating *participant roles* in bullying (Salmivalli, 1999; Salmivalli, Kaukiainen, Voeten, & Sinisammal, 2004;

Salmivalli, Lagerspetz, Björkqvist, Österman, & Kaukiainen, 1996; Salmivalli & Voeten, 2004). These studies investigated the different ways in which peers who are witnessing bullying (the 'bystanders'), respond, and how their responses influence the behaviour of the students who bully. The leading idea of KiVa was to influence the whole peer group, reducing the social rewards the peers were providing for the bullies and increasing their support to victimized students. We believed that improving the general school climate is not enough: bullying should be discussed with students, making them aware of how the group may be involved in bullying, maintaining or even fuelling it, and how everyone is needed to make the change. As learnt from previous intervention trials by Salmivalli and colleagues (Salmivalli, Kaukiainen, & Voeten, 2005; Salmivalli et al., 2004), schools also needed a systematic approach to address the students directly involved, that is, to tackle the cases of bullying that emerged. In addition, there was a recognized demand for tools to monitor the level of problems and changes taking place. The three key elements necessary for effective bullying prevention and intervention work included in KiVa were, therefore, universal actions (for all students), indicated actions (for those involved in bullying), and constant monitoring of the situation.

The team developing the programme included members from the Department of Teacher Education as well. Moreover, several teachers participated in the programme development by providing feedback to the teachers' manuals. This feedback ensured that the programme was sensible and usable for teachers in their practical work.

Key elements of KiVa

The universal actions are targeted to the whole school including all students, staff members, and parents. The KiVa lessons are delivered to the students three times during their basic education – first in Grade 1 (Unit 1), then in Grade 4 (Unit 2), and once more in Grade 7 (Unit 3) right after the middle school transition. The lesson plans are described in detail in teacher's manuals (Sainio et al., 2009; Salmivalli, Pöyhönen, & Kaukiainen, 2009; Salmivalli et al., 2009). The student lessons aim at raising awareness of bullying and of everyone's responsibility to respond constructively when witnessing bullying, increasing empathy towards the victimized peers, and providing safe strategies to stand up for these peers and support them. The working methods include discussions, short videos, and learning-by-doing exercises. The lessons are accompanied by individually played online games for the respective age groups.

For teachers, the programme provides an online training which introduces the programme. The schools are recommended to have an annual staff meeting to discuss how to implement KiVa and organize the anti-bullying work in the school; the programme materials include presentation graphics for the meeting to guide the discussion on the key issues. There are also presentation graphics to introduce the KiVa programme for parents in a back-to-school-night, as well as short information leaflets that can be sent homes for the parents. Additionally, there is an online parents' guide which is also available as a printed booklet (Kaukiainen & Salmivalli, 2009). Finally, KiVa posters as well as highly visible vests with the KiVa logo for recess supervisors aim to increase whole school awareness about KiVa.

The indicated actions consist of detailed guidelines for school staff on how to address emerging bullying cases. Schools nominate a KiVa team, whose task is, in collaboration with classroom teachers, to follow the step-wise procedure involving discussions with the bullies and the victimized students, as well as potential supporters for the latter. In each case, there are follow-up meetings to ensure that bullying has stopped. The follow-ups are strongly emphasized, and with good reason; they have turned out to be essential for effective intervention.

Finally, in order to monitor the situation in the school, the programme includes annual online surveys for both students and staff. The surveys for students include questions on bullying and victimization as well as on school well-being more generally. In addition, both students and staff members are asked questions on how the programme is implemented. The reports of the results are fed back to the schools so that they can follow the average bullying and victimization trends (both their own, and in all KiVa schools in Finland). The trends, along with the annual implementation feedback, serve as tools to improve the school's anti-bullying work.

Initial trials demonstrated evidence of efficacy

The development of the KiVa programme was followed by randomized controlled trials (RCT), first in Grade levels 4–6 in 2007–2008, and then in Grade levels 1–3 and 7–9 in 2008–2009. These trials, involving more than 30,000 students in 117 intervention and 117 control schools provided convincing evidence of the effectiveness of the programme in reducing bullying and victimization especially in elementary school Grades 1–6; the largest effects were seen in Grade 4, among 10-year-olds (Kärnä et al., 2013; Kärnä, Voeten, Little, Poskiparta, Kaljonen, et al., 2011). Across all grade levels, the average reductions in the prevalence of bullying students and their targets amounted to a 20–23% reduction during just one school year (i.e. nine months) of programme implementation – the reductions were twice that high in some elementary school grades.

The effects generalized across various forms of bullying, including cyber bullying and victimization (Salmivalli, Kärnä, & Poskiparta, 2011; Williford et al., 2013). Moreover, the programme influenced bystanders' behaviours, students' anti-bullying attitudes, and their empathy towards victimized peers (Kärnä, Voeten, Little, Poskiparta, Kaljonen, et al., 2011; Saarento, Boulton, & Salmivalli, 2015). The indicated actions appeared also an effective method in addressing emerging bullying cases (Garandeau, Poskiparta, & Salmivalli, 2014). In addition, KiVa influenced overall student well-being by reducing internalizing problems and improving peer group perceptions (Williford et al., 2012). Even academic motivation and school liking improved in KiVa schools, as compared with control schools (Salmivalli, Garandeau, & Veenstra, 2012).

There were some important effects on teachers as well. After the intervention, teachers felt more competent to tackle bullying (Ahtola, Haataja, Kärnä, Poskiparta, & Salmivalli, 2012). Importantly, students in KiVa schools (again, as compared with control schools) started perceiving their teachers as more disapproving of bullying (Saarento et al., 2015).

Overall, KiVa was considered a highly promising programme, which was worth investing in. Regular contact with the Ministry of Education and Culture, as well as the National Board of Education, in the form of steering group meetings during the development and initial evaluation of the programme ensured that stakeholders were aware of the experiences with the programme and the research findings obtained. Moreover, KiVa was represented in national conferences, and media briefs were released on the positive results. The positive attention and promising results encouraged the Ministry of Education to support the wide implementation of the programme: consequently, all programme materials and pre-implementation training were offered free of charge for all schools in Finland that registered as programme users during 2009–2011.

Scaling it up: nationwide implementation in 2009–2011

KiVa was provided to all basic education schools in Finland – and most of them adopted it

Information letters about the programme and the possibility to register were sent to all Finnish basic education schools in late 2008. There were 3,065 schools in Finland at that time (Official Statistics of Finland [OSF], 2010). Of these, 1,827 schools registered and wanted to start the programme implementation in the fall of 2009 (Kärnä, Voeten, Little, Poskiparta, Alanen, et al., 2011); thus 60% of Finnish schools were reached already in the first year of dissemination. Due to limited training resources, we were able to start with 1,400 schools in the first year, while the rest remained in the waiting list for next year. By 2011 the programme was adopted by as many as 92% of Finnish schools; now also schools in Åland Island came along.

The spread of the KiVa programme was quite unique, and it happened much faster than anyone could have foreseen. In just a couple of years, KiVa was in use in almost every basic education school in the country, with an estimated 450,000 school-aged children and youth as its potential target group – we say potential, acknowledging that programme adoption does not necessarily guarantee its implementation.

Several factors may have influenced the wide and fast spread of the KiVa programme in Finnish schools. First, school bullying received high-level political attention in general. Unfortunately, there also were again tragedies taking place, namely school massacres in Jokela (2007) and Kauhajoki (2008), which may have had an influence on the political priorities and schools' decision to adopt the KiVa programme. In the media, the former incident in Jokela especially was associated with prolonged bullying experienced by the 18-year-old perpetrator who killed seven peers and the school head teacher. These incidents brought bullying heavily in to the societal discussion and political agenda. Second, the political support for KiVa in particular was certainly a factor that made the dissemination of the programme possible. The funding enabled the face-to-face trainings around Finland and allowed all schools to receive the materials free of charge. In addition, we had the chance to conduct the large-scale evaluation studies, which with the positive results attracted also positive media attention when the trial results were published.

Pre-implementation training

Two-day pre-implementation trainings were organized in all provinces of Finland in 2009, 2010, and 2011. Each time, up to four staff members were invited from each registered elementary and middle school. From the comprehensive schools (including both elementary and middle school grades) up to six members could join the training. These participants were supposed to inform the rest of the staff in their schools how to implement the programme.

The first training day included an overall introduction to the programme, especially to the universal actions. This day was specifically targeted to teachers who would start to deliver the student lessons. The second day, in turn, was tailored to train the KiVa team members who were going to implement the indicated actions. During the initial trial the trainers, most of whom were also programme developers, had visited each participating school once and met the KiVa team members three times during the evaluation year. During the nationwide roll-out, there was no involvement with the participating schools from the developers' part besides the pre-implementation training.

An estimated 9,000 teachers and other staff members, such as school head teachers and school psychologists, participated in the pre-implementation training during the three years of broad roll-out. This has probably increased the awareness of bullying and ways to prevent and tackle it among Finnish professionals working in schools. Also many parents were informed about these issues, either through information leaflets, parents' guides, back-to-school nights, or through media coverage of the topic.

Effectiveness study during the first year of scale-up

The evaluation study during the first year of almost-nationwide implementation of the programme in 2009–2010 further accumulated evidence of programme effects (Kärnä, Voeten, Little, Poskiparta, Alanen, et al., 2011): using a cohort-longitudinal design similar to Olweus' evaluation of his programme in Norway (Olweus & Alsaker, 1991), after nine months (one school year) of programme implementation, both victimization and bullying were reduced compared with the initial levels. The effect sizes were considerably lower than during the randomized controlled trial, as could be expected. There was an average reduction of students bullying others as well as those being bullied of about 15%. Again, the effects were stronger in elementary rather than in middle schools, and they were strongest in Grade 4. Effects of this magnitude, if generalized to the Finnish population of roughly 500,000 basic education students, would mean a reduction of approximately 7,500 bullies and 12,500 victimized students – during just one year of programme implementation. Thus, the study demonstrated that the programme works even without additional support or involvement from the programme developers.

Keeping it running: the challenge of sustainability

In 2016, when there was a need to update the programme materials and add some new elements, a small licence fee was introduced to schools implementing the programme. At that point, many schools decided not to re-register. Since the academic year 2016–2017 there have been about 950 active KiVa schools who pay the annual fee and have access to all materials. As the number of schools providing basic education has decreased since 2009, being at present about 2,300 schools (Official Statistics of Finland [OSF], 2018), KiVa schools now represent about 40% of Finnish basic education schools. This can still be considered a very large proportion.

The annual fee was certainly a factor that influenced schools dropping out; however, before that we could already recognize schools with varying degrees of implementation. This was seen in our study utilizing survey data from 2009 to 2016. Through latent class analysis, we identified four different school profiles based on the patterns of responding to student surveys across these years (Sainio et al., 2018): 1) *persistent* (43%) schools maintained a high likelihood of annual responding; 2) *awakened* (14%) schools increased the likelihood of responding after an initial decrease; 3) *drop-offs* (23%) seemed to abandon the programme already after the first year; and 4) *tail-offs* (20%) decreased the likelihood of responding after the third KiVa year. Although until 2016 there were very few schools that officially dropped out from the programme, utilizing the student survey (a central element of the programme) can be regarded as a proxy for active use of the other elements of the programme (cf. Olweus, Solberg, & Breivik, 2018). Thus, although the programme was disseminated nationwide, and it was available for all schools, not all schools implemented it systematically.

It is important to understand why some schools continue to use the programme while others seem to abandon it. What are the factors predicting and supporting sustainable implementation of evidence-based anti-bullying programmes such as KiVa? With our ongoing research, we aim to answer this question (Herkama et al., in prep.): in spring 2017, we selected primary schools that had been actively responding to the surveys from the very beginning on with promising results. We conducted focus group interviews with teachers who had actively taken part in the implementation of the KiVa programme in 15 schools. In the following section we provide an overview on this ongoing qualitative research on sustainability of KiVa including also some findings from the early research on implementation of the programme (Ahtola et al., 2012; Haataja, Ahtola, Poskiparta, & Salmivalli, 2015).

We focus on three aspects of sustainable programme implementation that have been brought up in previous literature (Shediac-Rizkallah & Bone, 1998): (1) the programme itself, (2) the organizational level factors, and (3) the political and societal factors.

The KiVa programme as the framework for sustained anti-bullying work

The original goal of the developers of the KiVa programme was to create research-based concrete tools to tackle bullying that are motivating and easy-to-use. This indeed seemed to be an important factor contributing to the adoption of the programme in the first place but also to the delivery of it in the long run (Herkama et al., in prep.). The teachers participating in focus group interviews referred to various features of KiVa that created a solid base for their anti-bullying work. For example, in the teachers' opinion, the systematic approach of KiVa including both universal and indicated actions offered clear guidelines in regard to what to do, how to do it, and when to do it. This was considered to be an important feature of the programme supporting the initial start.

Additionally, it seems that a systematic anti-bullying programme, such as KiVa, can serve as an educational tool for teachers, especially among those who are engaged with the programme activities. Building knowledge on bullying as a phenomenon and on its prevention increases the confidence of individual teachers to tackle bullying, as found also in an earlier study by Ahtola et al. (2012): teachers felt more competent in addressing bullying after the first KiVa year, and especially the teachers involved with programme activities were more inclined to view bullying as something that can be influenced. In the focus group interviews this was brought up by teachers when they described how the programme actually changed their whole thinking and mindset connected to bullying (Herkama et al., in prep.). As one teacher put it, 'KiVa programme opened teachers' eyes and gave courage to intervene in emerging bullying case as a whole … that you are able to see the situation more broadly, who is in which role …'

Furthermore, the teachers in the focus group interviews seemed to value the fact that the programme was being researched and that rigorous scientific studies conducted offered evidence of effectiveness (Herkama et al., in prep.). Valuing evidence was also as seen in an earlier study by Haataja et al. (2015): teachers' beliefs in programme effectiveness predicted high implementation in the beginning. However, for the long-term commitment, as the interviewed teachers stressed, they also need to 'evidence the effectiveness themselves in their own classrooms' in order to be motivated to continue with the programme (Herkama et al., in prep.). If they have a feeling the programme does not work in real life, they do not continue to deliver it. The enthusiasm of children combined with a more peaceful working environment and successfully solved bullying cases are certainly reasons to continue. Some teachers also mentioned the trend data on the prevalence of students being bullied and of students bullying others, from the annual KiVa surveys, as motivators to continue with the programme.

Finally, it seems that sustainability of anti-bullying practices is also about support, sharing, and connecting with others. The ones in charge of the implementation and actually delivering the programme long for possibilities to share experiences and best practices, learn more, and receive confirmation and support for their own actions. Although, interestingly, the initial teacher training provided for the school personnel was not a significant predictor of programme maintenance during the first year of implementation (Haataja et al., 2015), the interviewed teachers still, after eight years since the initial trainings, remembered the motivation and enthusiasm they experienced and how this was an important boost for implementing the programme in the beginning (Herkama et al., in prep.).

In the focus group interviews, teachers brought up challenges as well (Herkama et al., in prep.). For instance, although the students' enthusiasm and the positive results of programme delivery observed in everyday life at school encouraged many teachers to continue, some teachers were reporting getting bored with using the same manuals year after year. This can lead to lack of motivation over time, and eventually to programme abandonment. Therefore, some refreshing updates are needed when anti-bullying programmes are implemented for a longer period of time. Similarly, the teachers expressed that a motivation boost once in a while would be welcomed from the part of programme developers or from own school community. Some of the schools participating in the focus group interviews had managed to incorporate the programme very well in their school activities with a systematic way of introducing the practices to new teachers, for instance using an apprentice or mentoring model. However, not all schools may have the capacity for such self-direction. Therefore, to sustain anti-bullying practices nationwide, some training may be needed also after the initial trainings.

Another challenge, as we view it, is related to programme adaptation versus implementation fidelity. The teachers participating in the focus group interviews spoke about the flexibility of the programme for local modifications (Herkama et al., in prep.). This is in accordance with previous literature in which adaptations are viewed as natural and even necessary for sustainability (Andreou, McIntosh, Ross, & Kahn, 2015; Harn, Parisi, & Stoolmiller, 2013; Sanford DeRousie & Bierman, 2012). The challenge is that it is not always clear what are the essential components and elements of the programme, and what can be modified. The schools selected for the focus group interviews were not the best references for understanding this aspect as it appeared during the interviews that most of these schools had chosen to implement the programme by the book in the beginning, and the modifications they made, were eventually minor (Herkama et al., in prep.). Starting as recommended may indeed be a good strategy to adopt the essence of the programme, as it is often only at the end of the first KiVa year that teachers start to see what the programme is really about (as expressed by teachers after the initial trails of KiVa, see Ahtola et al., 2012). It is possible that many schools start modifying the programme from the programme launch on, which may risk the implementation fidelity and the possible outcomes as well. In previous studies on KiVa, the implementation fidelity has, indeed, been related positively to programme outcomes (Haataja et al., 2014; Swift et al., 2017). Thus, a strong emphasis for the recommendation to start 'by the book' may facilitate long-term adoption of the programme accompanied with understanding of the essence of the programme. Also more emphasis could be placed on monitoring not only the outcomes but also the implementation process. Especially staff surveys are underused by the schools with much lower response rates as compared with student surveys (Sainio et al., 2018). When the outcomes, such as rates of being bullied or bullying others, are going in a wrong direction, the implementation data could help school staff to recognize whether this could be due to poor implementation.

Programme implementation requires commitment within the school community

Even a good programme can fail in some school communities. First, the organizational features such as demographic factors, resources available, and overall values and working culture may influence whether the programme is sustained. Second, the head teacher and individual teachers in the organization bringing their knowledge, values, and ways of working to the organization can inhibit or promote sustainable programme implementation. And third, the situational or environmental factors such as renovations in the school building and staff turnover can influence in many ways the sustainability of the anti-bullying practices.

Among the organizational features, one of the keys for success in the anti-bullying programme implementation lay in the underlying *values and priorities of the school*, as has been brought up in previous studies (Andreou et al., 2015; Leadbeater, Gladstone, & Sukhawathanakul, 2015; Sanford DeRousie & Bierman, 2012). Also the teachers interviewed in our ongoing research emphasized the importance of children's well-being and healthy relationships, and considered anti-bullying work as essential part of their work (Herkama et al., in prep.). In addition, the values should be realized through actual implementation, which requires *time and resources* allocated for the anti-bullying work. The issue of time was mentioned in each and every focus group interview conducted. As time is limited there is a constant need to prioritize and make decisions on what to teach, and how to utilize the current curriculum. It also seemed that in order to deliver the programme components, it is necessary to place emphasis on *planning and coordination*. This meant, according to the teachers, for example, reminding the staff of the importance of anti-bullying work regularly, discussing the anti-bullying values shared and promoted within the school, and also annually sharing information on the schools' anti-bullying plan.

In regard to the individuals within the organization, *head teacher support* has been found to be an important factor predicting implementation and sustainability of the KiVa programme (Ahtola et al., 2012; Haataja et al., 2015; Herkama et al., in prep.) as well as of other school-based programmes (Andreou et al., 2015; Leadbeater et al., 2015; Sanford DeRousie & Bierman, 2012; Woodbridge et al., 2014). The head teacher of the school is an important opinion leader setting up anti-bullying values, and in determining how the resources are directed. However, although leadership is important, the programme does not exist without the work by the individual teachers. Previous studies on programme sustainability have referred to staff buy-in or ownership as a crucial factor for long-term maintenance of the programme (Andreou et al., 2015; Leadbeater et al., 2015; Woodbridge et al., 2014). Similarly, the studies on KiVa suggest that *active staff* members are needed to advocate the programme within the schools (Herkama et al., in prep.; Sainio et al., 2018): there is typically a person in charge of KiVa activities, or a small team whose task is to coordinate KiVa activities. These active implementation agents play an important role in incorporating the programmes like KiVa to the everyday practices of the school community.

Finally, any work can be harmed by unexpected changes that burden the school staff. This was also brought up by the teachers interviewed (Herkama et al., in prep.): staff turnover including change of the head teacher, problems with the school building, challenging classrooms, and so forth, can be factors that temporarily inhibit anti-bullying work. Sometimes the work needs to be re-build and the anti-bullying practices started over again. However, a well-done ground work and established commitment facilitates the process of adopting the programme again.

Overall, it is important to keep in mind that anti-bullying work is a long-term process from early programme adoption to sustained implementation. As stated by one of the teachers interviewed, 'it takes a couple of years to become a KiVa school' (Herkama et al., in prep.). Typically, the teachers interviewed considered that resources and persistent work is needed for a couple of years in the beginning before the programme is incorporated in the school system. The teachers interviewed from one school explicitly stated that when KiVa was adopted, they put conscious effort to commit with the programme instead of considering it as a short-term project. They had brought this principle from the initial training where it was highlighted that *KiVa should not be a 100-metre race, but a marathon*. These interview statements corroborate the findings by Sainio et al. (2018), which indicated that the first and third year of implementation are the critical points for the programme abandonment. Thus, when aiming towards sustained anti-bullying work, effort needs to be put into overcoming 'project mentality', which in previous literature also has been considered as a significant barrier to sustained programme implementation (Adelman & Taylor, 2003).

Political and societal awareness offers a fertile ground for sustained anti-bullying work

The initial phases of KiVa can be described as optimal in regard to the societal and political landscape for the time being. Indeed, some teachers in the focus group interviews mentioned the optimal timing for adopting the programme, and also brought up the fact that there were few anti-bullying programmes, or programmes on social-emotional skills in general, available in Finland at the time (Herkama et al., in prep.). The curriculum changes a few years after the launch of the programme, in turn, were also mentioned in the teachers' interviews as an important factor supporting the programme implementation; the curriculum emphasized even more the students' well-being and social-emotional skills, which gave room especially for the preventive anti-bullying work, and encouraged the use of the KiVa materials to teach social-emotional skills. The more recent curriculum demands and priorities, along with new programmes, on the other hand, have probably shifted teachers' attention from the KiVa programme to other newer projects and programmes (Herkama et al., in prep.). This can, unfortunately, also mean a lower level implementation of the KiVa programme, various modifications being made to the programme (e.g. combining lesson goals and contents with other programmes), or even reducing anti-bullying work in general. The programme compatibility with the curriculum has been mentioned also in previous literature on sustainability (Andreou et al., 2015; Cunningham et al., 2016; Leadbeater et al., 2015).

Even though most teachers view anti-bullying work as important, the busy curriculum work rarely allows time for anything extra. Therefore, the message from politicians and education providers should be that anti-bullying work is essential, and it should be embedded in the curriculum.

The impact and legacy

The KiVa anti-bullying programme has now been implemented for 9 years in numerous Finnish schools providing basic education, and for 11 years in the schools that participated in the initial trial. KiVa has also been exported to numerous other countries where international partners provide the programme for local schools and certified KiVa trainers train and support the school personnel. At present, KiVa is being implemented in 19 countries (see www.kivaprogram.net), and promising results have been achieved in the countries where evaluation studies have been conducted (e.g. Nocentini & Menesini, 2016; Swift et al., 2017; Treial, 2016).

In Finland, thousands of teachers have participated in the pre-implementation training or other training days organized by programme developers. The key message of KiVa, the idea that bystanders are the key in putting an end to bullying, is widespread among educators as well as students. Finnish teachers' knowledge about bullying and its mechanisms has increased to some extent and possibly they are better equipped to prevent and tackle it. Moreover, they have concrete tools for doing so, and an understanding of the need for systematic work against bullying.

Importantly, the levels of bullying and victimization have continued to decrease in KiVa schools responding to the annual student surveys. It can be seen in Figure 3.1, based on annual student survey data collected during 2009–2017 from Grades 1–9, that the number of years a school has implemented the KiVa programme is associated with lower prevalence rates of students being bullied and those bullying others. In other words, the baseline

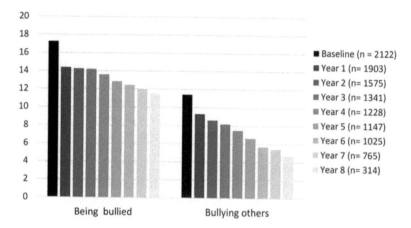

FIGURE 3.1 The percentages of students being bullied and bullying others in KiVa schools, by the number of years a school has implemented the KiVa programme (*n* = numbers of schools responding to annual student surveys; both elementary and middle schools included).

rates (data collected in the spring before starting to implement the programme) are the highest, whereas the rates in schools that have implemented KiVa for eight years are the lowest. In addition, data from the nationwide School Health Promotion Study by the Centre for Health and Welfare indicate that a turning point on victimization took place in 2009, that is, when the KiVa programme was disseminated across Finland: a slight upward trend in victimization in middle schools (until 2017, this survey only concerned middle school students, i.e. Grades 7–9) turned into a downward trend, and this trend has continued (Halme, Hedman, Ikonen, & Rajala, 2018).

There are negative voices as well. The once-so-positive media attention has also included criticism directed towards the KiVa programme. For instance, cases of bullying are brought up and discussed in the media in a sceptical tone: 'How come there is still bullying, if KiVa is effective?' In other words, news on the findings regarding the effects of KiVa have set the expectations high, and this leads to disappointments when bullying is observed. It is natural that the statistics showing decreases in the overall levels of bullying are neither helpful nor convincing for students who are still bullied – or to their parents. Research actually suggests that victimized students may be especially maladjusted in contexts where the overall level of victimization decreases (Garandeau, Lee, & Salmivalli, 2018), a phenomenon which has been referred to as 'healthy context paradox' (Salmivalli, 2018). This is certainly a concern, and it implies that we should find better ways to tackle the cases of bullying that are particularly challenging. Moreover, school staff need to be informed about this finding, so that they would be more discreet when discussing with students and parents about the positive trends in victimization in their school.

In order for implementation to be sustained, a programme needs to be updated and developed. We have updated the materials in 2017–18 and included new elements such as face-to-face games played in student teams utilizing mobile devices. These games are designed to stimulate discussion among students about key topics involved in KiVa lessons. We have also introduced an application (KiVApp) to guide KiVa team members as they are tackling the cases of bullying. Moreover, we have sought for cost-effective ways to train and motivate teachers; thus, since spring 2017, we have been organizing short webinars from two to four times a year for teachers on different topics. This way, we can offer tips for KiVa teams and teachers who deliver lessons, provide information based on our ongoing research, spread information on important topics such as cyberbullying, and boost the schools in their anti-bullying work in general.

It is also clear that face-to-face trainings are called for. After the initial trainings, we provided kick-off trainings around Finland in 2012. The biennial KiVa Days in Turku, in turn, offer possibilities for connecting and sharing ideas with other KiVa-teachers. By offering both basic and advanced training during the KiVa Days, teachers with different backgrounds gain motivation to continue with the programme. In 2018–19, with funding from the National Board of Education, we plan to organize training in various provinces in Finland on tackling challenging bullying cases.

Lessons learnt

Rigorous evaluation studies, years of successful implementation in Finland, and increasing use abroad show that a programme like KiVa can be effective and feasible, as it guides and facilitates successful anti-bullying work in schools. It is clear that the success of KiVa would have not been possible without the collaboration between policy-makers, researchers, and practitioners. Effort from all of these parties has been crucial in all phases of implementation, that is in developing, evaluating, disseminating, and sustaining the programme. Moreover, the way the programme is presented in the media can be important. This image can, at least to some degree, be influenced by the conscious effort by politicians and researchers, as well as by the educators using the programme. The programme misuse, in turn, may threaten the positive image. For instance, a school using the label of KiVa while not actually using the programme properly may lead to negative views concerning the programme. Schools, in turn, should have, from the beginning, realistic expectations of the programme, and also deliver these expectations to parents: the programme is not a magic wand, but requires hard work and everyone's involvement in anti-bullying actions. Importantly, it is crucial to understand that being a KiVa school does not mean that bullying does not occur at all. The programme offers tools for the school personnel, whose responsibility is to do their best in utilizing the tools appropriately.

During the past years, we have learnt that although school staff typically state that anti-bullying work is one of their priorities, several other responsibilities may prevent the individual staff members working accordingly. Therefore, it is important that explicit education policies are set to guide both preventive and interventive anti-bullying work, and also the usage of appropriate tools is required. Clear recommendation to use evidence-based programmes while also making them available for schools would be important. Moreover, emphasizing the need for schools to monitor and reflect on the possible positive steps taken in anti-bullying work over the years could also be done through education policies. Following the trends of being bullied and bullying others in relation to clear measures of implementation of specific anti-bullying practices may be motivating for schools, and also guide individual schools in the right direction.

Research is naturally needed to develop and evaluate evidence-based programmes. Looking back, if we had more time in the development phase, it would have been ideal to test the unique elements of KiVa (such as particular student lessons, even particular activities within lessons) separately from each other and optimize the programme contents before evaluating it as a whole. Schools have limited time and resources, thus asking less would reduce the burden and could even enhance programme implementation. More research is also needed on how individual students and classrooms moderate the effects of different programme components in order to understand under which conditions the programme is effective. Moreover, although some research is available supporting the theory behind the KiVa programme (e.g. Saarento et al., 2015), it would be important to examine more extensively what are the essential elements that effective anti-bullying work requires.

It is also clear that to achieve long-term benefits from anti-bullying work, just developing an evidence-based programme is insufficient. The problem is that many prevention programmes that were proven to be effective in short-term trials are never scaled up or sustained. Funding is typically available for programme development and evaluation; and politicians and policy-makers are often eager to introduce new innovations rather than making the best of the already existing ones by supporting their implementation and development. While the broad dissemination of KiVa was possible with the support by the Ministry, this initial support may not be enough as highlighted in our current research; in many schools additional support is needed during the first couple of years so that the programme gets well incorporated in the school activities. Thus, allocating funding additionally to support sustainable implementation would be advisable. Within the school communities, in turn, the school staff should, from the beginning on, avoid considering the programmes introduced as passing projects, but commit from the programme launch on, and make an explicit attempt to incorporate the chosen practices into schools' everyday activities. Raising anti-bullying values and putting effort in to planning and coordinating the activities in the beginning are crucial for sustained anti-bullying work.

Also research should be extended from initial evaluation trials to examine factors predicting sustainability. There are still plenty of questions waiting to be investigated. For instance, we have little understanding about the schools that abandon anti-bullying practices that they have once chosen to implement. Although the annual surveys of the KiVa programme include questions on implementation of the programme, these were added only one or two years after the schools started, thus basically lacking responses from the drop-outs. Organizational factors should be examined already before the implementation starts, in order to better understand the factors related to programme sustainability, and to find ways to support the schools on the way. Moreover, motivating school staff to monitor their implementation (i.e. systematically respond to staff surveys) and to regularly reflect on their own practices could enhance their competence to self-direct their anti-bullying work. And overall, by putting more effort in collecting implementation data, it would be possible to gain deeper understanding on the critical elements of the programme as well as on programme adaptability, that is, to what extent the programme can be modified without compromising effectiveness.

All in all, many promising anti-bullying initiatives have been introduced in recent years but less is known about their sustainability in the long run. Research could offer important standpoints for school staff and policy-makers on what is needed when effective anti-bullying practices are sought, chosen, implemented, and finally sustained. Clearly, given the efforts invested in developing various programmes, research addressing how to best capitalize on these investments would be a worthwhile effort.

Acknowledgment

The writing of this chapter was supported by the Academy of Finland Research Flagship INVEST (decision number: 320162).

References

Adelman, H. S., & Taylor, L. (2003). On sustainability of project innovations as systemic change. *Journal of Educational and Psychological Consultation*, 14(1), 1–25. https://doi:10.1207/S1532768XJEPC1401_01.

Ahtola, A., Haataja, A., Kärnä, A., Poskiparta, E., & Salmivalli, C. (2012). For children only? Effects of the KiVa antibullying program on teachers. *Teaching and Teacher Education*, 28(6), 851–859. https://doi:10.1016/j.tate.2012.03.006.

Andreou, T. E., McIntosh, K., Ross, S. W., & Kahn, J. D. (2015). Critical incidents in sustaining school-wide positive behavioral interventions and supports. *Journal of Special Education*, 49(3), 157–167.

Cunningham, C. E., Rimas, H., Mielko, S., Mapp, C., Cunningham, L., Buchanan, D., Vaillancourt, T., Chen, Y., Deal, K., & Marcus, M. (2016). What limits the effectiveness of antibullying programs? A thematic analysis of the perspective of teachers. *Journal of School Violence*, 15(4), 460–482. https://doi:10.1080/15388220.2015.1095100.

Finlex (2010). Basic Education Act 628/1998: Amendments up to 1136/2010. Retrieved from www.finlex.fi/en/laki/kaannokset/1998/en19980628.pdf.

Garandeau, C. F., Lee, I. A., & Salmivalli, C. (2018). Decreases in the proportion of bullying victims in the classroom: Effects on the adjustment of remaining victims. *International Journal of Behavioral Development*, 42(1), 64–72. https://doi:10.1177/0165025416667492.

Garandeau, C. F., Poskiparta, E., & Salmivalli, C. (2014). Tackling acute cases of school bullying in the KiVa anti-bullying program: A comparison of two approaches. *Journal of Abnormal Child Psychology*, 42(6), 981–991. https://doi:10.1007/s10802-014-9861-1.

Haataja, A., Ahtola, A., Poskiparta, E., & Salmivalli, C. (2015). A process view on implementing an antibullying curriculum: How teachers differ and what explains the variation. *School Psychology Quarterly*, 30(4), 564–576. https://doi:10.1037/spq0000121.

Haataja, A., Voeten, M., Boulton, A. J., Ahtola, A., Poskiparta, E., & Salmivalli, C. (2014). The KiVa antibullying curriculum and outcome: Does fidelity matter? *Journal of School Psychology*, 52(5), 479–493. http://dx.doi:10.1016/j.jsp.2014.07.001.

Halme, N., Hedman, L., Ikonen, R., & Rajala, R. (2018). *Lasten ja nuorten hyvinvointi 2017 – Kouluterveyskyselyn tuloksia* [Welfare of children and youth 2017 – Results from the School Health Promotion Study]. Helsinki: Center of Health and Welfare.

Harjunkoski, S.-M., & Harjunkoski, R. (1994). *Kiusanhenki lapsen kengissä: koulukiusaaminen - haaste kasvattajalle* [A bully in a child's shoes. Bullying at school – a challenge to an educator]. Helsinki: Kirjapaja.

Harn, B., Parisi, D., & Stoolmiller, M. (2013). Balancing fidelity with flexibility and fit: What do we really know about fidelity of implementation in schools? *Exceptional Children*, 79(2), 181–193. https://doi:10.1177/001440291307900204.

Herkama, S., Kontio, M., Sainio, M., Turunen, T., Poskiparta, E., & Salmivalli, C. (in prep.). Promoting and inhibiting factors of sustainable implementation: The case KiVa antibullying program. Manuscript in preparation.

Kärnä, A., Voeten, M., Little, T. D., Alanen, E., Poskiparta, E., & Salmivalli, C. (2013). Effectiveness of the KiVa antibullying program: Grades 1–3 and 7–9. *Journal of Educational Psychology*, 105(2), 535–551. https://doi:10.1037/a0030417.

Kärnä, A., Voeten, M., Little, T. D., Poskiparta, E., Alanen, E., & Salmivalli, C. (2011). Going to scale: A nonrandomized nationwide trial of the KiVa anti-bullying program for grades 1–9. *Journal of Consulting and Clinical Psychology*, 79(6), 796–805. https://doi:10.1037/a0029174.

Kärnä, A., Voeten, M., Little, T. D., Poskiparta, E., Kaljonen, A., & Salmivalli, C. (2011). A large-scale evaluation of the KiVa antibullying program: Grades 4–6. *Child Development*, 82(1), 311–330. https://doi:10.1111/j.1467-8624.2010.01557.x.

Kaukiainen, A., & Salmivalli, C. (2009). *KiVa: Parents' guide*. Turku, Finland: Finnish Ministry of Education and Culture.

Lagerspetz, K. M. J., Björkqvist, K., Berts, M., & King, E. (1982). Group aggression among school children in three schools. *Scandinavian Journal of Psychology*, 23(1), 45–52. https://doi:10.1111/j.1467-9450.1982.tb00412.x.

Leadbeater, B. J., Gladstone, E. J., & Sukhawathanakul, P. (2015). Planning for sustainability of an evidence-based mental health promotion program in Canadian elementary schools. *American Journal of Community Psychology*, 56(1–2), 120–133. https://doi:10.1007/s10464-015-9737-8.

Nocentini, A., & Menesini, E. (2016). KiVa anti-bullying program in Italy: Evidence of effectiveness in a randomized control trial. *Prevention Science*, 17(8), 1012–1023. https://doi:10.1007/s11121-016-0690-z.

Official Statistics of Finland [OSF]. (2010). Providers of education and educational institutions [e-publication]. Retrieved 19 January 2017, from wwwstat.fi/til/kjarj/2009/kjarj_2009_2010-02-18_tie_001_fi.html.

Official Statistics of Finland [OSF]. (2018). Providers of education and educational institutions [e-publication]. Retrieved 22 June 2018, from wwwstat.fi/til/kjarj/index_en.html.

Olweus, D. (1986). *Mobbning: Vad vi vet och vad vi kan göra* [Bullying: What we know and what we can do]. Falköping: Liber Utbildningsförlaget.

Olweus, D., & Alsaker, F. D. (1991). Assessing change in a cohort-longitudinal study with hierarchical data. In B. Torestad, D. Magnusson, L. R. Bergman, & G. Rudinger (Eds.), *Problems and methods in longitudinal research* (pp. 107–132). Cambridge: Cambridge University Press. https://doi:10.1017/CBO9780511663260.008.

Olweus, D., Solberg, M. E., & Breivik, K. (2018). Long-term school-level effects of the Olweus Bullying Prevention Program (OBPP). *Scandinavian Journal of Psychology*. Advanced online publication. https://doi:10.1111/sjop.12486.

Pikas, A. (1987). *Så bekämpar vi mobbning i skolan* [So we fight bullying in school]. Uppsala: AMA dataservice.

Roland, E. (1983). *Strategi mot mobbing* [Stragety against bullying] (2. oppl). Stavanger: Universitetsforlaget.

Saarento, S., Boulton, A. J., & Salmivalli, C. (2015). Reducing bullying and victimization: Student- and classroom-level mechanisms of change. *Journal of Abnormal Child Psychology*, 43(1), 61–76. https://doi:10.1007/s10802-013-9841-x.

Sainio, M., Herkama, S., Turunen, T., Rönkkö, M., Kontio, M., Poskiparta, E., & Salmivalli, C. (2018). Sustainable antibullying program implementation: School profiles and predictors. Advanced online publication. *Scandinavian Journal of Psychology*. https://doi:10.1111/sjop.12487.

Sainio, M., Kaukiainen, A., Willför-Nyman, U., Annevirta, T., Pöyhönen, V., & Salmivalli, C. (2009). *KiVa: Teacher's guide, unit 3*. Turku, Finland: University of Turku, Psychology Department.

Salmivalli, C. (1999). Participant role approach to school bullying: Implications for interventions. *Journal of Adolescence*, 22(4), 453–459. https://doi:10.1006/jado.1999.0239.

Salmivalli, C. (2018). Peer victimization and adjustment in young adulthood: Commentary on the special section. *Journal of Abnormal Child Psychology*, 46(1), 67–72. https://doi:10.1007/s10802-017-0372-8.

Salmivalli, C., & Voeten, M. (2004). Connections between attitudes, group norms, and behaviour in bullying situations. *International Journal of Behavioral Development*, 28(3), 246–258.

Salmivalli, C., Garandeau, C. F., & Veenstra, R. (2012). KiVa anti-bullying program: Implications for school adjustment. In A. M. Ryan & G. W. Ladd (Eds.), *Peer relationships and adjustment at school* (pp. 279–307). Charlotte, NC: Information Age Pub.

Salmivalli, C., Kärnä, A., & Poskiparta, E. (2011). Counteracting bullying in Finland: The KiVa program and its effects on different forms of being bullied. *International Journal of Behavioral Development*, 35(5), 405–411. https://doi:10.1177/0165025411407457.

Salmivalli, C., Kaukiainen, A., & Voeten, M. (2005). Anti-bullying intervention: Implementation and outcome. *British Journal of Educational Psychology*, 75(3), 465–487. https://doi:10.1348/000709905X26011.

Salmivalli, C., Kaukiainen, A., Voeten, M., & Sinisammal, M. (2004). Targeting the group as a whole: The Finnish anti-bullying intervention. In P. K. Smith, D. Pepler, & K. Rigby (Eds.), *Bullying in schools: How successful can interventions be* (pp. 251–274). Cambridge: Cambridge University Press. https://doi:10.1017/CBO9780511584466.014.

Salmivalli, C., Lagerspetz, K., Björkqvist, K., Österman, K., & Kaukiainen, A. (1996). Bullying as a group process: Participant roles and their relations to social status within the group. *Aggressive Behavior*, 22(1), 1–15.

Salmivalli, C., Pöyhönen, V., & Kaukiainen, A. (2009). *KiVa: Teacher's guide, unit 2.* Turku, Finland: University of Turku, Psychology Department.

Sanford DeRousie, R. M., & Bierman, K. L. (2012). Examining the sustainability of an evidence-based preschool curriculum: The REDI program. *Early Childhood Research Quarterly*, 27(1), 55–65. https://doi:10.1016/j.ecresq.2011.07.003.

Shediac-Rizkallah, M. C., & Bone, L. R. (1998). Planning for the sustainability of community-based health programs: Conceptual frameworks and future directions for research, practice and policy. *Health Education Research*, 13(1), 87–108.

Swift, L. E., Hubbard, J. A., Bookhout, M. K., Grassetti, S. N., Smith, M. A., & Morrow, M. T. (2017). Teacher factors contributing to dosage of the KiVa anti-bullying program. *Journal of School Psychology*, 65, 102–115.

Treial, K. (2016). KiVa kiusamisvastase programmi prooviuuring Eestis: kaheaastase klaster-randomiseeritud kontrollkatse tulemused [Pilot study on the KiVa anti-bullying program in Estonia: Results of a two-year cluster-randomized control study]. *Eesti Haridusteaduste Ajakiri. Estonian Journal of Education*, 4(2), 191–222. https://doi:10.12697/eha.2016.4.2.08.

Williford, A., Boulton, A., Noland, B., Little, T. D., Kärnä, A., & Salmivalli, C. (2012). Effects of the KiVa anti-bullying program on adolescents' depression, anxiety, and perception of peers. *Journal of Abnormal Child Psychology*, 40(2), 289–300. https://doi:10.1007/s10802-011-9551-1.

Williford, A., Elledge, L. C., Boulton, A. J., DePaolis, K. J., Little, T. D., & Salmivalli, C. (2013). Effects of the KiVa antibullying program on cyberbullying and cybervictimization frequency among Finnish youth. *Journal of Clinical Child & Adolescent Psychology*, 42(6), 820–833. https://doi:10.1080/15374416.2013.787623.

Woodbridge, M. W., Sumi, W. C., Yu, J., Rouspil, K., Javitz, H. S., Seeley, J. R., & Walker, H. M. (2014). Implementation and sustainability of an evidence-based program: Lessons learned from the PRISM applied to First Step to Success. *Journal of Emotional and Behavioral Disorders*, 22(2), 95–106. https://doi:10.1177/1063426613520456.

4

LESSONS LEARNED FROM THE NATIONAL IMPLEMENTATION AND INTERNATIONAL DISSEMINATION OF THE ViSC SOCIAL COMPETENCE PROGRAMME

Dagmar Strohmeier and Christiane Spiel

International research on bullying has grown considerably in the last decades (Smith, 2016) demonstrating that bullying is a severe problem in schools all over the world (Inchley et al., 2016). Bullying is characterized by (1) intentional harm doing, (2) repetition, and (3) imbalance of power (e.g. Olweus, 1978; 1991; Roland, 1989) and includes a variety of negative acts that can be carried out face-to-face, by indirect or relational means or by electronic forms of contact (Smith et al., 2008). From a socio-ecological perspective, bullying is understood as a complex systemic problem with mechanisms operating on several interacting levels (Bronfenbrenner, 1979; Swearer & Espelage, 2004). Consequently, socio-ecological preventive intervention programmes not only target individual students but also aim to change the class and school environment within a whole school transformation process (Gradinger & Strohmeier, 2018). Competencies on various systemic levels need to be developed, and measures for multipliers, teachers, students, and parents have to be implemented simultaneously to reduce the various forms of bullying and victimization.

The ViSC programme is a socio-ecological whole school anti-bullying programme that was originally developed, implemented, and evaluated in Austria (Atria & Spiel, 2007; Spiel & Strohmeier, 2011, 2012; Strohmeier, Atria, & Spiel, 2008; Strohmeier & Spiel, 2016). Later on, the programme has also been implemented in Romania, Cyprus, Turkey, and Kosovo (Arenliu, Strohmeier, Konjufca, Yanagida, Burger, 2019; Dogan, Keser,

Şen, Yanagida, Gradinger, & Strohmeier, 2017; Solomontos-Kountouri, Gradinger, Yanagida, & Strohmeier, 2016; Trip et al., 2015). Special features of the ViSC programme are (1) the implementation model, which in addition to bullying prevention, fosters knowledge transfer between research and practice and promotes preventive attitudes and behaviours in teachers, and (2) its adaptability and flexibility, which allow the cross-national dissemination in low-resource settings. In the following, the ViSC programme is briefly described with a focus on the implementation model and the cross-national dissemination. Then, a summary of the Austrian and international evaluation results are given. Finally, we described lessons learned from the development and the national and international evaluation and implementation of the ViSC programme for translating research findings into public policy.

The ViSC social competence program

The ViSC social competence programme was developed, implemented and evaluated as one component of the Austrian national strategy 'Together against violence' in Austrian secondary schools between 2008 and 2013 (Spiel & Strohmeier, 2011, 2012; Spiel, Wagner, & Strohmeier, 2012). In line with the socio-ecological perspective on bullying (Swearer & Espelage, 2004), the programme defines the prevention of aggressive behaviour and victimization as a whole school task. Thus, the programme not only aims to change the behaviour of the students (at individual and class level), but also to foster knowledge and competences among teachers to empower them for initiating change processes on the school level. During programme implementation, several routines on the school level (e.g. the handling of acute bullying cases) are changed. The programme is implemented via several in-school-teacher trainings and a class project for students (Strohmeier, Hoffmann, Schiller, Stefanek, & Spiel, 2012).

Programme structure and target groups

The main goal of the ViSC programme is to reduce aggressive behaviour and bullying and foster social and intercultural competencies in secondary schools. In Austria, secondary schools serve Grades 5 to 8, with students aged 11 to 15 years. The ViSC programme intends to install the mission of the national strategy 'Together against violence' as a commonly shared principle in schools and approaches the school as a whole using a systemic perspective. The prevention of aggression and bullying is defined as a school development task, and the initial implementation of the programme lasts one school year (Strohmeier, Hoffmann, Schiller, Stefanek, & Spiel, 2012). During the first semester, the programme covers preventive measures and interventions at the school, and teachers are the primary target group for change (see Table 4.1). Preventive measures at the class level are introduced to the teachers during the second semester. During this semester, the target groups are both teachers and students, as teachers train their students during the ViSC class project.

Implementation model

To foster knowledge transfer between research and practice and to empower sustainable preventive attitudes and behaviours in teachers, a cascaded train-the-trainer model has been developed and applied: scientists train multipliers (so-called ViSC coaches), multipliers train teachers, and teachers train their students (see Figure 4.1). Scientists are the programme developers in Austria, or certified scientists located in the partner countries. ViSC coaches are professionals working in the school or in a support system surrounding the school, e.g. school psychologists, specialized teachers, counsellors, school social workers, etc. This approach ensures the training of professionals who are potentially able to support teachers even after the initial programme implementation. It is well known that support systems are especially relevant to initiate sustainable change, as otherwise programmes are initially implemented but then quickly abandoned (Fixsen, Schultes, & Blase, 2016). Teachers are the most important change agents and the goal is to foster their knowledge about bullying and to change their attitudes and behaviours towards the students. When delivering the structured programme modules and the student-centred interactions, the teachers reflect their own teaching style.

The main goal during the programme implementation is to create a school development process during which as many teachers as possible are committed to work together against violence. The ViSC programme aims to foster shared responsibility among teachers, which in turn implies that as many teachers in the school as possible have worked out a common understanding of the problem, agreed on procedures for tackling acute cases, and jointly implement preventive measures at the school and class levels. The theorizing behind this approach is (1) that bullying is promoted in an environment where the problem is not taken seriously or is overlooked; and (2) that bullying can be stopped in an environment where there is a consensus that such behaviour will

TABLE 4.1 ViSC course for ViSC coaches

Semester	Month	Target Group	Activity	Content	School Level	Class Level	Individual Level
1 Semester	September	ViSC Coaches	Two-day workshop at university	State-of-the-art knowledge about bullying research. Knowledge about standards of evidence. Overview of the ViSC program. Detailed instructions on how to implement the program at the school level	School Poster, Parents Meetings, Teacher Trainings, Supervision		Recognizing and Handling Acute Bullying Cases
	September	Teachers	First pedagogical conference in the school	General information about the program to all teachers			
	September–October	Teachers	In-school training	Definition and recognition of the problem. Tackling acute cases. How best to implement preventive measures at the school level			
	October–February	Teachers	Coaching of the school team	How to engage as many people as possible in the school. How to involve parents. Parents meeting			
	February	Teachers	Second pedagogical conference in the school	Reflection about the implementation process at school level and how best to continue the activities			

2 Semester	February	ViSC Coaches	Two-day workshop at the university	Reflection on the implementation processes in the schools and the professional role of the ViSC coaches. Detailed instructions on how to implement the program at the class level. Continuation of the implementation at the school level	Teacher Trainings, Supervision	Class Project	Recognizing and Handling Acute Cases
	February–March	Teachers	In-school training	Preventive measures at the class level: Content and implementation of the class project			
	March–June	Teachers	Class and school team coaching	How to continue activities at the school level. How best to implement the units of the class project			
	June	ViSC Coaches	One-day workshop at the university	Reflection on the implementation processes in the schools and the professional role of the ViSC coaches			
	June	Teachers	Third pedagogical conference in school	Reflection on implementation of the program and how best to continue the activities in the next school year without the help of the ViSC coach			

Note. Activities during one school year starting between September and July.

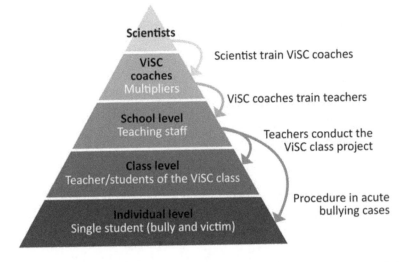

FIGURE 4.1. *Implementation model of the ViSC programme.* Note: Cascaded train-the-trainer model.

not be tolerated (for more on the theoretical background of the ViSC programme see Spiel & Strohmeier, 2012; Strohmeier et al., 2012).

The ViSC coach has a central role during this process. This person is an expert who provides state-of-the-art knowledge and introduces specific procedures for how to best tackle the problem and implement concrete preventive measures at the school and class levels. This person is also a coach who must be able to integrate the existing expertise of the teachers in order to commit and empower as many of them as possible. The ability of the ViSC coach to foster ownership of the programme by the school staff is considered central to initiate a sustainable school development process. Besides the implementation of this philosophy of the programme, the ViSC coach also offers many practical tools during the in-school training for the teachers.

ViSC teacher training

Two in-school teacher trainings are offered during programme implementation (see Table 4.1). During the first training that is offered at the beginning of the first semester, teachers are trained on how to recognize bullying, how to tackle acute bullying cases, and how to implement preventive measures at the school level. The second training is offered at the beginning of the second semester and the goal is to introduce the philosophy and materials of the ViSC class project to enable them to implement it in their classes. In accordance with the philosophy of the programme, the trainings contain many interactive elements to foster the development of a commonly shared perspective among as many teachers as possible. In total, the in-school trainings consist of four modules, as outlined below.

Module 1: Definition and recognition of the problem

To provide an overview of the lay definitions of violence, aggression, and bullying versus social and intercultural competencies, the ViSC coach prompts a brainstorming discussion among the teachers. The goal is to collect ideas without judging them as right or wrong. During this discussion, it becomes clear whether there are contradictory opinions among the teachers and whether and to what extent teachers have already worked on these topics. Next, the coach introduces the scientific perspective by discussing the broad definition of violence from the World Health Organization and the much narrower definition of bullying. The scientific definitions of social competence are also discussed. By acknowledging the previous knowledge of the teachers, the ViSC coach leads them to the insight that it is very helpful for prevention and intervention to have a common understanding of the problem and that bullying is a serious issue that needs to be tackled. Next, the teachers work in small groups and analyse hypothetical bullying cases. The goal is to discuss how to detect bullying and how to differentiate it from reactive aggression, rejection, shyness, or voluntary solitude. These discussions usually reveal that it is not always easy to detect bullying and that it is very helpful that teachers work together to get the information needed.

Module 2: Tackling acute bullying cases

It is very important for both intervention and prevention that the teachers follow a common procedure in addressing acute bullying cases. Based on the work of Roland and Vaaland (2006) and in line with their suggestions, a manualized best practice procedure is introduced to the teachers. To tackle a bullying case, the teachers need to talk with the victimized student first. Second, they need to talk with the bullying students by clearly stating that this behaviour is wrong and needs to be stopped immediately. These conversations need to be firm but respectful. If a group of students has bullied another student, the conversations need to be conducted in such a way as to weaken the social bonds of the bullying students. Third, it is necessary to inform the parents. The teachers are provided with a detailed manual including examples of scripts for how to conduct these conversations. Extending the work from Roland and Vaaland (2006), the manual also covers sample conversations with students who both bully others and are victimized by others, and their parents.

Module 3: Preventive measures at school level

Even before participating in the ViSC programme, many schools have already implemented some preventive measures. The ViSC coach aims to integrate these existing measures in a common school-wide approach to prevent violence. For instance, some schools have already implemented peer education approaches that are suitable complementary methods to the ViSC programme. Some teachers are experts in peer mediation techniques; these are not suitable for tackling bullying cases, but they can be integrated in a school-wide approach to solve conflicts between parties of equal strength. The task of the ViSC coach is to clarify which method is suitable for which goals. The coach aims to commit teachers to tackle acute bullying cases according to the guidelines presented in the manual and works on an agreement that clarifies who in the school will be responsible for conducting these conversations. The teachers who are willing to coordinate the activities at the school level are nominated as members of the school team. These teachers also prepare information sheets about the ViSC programme for students and parents. Finally, the ViSC coach works on an agreement to how best to implement a ViSC class project during the second semester. The team needs to clarify which classes will participate in the class project, which teachers will implement it, and how the teaching units needed for the class project can best be integrated in the academic curriculum of these classes.

Module 4: ViSC class project

The class project consists of 13 units divided into two main parts (see Table 4.2). During units 1 to 8, the students are trained in various social skills while during units 9 to 13, they work together to achieve a positive, common goal. Thus, the class project is not an anti-bullying programme in a

TABLE 4.2 ViSC class project: phases, units, and contents

Phase	Unit	Content
Impulse	Unit 1	What is the class project, and why are we participating? Why are rules important in our lives, and what rules do we want in our class?
	Unit 2	How can we recognize critical social situations, and what can we do to help improve the situation?
	Unit 3	How can we recognize the emotions of others, and what can we do to help them feel better?
	Unit 4	How can we recognize our own emotions, and what can we do to cope with them to feel better?
	Unit 5–6	What can we do if we are treated in a mean and unfair way by others? What is the best thing to do in such situations, and why?
	Unit 7–8	What can we do if we don't understand the behaviour of our classmates who come from another country? What is the best thing to do in such situations, and why?
Reflection	Unit 9	What have we learned during the project so far, and what do we want to learn in the remaining units? Which common activity do we want to carry out during our project day? How can we plan and organize the common activity in a way that every classmate is able to make a valuable contribution?
Action	Unit 10–13	Carrying out the common activity by creating a process that leads to the experience of a common success.

narrow sense. Instead, the programme trains a broad spectrum of competencies considered important for the development of social and intercultural competencies. In many classes, a rather large group of students neither feels responsible for what happens around them nor intervenes in critical situations. Therefore, the students are trained to feel responsible when something negative is going on in their class and to react in a way that is likely to improve the situation. Furthermore, in many lower secondary school classes there is a group of preadolescents, who are not able to manage their negative emotions in a non-aggressive way. Therefore, the students are trained to recognize their own emotions and the emotions of others and to cope with these emotions in a positive, non-aggressive way. Third, it is necessary to empower students who might be victimized easily because they might invite attacks with their unassertive behaviour. Thus, the students are trained how best to react when others are picking on them. Taken together, the programme empowers victims and bystanders, and helps bullies and bully victims to cope with anger and frustration in a socially competent way. The class project does not include units to directly change the behaviour of bullying students; instead, the class project aims to create an encouraging, structured, and friendly environment where students are able to feel part of a group and are able to create common successes.

To train these competencies, concrete materials are provided in the class manual. Each unit is designed for a two-hour lesson and consists of worksheets for individual students, sheets for small group work, summary sheets, and a detailed implementation plan. The task of the teacher is to lead the class and work with the materials provided in the manual. The units are designed to foster exchange and discussions among the students. The teacher is encouraged to use interactive games, role-plays, and other interactive pedagogical methods. During unit 9, the focus of the class project changes. To transfer the trained social competencies into real life, the class is assigned to find a common, positive, and realistic activity that can be carried out together during a project day. The role of the teacher is to create a group process that enables cooperative learning and the experience of a common success. Thus, the teacher helps the students find a cooperative structure and supervises them as they plan and carry out the activity. A huge variety of activities has been carried out during ViSC project days. Some classes produced photos, short films, songs, or newspapers. Others conducted interviews with students in other classes, people on the street, and local politicians, and asked them about their contribution to prevent violence. Still others organized parents' meetings demonstrating what they had learned during the class project.

Cross-national dissemination in low-resource settings

Although there is an ongoing scientific debate about the cross-national transportability of evidence-based anti-bullying programmes (e.g. Nocentini & Menesini, 2016; Malti, Noam, Beelmann, & Sommer, 2016), the manifold challenges of implementing prevention programmes in low-resource settings have not been adequately addressed yet. Socio-ecological anti-bullying programmes consist of a variety of measures on the school, class, and individual level; therefore, their implementation requires extensive amounts of resources that are not available in all settings. Consequently, socio-ecological anti-bullying interventions are rarely implemented in low-resource settings although bullying prevention is also needed there. As Flay and colleagues (2005) point out, dissemination is the ultimate purpose for which evidence-based prevention programmes are developed, yet little knowledge exists on the processes through which high-quality programmes are adopted, implemented, and sustained. Cross-national implementation studies offer unique possibilities to investigate (a) whether the original implementation model is universally applicable or needs to be changed, (b) whether the programme outcomes can be replicated in a different national context and (c) whether the theoretical model is universally valid.

To be able to implement the programme in low-resource settings like Romania, Cyprus, Turkey, and Kosovo, it was therefore necessary to adapt the programme. The adaptations were guided primarily by available resources but also by theoretical considerations to overcome several practical obstacles. In Romania and Kosovo, the Austrian programme developers trained volunteer assistants who were undergraduate students of the universities of Oradea and Prishtina, instead of training professional multipliers who were not available in the educational systems of these two countries. A team consisting of two volunteer assistants then implemented a shortened class project to not overburden the schools and the volunteer assistants (for more details see Arenliu et al., 2019; Trip et al., 2015). In Cyprus and Turkey, it was possible to train existing multipliers. However, these multipliers needed several follow-up training sessions in their native language in addition to the training that was provided by the Austrian programme developers (for more details see Dogan et al., 2017; Solomontos-Kountouri et al., 2016). In all four countries, the national scientific coordinator had an important role to ensure a programme adaptation suitable for the national circumstances and a high-quality programme implementation.

Program evaluation

The ViSC programme was developed in several phases. During the years 1999 to 2005, the programme consisted of the class project only and was implemented by external experts and not by teachers (Atria & Spiel, 2007). Evaluation results showed encouraging short-term effects but failed to produce any long-term changes (Atria & Spiel, 2007; Gollwitzer, 2005; Gollwitzer, Banse, Eisenbach, & Naumann, 2007; Gollwitzer, Eisenbach, Atria, Strohmeier, & Banse, 2006). During 2008 and 2013, the programme was substantially improved and rolled out in about 100 secondary schools in Austria. This large rollout was possible because of available funding from the Austrian Ministry of Education. In total, three consecutive train-the-trainer seminars for ViSC coaches were organized at the University of Vienna during these years. Furthermore, it was possible to evaluate the programme with the highest possible research standards to gain evaluation results with high statistical conclusion validity (Gradinger, Yanagida, Strohmeier, & Spiel, 2014, 2016; Yanagida, Strohmeier, & Spiel, 2016). In Austria, the effectiveness of the ViSC programme has been demonstrated in various studies and it has been shown that the programme is effective in reducing victimization, cyber-victimization, and cyberbullying (Gollwitzer et al., 2006; 2007; Gradinger et al., 2014; 2016; Yanagida et al., 2016). In Cyprus, evaluation results revealed that Grade 7 students profited more from the programme compared to Grade 8 students (Solomontos-Kountouri et al., 2016). In Romania, where only the class project was implemented by external research assistants and no teacher trainings were provided, no intervention effects on victimization and bullying were found but changes regarding dysfunctional cognitions and emotions were observed (Trip et al., 2015). In Turkey, evaluation results demonstrated that perpetration and victimization increased in the intervention group compared to control group between pre- and post-test, but also decreased between post-test and follow-up indicating a sensitizing effect of the programme (Dogan et al., 2017). In Kosovo, where it was only possible to compare an ultra-short and a short version of the class project consisting of 4 and 6 units, training effects for direct victimization were found (Arenliu et al., 2019).

Summary and discussion

The ViSC programme has several strengths. To begin with, the ViSC programme is well grounded in the socio-ecological framework of bullying and uses state-of-the art methods to initiate change processes to prevent bullying on several systemic levels (Farrington, Gaffney, Lösel, & Ttofi, 2017; Fox, Farrington, & Ttofi, 2012; Swearer & Espelage, 2004). In Austria, the programme was implemented within a national strategy, and it was possible to investigate programme effectiveness on the class and the individual level within a large cluster randomized control study (Gradinger et al. 2014; 2016; Yanagida et al., 2016). Thus, evaluation results from Austria are solid and provide insights regarding the mechanisms of change on class level and regarding teachers' behaviour (Schultes, Stefanek, van de Schoot, Strohmeier, & Spiel, 2014). Furthermore, the ViSC programme was transported to four other countries (Arenliu et al., 2018; Dogan et al., 2017; Trip et al., 2015; Solomontos-Kountouri et al., 2016). To summarize, the programme is both highly structured including a large number of materials but also adaptive to create ownership and a sustainable change process on school level.

Regardless of the benefits of ViSC programme, there are several drawbacks. To begin with, programme implementation is a very complex task because the whole school needs to engage in a developmental process. Because sustainable changes need time, it is not always possible that teachers see changes among their students quickly (see Trip et al., 2015). Consequently, several schools started disengaging with bullying prevention after the initial implementation. In Cyprus and Turkey, we also found sensitizing effects, and preventive effects were detected only in the long run (Dogan et al. 2017; Solomontos-Kountouri et al., 2016). However, our studies clearly demonstrate that schools where teachers show high programme responsiveness profited most (Schultes et al., 2012).

To summarize, the ViSC programme is effective and shows sustainable effects regarding different forms of bullying and victimization, and can be adapted to new countries. However, it is important that well-designed, theoretically sound programmes like ViSC are implemented sustainably and with high fidelity in practice.

However, intervention research and implementation research have not yet been connected systematically and different traditions and research groups are involved. This presently prevailing separation of intervention and implementation research leads to gaps within a coherent improvement process and might be the reason for diverse barriers for a successful transfer of scientific knowledge to practice (Fixsen, Blase, & van Dyke, 2011). Based on our experience with implementing different evidence-based intervention programmes including the ViSC into educational settings (see Spiel, Schober, & Strohmeier, 2018) we argue for a systematic integration of intervention and implementation.

Lessons learned for policy impact through research

The systematic integration of intervention and implementation research requires that researchers design and develop intervention programmes using a field-oriented and participative approach. How this systematic connection between intervention and implementation research can be realized is illustrated by a six-step procedure for policy impact from research we have proposed. The six steps together should be considered as parts of a dynamic process with many sub-processes, feedback loops, and interdependencies. The following brief description is based on previous presentations (Schober & Spiel, 2016; Spiel & Schober, 2017; Spiel et al., 2018).

Step 1: Identify where support is needed

Intervention researchers must not only be curiosity-driven but also mission-driven because they need to combine their quest for fundamental understanding with considerations of practical applications (Stokes, 1997). If researchers intend to prevent bullying in schools and to transfer their research findings into educational settings via evidence-based intervention programmes, they require socio-political responsibility as a basic mindset.

Step 2: Ensure availability of robust knowledge

The availability of robust evidence and sound scientific knowledge is a fundamental precondition for designing evidence-based intervention programmes. Consequently, researchers have to be experts in the relevant field with excellent knowledge of theory, methods, empirical findings, and limitations. This also includes the political dimension of research in the sense of defining and financing corresponding research topics. Obviously, within bullying research a large body of theoretical and empirical knowledge has been produced that is ready for being translated into educational settings.

Step 3: Identify reasonable starting points for action

A wide body of research made it clear that intervention programmes do not work everywhere and at all times (Meyers, Durlak, & Wandersmann, 2012). Therefore, it is necessary to combine scientific knowledge with prevailing cultural and political conditions. Intervention researchers need knowledge and experience in the relevant practical field and its contextual conditions. Intervention researchers need to know whether schools are ready for implementing an evidence-based anti-bullying programme and if not, how to prepare them (Spiel & Schober, 2017). For example, it is important that the principals are respected for their educational leadership. Readiness for intervention also requires responsibility and willingness for engagement both on the school and the single teacher level as precondition for establishing the ViSC school teams with a majority of consensus in the institution and with administrative support (see e.g. Spiel & Strohmeier, 2011). Promotable conditions for success are the establishment of basic evaluation attitudes in teachers and a school culture where failures are seen as learning opportunities (see Spiel & Schober, 2016).

Step 4: Establish a cooperation process with policy-makers

This step is a very crucial one for several reasons. Successful development and implementation of evidence-based intervention in practical settings involves various stakeholders and requires cooperation, persistence, time, and money. Consequently, researchers are forced to communicate their research findings in the language of practitioners and politicians and to meet them as equals. In order to implement prevention and intervention research into public policy, stable alliances both with policy-makers and practitioners as well as with the relevant institutions e.g. schools are needed. Respective networks should be built in advance. We recommend also including people from the media in such networks. Furthermore, researchers have to be aware of policy-makers' scope of action. They have to consider that there are other influences on government and policy, beyond evidence, and that policy-making is always a matter of what works at what costs and with what outcomes (Davies, 2012). Usually, the decisions of policy-makers are driven by urgent and pressing societal demands. For instance, to start working on the Austrian national strategy to prevent violence was possible after a murder in a school that put policy-makers under urgent pressure to take action. Therefore, intervention researchers need to integrate their expertise with these factors. Consequently, the establishment of a cooperation process with policymakers requires that researchers make their voice heard (see also Spiel & Schober, 2017).

Step 5: Coordinate development of intervention and implementation

Different research groups with different research traditions are usually involved in intervention research and in implementation research and these two research fields are poorly connected. Therefore, a systematic integration of intervention and implementation research is urgently needed (Spiel et al., 2018; Schober & Spiel, 2016). The whole conceptualization of an intervention as well as its evaluation and implementation should systematically consider the needs of the field in an integrated way (Beelmann & Karing, 2014). The implementation model of the ViSC programme clearly considers these demands.

Step 6: Transfer of programme implementation

Implementation science has emerged in the early 1980s of the last century and has been defined as 'the scientific study of methods to promote the systemic uptake of research findings and evidence-based practices into professional practice and public policy' (Forman et al., 2013, p. 80). In the last decades, many implementation studies have been conducted and several conceptual models and implementation frameworks have been presented. According to the synthesis of Meyers and colleagues (2012), the implementation process consists of a temporal series of interrelated steps, which are critical to quality implementation of anti-bullying programmes. These steps are considered for the ViSC programme implementation (Spiel et al., 2018).

Based on our experiences, we strongly recommend researchers to applying the proposed six-steps-procedure for getting policy impact from research and interventions in particular in the field of bullying intervention.

Acknowledgements

The implementation and evaluation of the ViSC programme in Austria was funded by the Austrian Federal Ministry for Education, Arts and Cultural Affairs between 2008 and 2011. The writing of the present study was funded by the Platform for Intercultural Competences, University of Applied Sciences Upper Austria in 2018. We are very grateful to the whole ViSC project team consisting, besides the authors, of Eva-Maria Schiller, Elisabeth Stefanek, Petra Gradinger, Takuya Yanagida, Christoph Burger, Bianca Pollhammer, Katharina Derndarsky, Marie Therese Schultes, and Christine Hoffmann for their invaluable work during the intervention studies conducted in Austria. We also want to thank our international collaborators who were willing to implement the programme in their countries. Finally, we want to thank all ViSC coaches and teachers who implemented the programme in their schools and classes. Last but not least, we thank all schools and students who participated in the studies in Austria, Cyprus, Romania, Turkey, and Kosovo.

References

Arenliu, A., Strohmeier, D., Konjufca, J., Yanagida, T., & Burger, C. (2019, under review). Empowering the peer group to prevent school bullying in Kosovo: effectiveness of a short and ultra-short version of the ViSC Social Competence Program. *International Journal of Bullying Prevention*.

Atria, M., & Spiel, C. (2007). The Viennese Social Competence (ViSC) training for students: program and evaluation. In J. E. Zins, M. J. Elias, & C. A. Maher (Eds.), *Bullying, victimization and peer harassment: A handbook of prevention and intervention* (pp. 179–198). New York: The Haworth Press.

Beelmann, A., & Karing, C. (2014). Implementationsfaktoren und -prozesse in der Präventionsforschung: Strategien, Probleme, Ergebnisse, Perspektiven [Implementation factors and processes in prevention research: Strategies, problems, findings, prospects]. *Psychologische Rundschau*, 65(3), 129–139. doi:10.1026/0033-3042/a000215.

Bronfenbrenner, U. (1979). *The ecology of human development: Experiments by nature and design*. Cambridge, MA: Harvard University Press.

Davies, P. (2012). The state of evidence-based policy evaluation and its role in policy formation. *National Institute Economic Review*, 219, 41–52. doi:10.1177/002795011221900105.

Dogan, A., Keser, E., Şen, Z., Yanagida, T., Gradinger, P., & Strohmeier, D. (2017). Evidence based bullying prevention in Turkey: Implementation of the ViSC Social Competence Program. *International Journal of Developmental Science*, 11, 93–108. doi:10.3233/DEV-170223.

Farrington, D., Gaffney, H., Lösel, F., & Ttofi, M. M. (2017). Systematic reviews of the effectiveness of developmental prevention programs in reducing delinquency, aggression, and bullying. *Aggression and Violent Behavior*, 33, 91–106. doi:10.1016/j.avb.2016.11.003.

Fixsen, D. L., Schultes, M.-T., & Blase, K. A. (2016). Bildung-Psychology and Implementation Science. *European Journal of Developmental Psychology*, 13, 666–680. doi:10.1080/17405629.2016.1204292.

Flay, B. R., Biglan, A., Boruch, R. F., Castro, F. G., Gottfredson, D., Kellam, S., Mościcki, E. K., Schinke, S., Valentine, J. C., & Ji, P. (2005). Standards of evidence: Criteria for efficacy, effectiveness, and dissemination. *Prevention Science*, 6, 151–175. doi:10.1007/s11121–11005–5553-y.

Forman, S. G., Shapiro, E. S., Codding, R. S., Gonzales, J. E., Reddy, L. A., Rosenfield, S. A., Sanetti, L.M., & Stoiber, K. C. (2013). Implementation science and school psychology. *School Psychology Quarterly*, 28, 77–100. doi:10.1037/spq0000019.

Fox, B. H., Farrington, D. P., & Ttofi, M. M. (2012). Successful bullying prevention programs: Influence of research design, implementation features, and program components. *International Journal of Conflict and Violence*, 6, 27–56. doi:245/pdf_65.

Gollwitzer, M. (2005). Könnten Anti-Aggressions-Trainings in der Schule wirksamer sein, wenn sie weniger standardisiert wären? [Could anti-aggression trainings in schools more effective, if they would be less standardized?] In A. Ittel & M. von Salisch (Eds.), *Lästern, Lügen, Leiden lassen: Aggressives Verhalten von Kindern und Jugendlichen* [Bullying, harassing, suffering: Aggressive behaviour among children and adolescents] (pp. 276–312). Stuttgart: Kohlhammer.

Gollwitzer, M., Banse, R., Eisenbach, K., & Naumann, E. (2007). Effectiveness of the Vienna social competence training on implicit and explicit aggression. Evidence from an Aggressiveness IAT. *European Journal of Psychological Assessment*, 23, 150–156. doi:10.1027/1015–5759.23.3.150.

Gollwitzer, M., Eisenbach, K., Atria, M., Strohmeier, D., & Banse, R. (2006). Evaluation of aggression-reducing effects of the 'Viennese Social Competence

Training'. *Swiss Journal of Psychology*, 65(2), 125–135. doi:10.1024/1421–0185.65.2.125.

Gradinger, P. & Strohmeier, D. (2018). Cyberbullying prevention within a socio-ecological framework: The ViSC social competence program. In M. Campbell & S. Bauman (Eds.). *Reducing cyberbullying in schools: International evidence-based best practices* (pp. 189–202). London: Elsevier Academic Press.

Gradinger, P., Yanagida, T., Strohmeier, D., & Spiel, C. (2014). Prevention of cyberbullying and cyber victimization: Evaluation of the ViSC Social Competence Program. *Journal of School Violence*, 14, 87–110. doi:10.1080/15388220.2014.963231.

Gradinger, P., Yanagida, T., Strohmeier, D., & Spiel, C. (2016). Effectiveness and sustainability of the ViSC Social Competence Program to prevent cyberbullying and cyber-victimization: Class and individual level moderators. *Aggressive Behavior*, 42, 181–193. doi:10.1002/ab.21631.

Inchley, J., Currie, D., Young, T., Samdal, O., Torsheim, T., Auguston, L., Mathison, F., Aleman-Diaz, A., Molcho, M., Weber, M., & Barnekov, V. (2016). *Growing up unequal: gender and socioeconomic differences in young people's health and well-being. Health behavior in school-aged children (HBSC) study: International report from the 2013/2014 survey.* Copenhagen: WHO Regional Office for Europe.

Malti, T., Noam, G. G., Beelmann, A., & Sommer, S. (2016). Toward dynamic adaptation of psychological interventions for child and adolescent development and mental health. *Journal of Clinical Child & Adolescent Psychology*, 45(6), 827–836. doi:10.1080/15374416.2016.1239539.

Menesini, E., Nocentini, A., & Palladino, B. (2012). Empowering students against bullying and cyberbullying: Evaluation of an Italian peer-led model. *International Journal of Conflict and Violence*, 6(2), 314–321. doi:10.4119/UNIBI/ijcv.253.

Meyers, D. C., Durlak, J. A., & Wandersmann, A. (2012). The quality implementation framework: A synthesis of critical steps in the implementation process. *American Journal of Community Psychology*, 50(3–4), 462–480. doi:10.1007/s10464-012-9522-x.

Nocentini, A., & Menesini, E. (2016). KiVa anti-bullying program in Italy: Evidence of effectiveness in a randomized control trial. *Prevention Science*, 17(8), 1012–1023. doi:10.1007/s11121–11016–0690-z.

Olweus, D. (1978). *Aggression in the schools: Bullies and whipping boys.* Washington, DC: Hemispere Press (Wiley).

Olweus, D. (1993). *Bullying at school: What we know and what we can do.* Oxford: Blackwell.

Roland, E. (1989). A system oriented strategy against bullying. In E. Roland & E. Munthe (Eds.), *Bullying: An international perspective* (pp. 1–12). London: David Fulton.

Roland, E., & Vaaland, G. (2006). *ZERO teacher's guide to the Zero Anti-Bullying Programme.* Stavanger: Centre for Behavioural Research, University of Stavanger.

Schober, B., & Spiel, C. (2016). Enabling improvements: Combining intervention and implementation research. In R.A. Scott, S.M. Kosslyn, & M. Buchmann (Eds.),

Emerging trends in the social and behavioral sciences: An interdisciplinary, searchable, and linkable resource (pp.286–296). New York: John Wiley & Sons. doi:10.1002/9781118900772.

Schultes, M.-T., Stefanek, E., van de Schoot, R., Strohmeier, D., & Spiel, C. (2014). Measuring implementation of a school-based violence prevention program. Fidelity and teachers' responsiveness as predictors of proximal outcomes. *Zeitschrift für Psychologie, 222,* 49–57. doi:10.1027/2151-2604/a000165.

Smith, P. K. (2016). Bullying: Definition, types, causes, consequences and intervention. *Social & Personality Psychology Compass,* 10(9), 519–532. doi:10.1111/spc3.12266.

Smith, P.K., Mahdavi, J., Carvalho, M., Fisher, S., Russell, S., & Tippett, N. (2008). Cyberbullying: its nature and impact on secondary school pupils. *Journal of Child Psychology and Psychiatry,* 49, 376–385. doi:10.1111/j.1469-7610.2007.01846.x.

Solomontos-Kountouri, O., Gradinger, P., Yanagida, Y., & Strohmeier, D. (2016). The implementation and evaluation of the ViSC program in Cyprus: Challenges of cross-national dissemination and evaluation results. *European Journal of Developmental Psychology,* 13, 737–755. doi:10.1080/17405629.2015.1136618.

Spiel, C., & Schober, B. (2017). Lessons learned for policy impact from research and interventions. In A.C. Petersen, S.H. Koller, F. Motti-Stefanidi, & S. Verma (Eds.), *Positive youth development in global contexts of social and economic change* (pp. 267–278). London: Routledge Taylor & Francis.

Spiel, C., & Strohmeier, D. (2011). National strategy for violence prevention in the Austrian public school system: Development and implementation. *International Journal of Behavioral Development,* 35, 412–418. doi:10.1177/0165025411407458.

Spiel, C., & Strohmeier, D. (2012). Evidence-based practice and policy: When researchers, policy-makers, and practitioners learn how to work together. *European Journal of Developmental Psychology,* 9, 150–162. doi:10.1080/17405629.2011.616776.

Spiel, C., Schober, B., & Strohmeier, D. (2018). Implementing intervention research into public policy - the 'I3-Approach'. *Prevention Science,* 19, 337–346. doi:10.1007/s11121-11016-0638-0633.

Spiel, C., Wagner, P., & Strohmeier, D. (2012). Violence prevention in Austrian schools: Implementation and evaluation of a national strategy. *International Journal of Conflict and Violence,* 6(2), 176–186.

Stokes, D. E. (1997). *Pasteur's quadrant: Basic science and technological innovation.* Washington, DC: Brookings Institution Press.

Strohmeier, D., & Spiel, C. (2016). WiSK Programm: Förderung von sozialen und interkulturellen Kompetenzen in der Schule [ViSC program: Fostering social and intercultural competences in schools]. In T. Malti & S. Perren (Eds.). *Soziale Kompetenz bei Kindern und Jugendlichen: Entwicklungsprozesse und Fördermöglichkeiten* [Social competence among children and adolescents: Developmental processes and their promotion], (2nd ed., pp. 227–243). Stuttgart: Kohlhammer.

Strohmeier, D., Atria, M., & Spiel, C. (2008). WiSK: Ein ganzheitliches Schulprogramm zur Förderung sozialer Kompetenz und Prävention aggressiven Verhaltens. [The ViSC program: A whole school approach to foster social competences and to prevent aggressive behavior] In T. Malti & S. Perren (Hg.). *Soziale Kompetenzen bei Kindern und Jugendlichen: Entwicklungsprozesse und Fördermöglichkeiten* [Social competence among children and adolescents: Developmental processes and their promotion] (pp. 214–230). Stuttgart: Kohlhammer.

Strohmeier, D., Hoffmann, C., Schiller, E.M., Stefanek, E., & Spiel, C. (2012). ViSC social competence program. *New Directions for Youth Development*, 133, 71–84. doi:10.1002/yd.20008.

Swearer, S. M., & Espelage, D. L. (2004). Introduction: A social-ecological framework of bullying among youth. In D.L. Espelage & S. M. Swearer (Eds.), *Bullying in American schools: A social-ecological perspective on prevention and intervention* (pp. 1–12). Mahwah, NJ: Lawrence Erlbaum.

Trip, S., Bora, C., Sipos-Gug, S., Tocai, I., Gradinger, P., Yanagida, T., & Strohmeier, D. (2015). Bullying prevention in schools by targeting cognitions, emotions and behavior: Evaluating the Effectiveness of the REBE-ViSC Program. *Journal of Counseling Psychology*, 62, 732–740. doi:10.1037/cou0000084.

Ttofi, M. M., & Farrington, D. P. (2011). Effectiveness of school-based programs to reduce bullying: A systematic and meta-analytic review. *Journal of Experimental Criminology*, 7, 27–56. doi:10.1007/s11292–11010–9109–9101.

Yanagida, T., Strohmeier, D, & Spiel, C. (2016). Dynamic change of aggressive behavior and victimization among adolescents: Effectiveness of the ViSC Program. *Journal of Clinical Child & Adolescent Psychology*. doi:10.1080/15374416.2016.1233498.

5

ANTI-BULLYING PROGRAMMES IN THE UNITED STATES

What works and what doesn't?

Dorothy L. Espelage, Jun Sung Hong, Alberto Valido and Jeoung Min Lee

Introduction

Norwegian researcher Dan Olweus, a pioneer of bullying research, defined a *victim of bullying* as usually an individual who has been repeatedly and intentionally harassed over time by an individual or a group of individuals with significantly more power (Olweus, 1993). Although many scholars use Olweus' conceptualization of bullying, this definition provides limited explanations regarding the impact of various individual characteristics on bullying (Gladden, Vivolo-Kantor, Hamburger, & Lumpkin, 2014). In response, the Centers for Disease Control and Prevention, the Department of Education, and the Health Resources and Services Administration conceptualized the first uniform federal definition of bullying for research and surveillance in the US. *Bullying* is 'any unwanted aggressive behaviour(s) by another youth or group of youths who are not siblings or current dating partners that involves an observed or perceived power imbalance and is repeated multiple times or is highly likely to be repeated. Bullying may inflict harm or distress on the targeted youth including physical, psychological, social, or educational harm' (Gladden et al., 2014, p. 7).

Prevalence of bullying in the United States

The National Center for Education Statistics (NCES) of the Bureau of Justice Statistics (BJS) collected data from 12- to 18-year-old American students who were attending public schools during the 2015–2016 school year (Musu-Gillette et al., 2018). According to the NCES, 21.8% of middle schools, 14.7% of high schools, and 8.1% of elementary schools reported that bullying occurred among students at least once a week. Also, 25.9% of high schools, 25.6% of middle schools, and 4.2% of elementary schools reported that cyberbullying occurred among students at least once a week. During the 2015–2016 school year, 20.8% of students reported being bullied and 13.3% reported being made fun of, called names, or insulted. In addition, 12.3% reported being the subject of rumours; 5.1% reported being pushed, shoved, tripped, or spat on; 5% reported being excluded from activities on purpose; 3.9% reported being threatened; 2.5% reported being made to do things they did not want to do; and 1.8% reported that their property was destroyed on purpose.

Moreover, students reported they were being bullied because of their physical appearance (27%), race (10%), ethnicity (7%), gender (7%), disabilities (4%), religion (4%), and sexual orientation (3%). The report also indicated that public schools located in towns had the highest rate of bullying (18.3%), followed by schools in urban areas (12.9%), suburban areas (10.3%), and rural areas (9.7%). Students also reported that bullying occurred in various school locations, such as in a hallway or stairwell (41.7%), inside a classroom (33.6%), in the cafeteria (22.2%), outside on school grounds (19.3%), online or by text (11.5%), and on a school bus (10%) (Musu-Gillette et al., 2018).

Bullying appears to be a serious and persistent youth problem, which requires effective anti-bullying intervention and prevention efforts. Over the years, several programmes have been implemented in US school districts, including the Olweus Bullying Prevention Program (OBPP), Second Step, Steps to Respect, and other Social-Emotional Learning programmes. This chapter will provide an overview of the OBPP, one of the most widely implemented programmes in US schools, followed by the feasibility of the programme in US schools. We then review anti-bullying programmes that have demonstrated efficacy in US schools, such as Second Step, Steps to Respect, and other Social-Emotional Learning programs.

The social-ecological framework has long been applied to the conceptualization of bullying and peer victimization (Espelage & Swearer, 2003, 2010), and it is clear that bullying is influenced by factors at various levels: individual, family, peer group, school, community, and societal. Within this framework, the systems directly affecting individual youth also include interactions of teacher–student, parent–youth, parent–school (Hong & Espelage,

2012). This offers a holistic view of bullying, but within this framework are situated process-oriented theories of behavioural and attitude changes in youth (Hong & Espelage, 2012). A number of anti-bullying interventions, most notably, the OBPP, have been guided by the social-ecological framework.

Olweus Bullying Prevention Program

Background

The OBPP (see also Chapter 2) is one of the most well-recognized bullying prevention programmes, which has been implemented in school districts all over the world. The OBPP was first implemented in schools in Norway in 1983, was developed and evaluated in a large-scale project, and has since been refined, expanded, and further evaluated. A whole-school-based programme, the OBPP targets several levels of school ecology – individual characteristics, classroom settings, and the school environment (Kallestad & Olweus, 2003), and the goal is to improve students' relations with their peers and making the school a safer environment for students' learning and development.

The OBPPs are divided into four major components: individual level, classroom level, school level, and community level. Individual level includes: supervising students' activities, ensuring staff intervention, holding meetings with students involved in bullying and their parents, and developing individualized intervention plans. Classroom level includes posting and enforcing anti-bullying rules, holding regular class meetings, and holding meetings with parents. School level includes establishing a Bullying Prevention Coordinating Committee, conducting committee and staff training, administering the Olweus Bullying Questionnaire, holding staff discussions, introducing school rules, reviewing the school's supervisory system, and holding events to launch the programme, and involving parents. Community level includes involving community members, developing partnerships with community members, and helping to spread anti-bullying messages (Violence Prevention Works, 2016).

Effectiveness of the OBPP in American schools

The OBPP has been identified as one of a few programmes demonstrated to be effective in reducing bullying, fostering pro-social behaviour of students, and improving peer relationships among students (Blueprint for Violence

Prevention, 2002–2004). There have been several evaluations of the OBPP conducted in many different countries, although the data are limited in the US (Espelage, 2013). The studies have produced both positive and negative (null) results (Limber, 2010; Olweus & Limber, 2013). However, recently the developers published findings from the largest evaluation of the OBPP to date in the US (Limber, Olweus, Wang, Masiello, & Breivik, 2018). This study involved over 70,000 students in 214 schools (five cohorts, Grades 3–11). Findings from this quasi-experimental study of a sample of racially and ethnically diverse students demonstrated that participants of OBPP were less likely to report being involved in bullying. More specifically, they found a significant reduction of bullying victimization and perpetration. 'The average Absolute Change score over the two-year period amounted to somewhat 3%. This change score can be translated into a rough estimate of nearly 2,000 students who have escaped being bullied in the two-year period (and very likely, longer) and a similar number who have stopped bullying other students' (p. 69). Also, longitudinal analyses found that students who partici-pated in OBPP showed increases in empathy toward the victims, decreases in their willingness to participate in bullying, and increases in students perceptions that teachers had increased their efforts to address bullying. The authors also found that the effects were stronger the longer the programme was in place.

Although the OBPP showed promising results in Limber and colleagues' (2018) study, it is unclear whether the programme demonstrates efficacy in other US school districts, as study findings have been inconsistent. One non-randomized controlled trial study, which tested the effectiveness of the OBPP in ten public middle schools reported that the programme had some mixed positive effects, which varied by gender, race/ethnicity, and grade, but no overall effect (Bauer, Lozano, & Rivara, 2007). Another study, which utilized a quasi-experimental design, examined the impact of OBPP in urban/suburban middle schools (Bowllan, 2011). The study reported statistically significant findings for 7th grade female students who received one year of the OBPP on reports of prevalence of bullying and exclusion by peers. However, variability in the statistical findings was also observed for 8th grade females and no statistical findings were found for male students. Following one year of the programme, teachers reported significant improvement in their capacity to identify bullying, talks with students who bully, and talks with students who are bullied (Bowllan, 2011).

Another recent evaluation of OBPP in the US examined 1,791 middle school students from three communities with high rates of crime and poverty

(Farrell, Sullivan, Sutherland, Corona, & Masho, 2018). This five-year study found a decrease in teacher reported physical, verbal, and relational aggression after the third year of the programme but no significant effects on student's self-reported aggression. Paradoxically, there were significant increases in concerns regarding school safety problems during the first year ($d=.44$) and during subsequent years ($d=.66$ to 1.22). Student ratings of the frequency of school safety problems also increased during the initial year of the programme ($d=0.18$) (Farrell et al., 2018).

Other anti-bullying programmes in US school districts

Positive Behavior Intervention and Supports

Positive Behavioral Interventions and Supports (PBIS) was created by the U.S. Department of Education and is one of the largest bullying prevention programmes implemented in the US school districts (www.pbis. org). PBIS is a prevention-oriented, multi-tiered framework for school officials to utilize evidence-based practices, implement these practices with high degree of fidelity, and maximize academic success and pro-social behaviour for all students (Horner et al., 2000). PBIS aims to produce a systemic change in school climate by (a) using a consistent strategy to disciplinary action; (b) providing multi-tiered support to the school, school staff, and students; and (c) adopting empirically based practices to create positive behaviour change (Bradshaw, Koth, Bevans, Ialongo & Leaf, 2008). PBIS is a non-curricular intervention that takes a proactive rather than a reactive approach to school discipline (Bradshaw et al., 2008; Netzel & Eber, 2003). A PBIS team is assigned to the school which conducts training events, creates action plans, and provides support to the programme implementation (Bradshaw et al., 2008). The staff members involved are trained on how to disseminate the school's behavioural expectations and how to systematically reward students who engage in positive behaviour and follow a clear system to deal with disciplinary violations (Bradshaw et al., 2008). PBIS has shown some success, as demonstrated by a randomized clinical trial study, which found that the programme was associated with improvements in students' perceived safety and academic achievement (Horner et al., 2009). Additionally, Bradshaw, Mitchell, and Leaf (2010) documented a reduction of office discipline referrals and suspensions as well as improvement of 5th grade academic achievement in a randomized controlled trial of PBIS in elementary schools.

In 2008, the *Bullying Prevention-PBIS Program* (BP-PBIS; Ross, Horner, & Stiller, 2008) was designed in order to integrate the anti-bullying programme within a tiered, prevention-based approach that implements efficient, universal supports for all students, followed by more intensive supports for students who fail to respond. The goals were to prevent peer aggression before it escalates into bullying, to give all students clear, simple, and specific skills to manage conflicts, and to give all adults skills to respond to students' disrespectful behaviours. The curriculum includes lesson plans that teach students how to respond to disrespectful behaviours (e.g. 'Stop/Walk/ Talk'). Subsequent lessons promote the use of these skills with other types of behaviours (e.g. rumour-spreading, cyberbullying). The BP-PBIS universal intervention strategies were originally validated through an experimental trial across three elementary schools. Using a single-subject methodology and a multiple-baseline-across-schools design, Ross and Horner (2009) observed a 72% reduction in the bullying behaviours of at-risk students after the intervention was delivered. Furthermore, following implementation of BP-PBIS, bully victims were 19% less likely to cry or fight back, and bystanders were 22% less likely to laugh, cheer, or otherwise join in during incidents. Since the initial validation, over 1,500 schools across the world have implemented BP-PBIS. Follow-up studies in elementary and middle schools have also shown significant reductions in self-reported bullying (Ross & Horner, 2014) and bullying-related disciplinary referrals and suspensions (Good, McIntosh, & Gietz, 2011).

Programmes using the social-emotional learning approach

Social-emotional competency is increasingly recognized as a major factor for student success and constitute the main ingredient for numerous school violence prevention programmes (Moy, Polanin, McPherson, & Phan, 2018). Social-emotional learning (SEL), or the process of acquiring social-emotional skills, promotes positive emotional management, pro-social behaviours, and the establishment and maintenance of positive relationships. Researchers concur that the lack of such skills is associated with poor school connectedness, increased behavioural problems, negative health outcomes, and a detrimental impact on academic performance (Durlak, Weissberg, Dymnicki, Taylor, & Schellinger, 2011; Domitrovich, Durlak, Staley, & Weissberg, 2017; Jennings & Greenberg, 2009).

SEL is grounded in five core competencies: self-awareness, self-management, responsible decision-making, relationship skills, and social awareness (www.ca

sel.org). The SEL model maximizes the use of internal assets and moves outwardly towards building positive behaviours and human relationships. Raising *self-awareness*, or the ability to recognize one's thoughts and emotions, is the first step towards learning how to regulate one's impulses, behaviours, and set personal and academic goals (*self-management*). Responsible decision-making is focused on improving behaviour by making sensible decisions and weighting the consequences of each choice not only for oneself but also for their impact on others. SEL programmes aim to establish healthy relationships based on clear communication (*relations-skills*) and the appreciation of diversity and other's perspectives (*social awareness*). Teaching children these skills at an early age can have a lasting positive effect on their present and future life (Catalano et al., 2004; Domitrovich et al., 2017).

In the U.S, a move towards the inclusion of SEL in school-based programmes has been largely successful with educators who are advocating for its inclusion in education curricula (Durlak et al., 2011; Durlak & Weissberg, 2011). More specifically, often SEL programmes have become a part of the required health education curricula alongside other mandatory programming. An extensive body of research shows that mastering SEL skills such as grit, self-awareness, character, and relationship skills can strengthen student achievement (Greenberg, Domitrovich, Weissberg, & Durlak, 2017; Osher et al., 2016). Bullying prevention programmes that applied the SEL principles such as Second Step Middle School Prevention Program, Steps to Respect, Promoting Alternative Thinking Strategies, Ruler, and Positive Action have also been found to be effective in addressing and preventing bullying in schools.

Second Step middle school prevention programme

Second Step: Students Success Through Prevention (SS-SSTP) is a middle school social-emotional learning programme that targets bullying, sexual harassment, homophobic name-calling, among other outcomes (Committee for Children, n.d; Espelage, Low, Polanin, & Brown, 2015). The curriculum consists of 15 lessons at grade 6 and 13 lessons at grade 7 (Espelage et al., 2015). Students are coached in empathy, communication, problem solving, emotion regulation, and knowledge of bullying (Espelage et al., 2015). The programme aims to increase students' interactions by using rich content, dyadic exercises and small group discussions (Espelage et al., 2015). In a large randomized clinical trial of over 3,600 students across 36 middle schools, reductions in fighting were found after the 6th grade curriculum (Espelage, Low, Polanin, & Brown, 2013), sexual harassment and homophobic name-calling was reduced after two years of implementation (Espelage, Low, Polanin, & Brown, 2015), and bullying, homophobic name-calling, and cyberbullying were reduced after three years of implementation (Espelage, Van Ryzin, Low, & Polanin, 2015). Bully perpetration was also reduced for students with disabilities in the Second Step condition compared to students with disabilities in the control condition (Espelage, Rose, & Polanin, 2015). Furthermore, when teachers spent more time prepping the lesson and prepared the lesson as a group, reductions were found in a global statistic of aggression, including bullying (Polanin & Espelage, 2015).

The programme has been applied internationally in Germany, Greenland, Denmark, Sweden, Lithuania, Finland, Slovakia, and Norway (Moy et al., 2018). The results of Second Step, although promising, have been inconsistent in other countries. In a large meta-analysis of US and international programmes Second Step showed significant effects on knowledge about the content of the curriculum as well as moderate effect on pro-social behaviours, but no significant changes in antisocial behaviours (Moy et al., 2018). These results align with previous research in bullying prevention and speak about the challenges of implementation across diverse cultural and regional areas (Ttofi & Farrington, 2011).

Steps to respect

Steps to Respect is a school-wide bullying prevention programme based on the improvement of social-emotional competencies (Committee for Children, 2008). The programme has a three-level approach: providing school-wide guidelines for implementation, conducting staff trainings, and implementing classroom curricula for students in Grades 3 to 6 (Frey et al., 2005). This programme is based on the social-ecological framework which posits that multiple level factors contribute to an adolescents' involvement in bullying (Low, Van Ryzin, Brown, Smith, & Haggerty, 2014). The programme focuses on the roles that the school, staff, peers, and the student play in the maintenance of aggression (Low et al., 2014). The programme instructs children on adequate ways to respond and report bullying incidents as well as how to be assertive towards the bully (e.g. STOP!) (Frey et al., 2005). Participants are also taught strategies to cope with distress and how to remain calm when they are confronted with bullying situation (emotional management).

Steps to Respect has shown promising results among children in elementary schools. Frey and colleagues (2005) conducted a randomized controlled trial of Steps to Respect among 1,023 children in elementary school (grades 3–6).

The study used self-reports and teacher's observations to measure bullying in the playground social interactions, and attitudes related to bullying. Results showed intervention effects on increased bystander responsibilities, greater perception of adult's responses to bullying, and reduced acceptance of bullying behaviours. Other study results suggest that Steps to Respect showed significant improvements in school climate, reductions in bullying behaviours, and more negative attitudes towards bullying (Brown, Low, Smith & Haggerty, 2011; Low & Van Ryzin, 2014). In a large efficacy trial in 34 schools, Low and Van Ryzin (2014) found that the effect of Steps to Respect was moderated by staff's and students' perceptions of school climate The findings suggest that staff who feel part of a positive school community show greater adoption of bullying prevention curriculum and foment trusting relationships with their students, relationships that facilitate students application of the new skills learned in the programme.

Promoting Alternative Thinking Strategies (PATHS)

Promoting Alternative Thinking Strategies (PATHS) is a curriculum-based anti-bullying programme focused on the development of social-emotional competencies to reduce aggressive behaviour. Effective universal early childhood education programmes have been associated with positive outcomes later in life and greater return for time and resources spent during early development (Burger, 2010; Reynolds, Mathieson & Topitzes, 2009). A study of the Head Start programme which uses the PATH model showed that children from poor communities that participated in the programme were more likely to complete high school, attend college, and had lower levels of incarceration than children in similar socioeconomic context (Garces, Thomas & Currie, 2002). PATHS has also reached students with disabilities and those with conduct or mental health problems having promising results (Conduct Problems Prevention Research Group, 1999a, b; Greenberg & Kusche, 1998).

The PATHS curriculum has been successful in reducing bullying in early childhood education implemented in Head Start, a programme funded by the U.S Department of Health and Human Services (n.d.). Similar to other SEL programmes, PATHS is a programme that teaches children how to remain calm in peer conflicts, take others' perspectives, and increase their circle of friends. Domitrovich, Cortes, and Greenberg (2007) reported a randomized clinical trial, and found that children exposed to PATHS had higher emotional intelligence and were more socially competent compared with their control group.

Ruler

Ruler is an evidence-based SEL programme that is supported by the Yale Center for Emotional Intelligence (http://ei.yale.edu/). The programme provides training and coaching for school staff as well as materials and resources (Nathanson, Rivers, Flynn & Brackett, 2016). The multiple components of the programme target emotional intelligence (self-awareness) using activities designed for the classroom but also for the entire school as well as for parents (Nathanson et al., 2016). For example, students are taught to use 'emotional anchors' such as 'mood meter' to increase children's awareness of their own emotions in an everyday basis (Brackett, Caruso, & Stern, 2006). In another activity, children devise a plan about what to do when they face a conflict (a 'Meta-moment'). The plan outlines how to recognize when they are upset, how to remain calm, and try to have a conversation with the other person involved in the event (Nathanson et al., 2016).

Studies have documented the effectiveness of Ruler in increasing emotional intelligence among children aged 3 to 5 attending schools from low-income communities (Nathanson et al. 2016). In a quasi-experimental pilot study, the programme also showed a positive effect on educators who reported higher work engagement, positive teacher–student interactions and greater caring emotions towards their students (Castillo, Fernández-Berrocal, & Brackett, 2013). The effects of SEL on teachers is an important avenue of research for the implementation of bullying prevention programmes. A study of the implementation of Ruler found that students experienced more positive outcomes when teachers had received more training themselves (Reyes, Brackett, Rivers, Elberston, & Salovey, 2012). However, additional studies are needed to determine the effectiveness of Ruler.

Positive Action (PA)

Positive Action is a school-based programme that focuses on social-emotional and character development and social skill development among children and adolescents from grades K – 12 (Flay & Allred, 2010). The goal of the programme is to promote positive action (intellectual, physical, emotional development), prevent substance abuse and disruptive behaviour, and enhance school performance. Lessons of PA consist of a K-12 classroom curriculum, drug education, and conflict resolution supplements, self-training kits for school preparation and teacher training, school-wide climate development, counsellors for students, and family classes for parents. The programme focuses on six core concepts: (1) self-concept, (2) positive actions for body and mind, (3) positive actions focusing on getting along with others, (4) emotion and self-management, (5) being honest with oneself, and (6) continually improving oneself. Lessons are taught by classroom teachers in 15–20-minute sessions for a total of 35 hours throughout the school year. The programme is achieved through adults (teachers, administrators, and parents) to reinforce youths' positive actions.

Teachers and students are both given the 'Thought-Action-Feelings about Self' poster to help them understand the theory of three self-concepts: thoughts lead to actions, actions lead to feelings, and feelings lead to thoughts. Teachers are also given a kit to plan 15-minute activities and lessons for their students for four days of the week. The kit includes scripted lessons, suggested activities (e.g. role-playing, plays, games, music, stories, question-and-answer, etc.), and teaching methods (e.g. role-modelling positive behaviours, and reinforcement of positive behaviours). School principals are given the Climate Development Kit to learn about how to promote a positive school climate, and they are responsible for appointing the PA Committee in their school who are responsible for coordinating training and monitoring the progress of each grade level to make sure the rates of teaching and learning concepts are the same. A counsellor and family component are also included in the programme. The family and counsellor both receive lesson kits, consisting of 36 lessons to correspond with the number of weeks in a school year. The family's kit for parents is similar to those used by teachers at school, whereas the counsellor's kit primarily focuses on education, mentoring, and peer tutoring. The PA programme is administered for three years by a programme developer, who trains teachers and staff members for three to four hours before the first year, and then one to two hours in each of the subsequent years. They also visit schools at least once per year to provide an in-service training session and hold a mini-conference each February to train a small representative group of teachers from each school district.

Results of a large-scale randomized clinical trial by Li and colleagues' (2011) showed significant reductions in violent behaviour, substance use, and bullying. More specifically, approximately 510 racially and ethnically diverse 3rd grade students from 14 Chicago public elementary schools participated in this study. Schools in the PA group received a K-8 curriculum, training, and materials. The study found that at the end of Year 3 (at the completion of the programme), students in the PA group had significantly fewer endorsements of substance use (31% reduction), serious violence (37% reduction), and bullying behaviours (41% reduction) compared to the control group.

Challenges and future of SEL approaches to bullying prevention

Despite the significant reductions of bullying in behaviourally based (i.e. PBIS) and social-emotional learning programmes, results of these programmes in US school districts have been less significant relative to those outside the US. Student diversity and socioeconomic disparities across testing sites may be a moderator of the generalizability of bullying prevention programmes in the US (Rowe & Tricket, 2018). Even when these reductions are reported, there is concern that the effects are not sustainable when the researchers opt to leave and the highly controlled trials end. Further, the demographics of US classrooms are changing significantly, such that many of the programmes may not have been developed with youth and families who are in the schools. Thus, researchers and practitioners are attempting to understand how to tailor these programmes to fit the changing student demographics in US classrooms. There are many core common components to SEL, but these need to be modified to address the school and classroom dynamics in US school districts. SEL would look different in one classroom as opposed to another classroom and in one school as opposed to another school. Further, given the racial/ethnic and socioeconomic variations of US students, SEL may be effective in one school setting (e.g. suburban schools) as opposed to another school setting (e.g. urban schools). We have evidence-based, research-informed programmes that can range from classroom curriculum to after-school programmes to make SEL become embedded within the arts in our school. How can researchers and relevant stakeholders tailor SEL to address the existing challenges in the US school system, such as inequity and discipline problems?

For many of these programmes, teachers are the ones in charge of implementing them in their classrooms. However, it is also important to understand how to prepare teachers to develop their own SEL competencies so they can teach them to their students in the classroom. Many of our new teachers are ill-equipped with their own SEL competencies and to address this, pre-service and future teachers in recent years have been trained in SEL competencies in higher education institutions in the US.

Five Ps of effective school-based research (Espelage & Poteat, 2012): enter with caution

Patience and persistence

Teachers, school administrators, and other personnel are often slower to respond to communications, such as telephone calls and email correspondences, because of the many other tasks to which they must attend. Effective school-based research requires remembering and respecting what a day in the life of a teacher or school personnel entails. Teachers in the US teach all day, and, in some cases, they are provided with 20 to 30 minutes of prep time, which is quickly filled with lesson plans and grading. Consequently, contacting teachers may not always be the most effective strategy to initiate school-based research. Thus, it is suggested that first, identify other gatekeepers, such as principals who have and can provide access to schools. Some universities, especially within education departments, have staff members who have connections with school districts in surrounding communities. In such cases, researchers might consult with these staff members before initiating contacts with schools independently. Moreover, there are other informal mechanisms through which researchers can be connected to personnel in the school districts. For instance, many faculty members in the departments of education have established ongoing connections with teachers or school administrators in the community, and they may also teach a number of teachers or administrators in graduate-level classes. Often, these faculty members may be able to facilitate introductions with teachers and administrators in the local school districts.

Moreover, researchers might try to connect with parents who are involved in their children's school districts. In many cases, parents can be highly influential when they advocate for a school-based study, and their support may be critical prior to initiating a study. In addition, researchers might identify individuals who have the authority to provide permission for conducting research in the school settings. Although institutional review boards are required prior to conducting any studies in US universities, it is important that researchers receive permission from someone within the school system to conduct the study in the school setting. It is recommended that researchers first visit the school to introduce themselves and explain the importance of the study. Also, building rapport with staff members who can facilitate communication with school is very important. Overall, patience and persistence are needed to connect with school districts and school administrators are the gatekeepers to conducting successful research in the school settings.

Perspective-taking

School personnel needs to understand what is needed for students to be successful in US schools. School personnel, teachers in particular, work directly with students (and sometimes their families), especially those who experiences challenges and barriers to education. Teachers and school personnel are confronted with numerous challenges, including salary and budget constraints, mandates concerning test performances, school disciplinary problems, mental health problems, and social concerns. It is imperative that researchers recognize and communicate to teachers their respect and appreciation. Also, researchers must recognize that their experiences in academia differs tremendously from those of teachers and school administrators and should connect with teachers, parents, and other school personnel to take a team-based approach to making schools safer for students. Successful collaborative effort requires the researchers to be flexible in how they conduct their studies when collaborating with schools. For instance, although researchers often add their expertise in the focus of their study, we strongly advise that they include additional items in surveys or address other issues that the school personnel have identified as relevant and important.

Positive relationship-building

School psychologists are experts in students' relationship skills, rapport-building, and conflict management. Their clinical and counselling skills translate from therapy to research in the schools. Every meeting with school personnel, teachers, parents, and other stakeholders provides an opportunity to observe people's interactions, their body language, and their impression of the researchers. For instance, if a teacher in a meeting is disengaged, then it might be worthwhile to ask this teacher to share his or her thoughts or concerns related to the research project. Relationship-building also needs to be serious considered in school-based research. Researchers need to build rapport with not only teachers and school administrators (e.g. principals), but also superintendents, office staff, cafeteria workers, security guards, and other paraprofessional staff. This can be achieved by sampling asking questions and taking notes after each meeting, as well as by inquiring about their personal life, including family, education (diplomas on the wall), plans for the holidays, etc. Researchers can take food and refreshments to teacher meetings or invite teachers and school personnel to a meal. Most of all, it is crucial that researchers deliver or follow through on their promises.

Building long-term, sustainable, collaborative, and mutually beneficial partnerships with school districts is important. Researchers need to keep in mind that schools provide substantial resources and opportunities, and it would be unprofessional if they gather data without any long-term commitment, follow-up, or contribution to the participating school. This is a major disservice to not only the participating schools, but also to the image of the researcher. In the past, studies have been conducted among college students, which provided data with little time investment on the part of the researcher, and little benefit to the study participants. This approach would not work within the K-12 school districts today.

Professionalism

It is also essential to maintain professionalism by, for example, remaining objective in school politics or posturing. Also, some parents may display strong reaction to the study approach or topic or perceive school-based research as interfering with students' normal school activities. Researchers need to approach parents with utmost professionalism in order for the study to proceed. Most importantly, researchers need to demonstrate professionalism as this would reflect on the research profession. And finally, some individuals may be less familiar with research ethics and may request confidential information. To avoid this, researchers need to inform the stakeholders about the importance of adhering to research ethics and standards.

Politics

Bullying prevention, like many educational topics, has become a politicized topic of discussion over the last seven years in the US. On 10 March 2011, then-president of the United States Barack Obama held the first White House Conference on Bullying. More specifically, President Obama, the First Lady, the Department of Education, and the Department of Health and Human Services convened students, parents, and teachers in addition to non-profit leaders, advocates, and policy-makers to the White House for a Conference on Bullying Prevention. The conference brought together communities from across the nation that have been affected by bullying as well as those who are taking action to address it. Subsequently, a website was launched (www.stop bullying.gov) to provide evidence-based guidance for schools and communities. StopBullying.gov works closely with the Federal Partners in Bullying Prevention Steering Committee, an interagency effort co-led by the Department of Education and the Department of Health and Human Services that coordinates policy, research, and communications on topics related to bullying. The Federal Partners in Bullying Prevention Steering Committee includes representatives from the U.S. Departments of Agriculture, Defense, Education, Health and Human Services, Interior, and Justice, as well as the Federal Trade Commission and the White House Initiative on Asian Americans and Pacific Islanders. The Obama administration was committed to increasing federal funding for the development and evaluation of research-based prevention efforts.

The landscape for school safety and bullying prevention is quite different under President Donald Trump who was inaugurated in 2016. Much of the progress that had been made in bullying prevention has been stalled under the Trump administration. In the aftermath of school shootings, such as the Parkland shootings that occurred in February of 2016 in Florida, federal funding for school safety has been substantially cut as the priority shifted to 'get tough with' school violence with metal detectors, police officers, clear backpacks, and active shooter drills (https://thecrimereport.org/2018/02/27/trump-seeks-shutdown-of-new-school-safety-studies/). This leaves little room for social-emotional learning approaches to school safety and bullying prevention, as these programmes are seen as 'soft' approaches to school safety issues. The nation's focus on bullying prevention was re-energized with the First Lady of the United States, Melania Trump's 'Be Best' campaign to create kind and caring children and to end cyberbullying and cruelty on social media platforms. After almost two years into the Trump administration, Melania Trump organized and attended the first White House Cyberbullying Summit in 2018 (see wwwrefinery29.com/2018/08/207775/melania-trump-cyberbullying-be-best). Many attendees of both White House Conferences were struck by the differences between the two summits. The first conference had a long waiting list, standing room only attendance, and included discussions of both science and practice. The second conference did not have a waiting list, as there were hundreds of empty chairs, and the science was treated as an after-thought. Ironically, Melania Trump was talking as President Trump was tweeting messages on Twitter that appear to be indicative of bullying.

All aspects of education can be political. This is not likely to change anytime soon in the US. The current political climate has only energized prevention scientists to become creative in the ways in which scholars and other relevant stakeholders garner support for bullying prevention efforts. Scholars need to modify their research questions to fit the funding priorities in the federal agencies. For example, with a focus on armed police officers in the entire school schools, one research team has created professional development for these police officers to understand the importance of social-emotional learning and cultural competence in their work with youth.

Conclusion

Bullying has been recognized as a serious concern in US school districts, and many concerned parents, teachers, and school officials have called for anti-bullying approaches to address bullying and create a safe school climate in which students maximize their learning potentials. Although states are required by law to implement anti-bullying policies and programmes in their school districts, the effectiveness of anti-bullying programmes in US schools have been moderate. Although several anti-bullying programmes, especially those using the SEL approach are potentially impactful in addressing and reducing bullying, it is imperative that these programmes are effective across diverse groups of students in K-12 school districts. In order to create a bully free school, school officials need to consistently work with scholars and practitioners in developing and administering programmes that are developmentally appropriate, culturally relevant, and cost-effective. The first necessary step is to consistently monitor and evaluate the effectiveness of the existing programmes, which is the focus of this chapter.

References

Bauer, N. S., Lozano, P., & Rivara, F. P. (2007). The effectiveness of the Olweus Bullying Prevention Program in public middle schools: A controlled trial. *Journal of Adolescent Health*, 40(3), 266–274.

Blueprint for Violence Prevention. (2002–2004). Blueprints model programs: Olweus Bullying Prevention Program (BPP). Retrieved from www.colorado. edu/cspv/blueprints/model/ programs/BPP.html.

Bowllan, N. M. (2011). Implementation and evaluation of a comprehensive, school-wide bullying prevention program in an urban/suburban middle school. *Journal of School Health*, 81(4), 167–173.

Brackett, M. A., Caruso, D. R., & Stern, R. (2006). *Anchors of emotional intelligence*. New Haven, CT: Emotionally Intelligent Schools, LLC.

Bradshaw, C. P., Koth, C. W., Bevans, K. B., Ialongo, N., & Leaf, P. J. (2008). The impact of school-wide positive behavioral interventions and supports (PBIS) on the organizational health of elementary schools. *School Psychology Quarterly*, 23(4), 462–473.

Bradshaw, C. P., Mitchell, M. M., & Leaf, P. J. (2010). Examining the effects of schoolwide positive behavioral interventions and supports on student outcomes: Results from a randomized controlled effectiveness trial in elementary schools. *Journal of Positive Behavior Interventions*, 12(3), 133–148.

Brown, E. C., Low, S., Smith, B. H., & Haggerty, K. P. (2011). Outcomes of a randomized controlled trial of Steps to Respect: A Bullying Prevention Program. *School Psychology Review*, 40, 423–443.

Burger, K. (2010). How does early childhood care and education affect cognitive development? An international review of the effects of early interventions for children from different social backgrounds. *Early Childhood Research Quarterly*, 25(2), 140–165.

Casel. (n.d.). Retrieved 29 August 2018, from https://casel.org/.

Castillo, R., Fernández-Berrocal, P., & Brackett, M. A. (2013). Enhancing teacher effectiveness in Spain: A pilot study of the RULER approach to social and emotional learning. *Journal of Education and Training Studies*, 1(2), 263–272.

Catalano, R. F., Berglund, M. L., Ryan, J. A., Lonczak, H. S., & Hawkins, J. D. (2004). Positive youth development in the United States: Research findings on evaluations of positive youth development programs. *Annals of the American Academy of Political and Social Science*, 591(1), 98–124.

Committee for Children. (n.d.). Social-Emotional Learning Curriculum. Retrieved from wwwcfchildren.org/programs/social-emotional-learning/.

Conduct Problems Prevention Research Group. (1999a). Initial impact of the Fast Track prevention trial for conduct problems: I. The high-risk sample. *Journal of Consulting and Clinical Psychology*, 67, 631–647.

Conduct Problems Prevention Research Group. (1999b). Initial impact of the Fast Track prevention trial for conduct problems: II. Classroom effects. *Journal of Consulting and Clinical Psychology*, 67, 648–657.

Crime Report. (2018). Trump seeks shutdown of new school safety studies. Retrieved from https://thecrimereport.org/2018/02/27/trump-seeks-shutdown-of-new-school-safety-studies/.

Domitrovich, C. E., Cortes, R. C., & Greenberg, M. T. (2007). Improving young children's social and emotional competence: A randomized trial of the preschool 'PATHS' curriculum. *Journal of Primary Prevention*, 28(2), 67–91.

Domitrovich, C. E., Durlak, J. A., Staley, K. C., & Weissberg, R. P. (2017). Social-emotional competence: An essential factor for promoting positive adjustment and reducing risk in school children. *Child Development*, 88(2), 408–416.

Durlak, J. A., & Weissberg, R. P. (2011). Promoting social and emotional development is an essential part of students' education. *Human Development*, 54(1), 1–3.

Durlak, J. A., Weissberg, R. P., Dymnicki, A. B., Taylor, R. D., & Schellinger, K. B. (2011). The impact of enhancing students' social and emotional learning: A meta-analysis of school-based universal interventions. *Child Development*, 82(1), 405–432.

Espelage, D. L. (2013). Why are bully prevention programs failing in U.S. schools? *Journal of Curriculum and Pedagogy*, 10, 121–123. doi:10.1080/15505170.2013.8496299.

Espelage, D. L., & Poteat, V. P. (2012). School-based prevention of peer relationship problems. In Betsy Altmaier & Jo-Ida Hansen (Eds.), *Oxford handbook of counseling psychology* (pp. 703–722). New York: Oxford University Press.

Espelage, D. L., & Swearer, S. M. (2003). Research on school bullying and victimization: What have we learned and where do we go from here? *School Psychology Review*, 32(3), 365–383.

Espelage, D. L., & Swearer, S. M. (2010). A social-ecological model for bullying prevention and intervention: Understanding the impact of adults in the social ecology of youngsters. In S. R. Jimerson, S. M. Swearer, & D. L. Espelage (Eds.), *Handbook of bullying in schools: An international perspective* (pp. 61–72). New York: Routledge.

Espelage, D. L., Low, S., Polanin, J. R., & Brown, E. C. (2013). The impact of a middle school program to reduce aggression, victimization, and sexual violence. *Journal of Adolescent Health*, 53(2), 180–186.

Espelage, D. L., Low, S., Polanin, J. R., & Brown, E. C. (2015). Clinical trial of Second Step© middle-school program: Impact on aggression & victimization. *Journal of Applied Developmental Psychology*, 37, 52–63.

Espelage, D. L., Low, S., Van Ryzin, M. J.& Polanin J.R., (2015). Clinical trial of second step middle school program: Impact on bullying, cyberbullying, homophobic teasing, and sexual harassment perpetration. *School Psychology Review*, 44(4), 464–479.

Espelage, D. L., Rose, C. A., & Polanin, J. R. (2015). Social-emotional learning program to reduce bullying, fighting, and victimization among middle school students with disabilities. *Remedial and Special Education*, 36(5), 299–311.

Farrell, A. D., Sullivan, T. N., Sutherland, K. S., Corona, R., & Masho, S. (2018). Evaluation of the Olweus Bully Prevention Program in an urban school system in the USA. *Prevention Science*, 1–15.

Flay, B. R., & Allred, C. G. (2010). The positive action program: Improving academics, behavior, and character by teaching comprehensive skills for successful learning and living. In T. Lovat et al. (Eds.), *International research handbook on values education and student wellbeing* (pp. 471–501). Dordrecht: Springer.

Frey, K. S., Hirschstein, M. K., Snell, J. L., Edstrom, L. V. S., MacKenzie, E. P., & Broderick, C. J. (2005). Reducing playground bullying and supporting beliefs: An experimental trial of the steps to respect program. *Developmental Psychology*, 41(3), 479.

Garces, E., Thomas, D., & Currie, J. (2002). Longer-term effects of Head Start. *American Economic Review*, 92(4), 999–1012.

Gladden, R. M., Vivolo-Kantor, A. M., Hamburger, M. E., & Lumpkin, C. D. (2014). *Bullying surveillance among youths: Uniform definitions for public health and recommended data elements, version 1.0.* Atlanta, GA: National Center for Injury Prevention and Control, Centers for Disease Control and Prevention and U.S. Department of Education.

Gontcharova, N. (2018). Melania Trump talks cyberbullying while her husband lashes out on Twitter. Retrieved from wwwrefinery29.com/2018/08/207775/melania-trump- cyberbullying-be-best.

Good, C. P., McIntosh, K., & Gietz, C. (2011). Integrating bullying prevention into schoolwide positive behavior support. *Teaching Exceptional Children*, 44(1), 48–56.

Greenberg, M. T., & Kusché, C. A. (1998). Preventive intervention for school-age deaf children: The PATHS curriculum. *Journal of Deaf Studies and Deaf Education*, 3(1), 49–63.

Greenberg, M. T., Domitrovich, C. E., Weissberg, R. P., & Durlak, J. A. (2017). Social and emotional learning as a public health approach to education. *Future of Children, 27*(1), 13–32.

Hong, J. S., & Espelage, D. L. (2012). A review of research on bullying and peer victimization in school: An ecological system analysis. *Aggression and Violent Behavior,* 17(4), 311–322.

Horner, R. H., Dunlap, G., Hieneman, M., Nelson, C. M., Scott, T., Liaupsin, C., Sailor, W., Turnbull, H. R., Wickham, D., Wilcox, B., & Ruef, M. (2000). Applying positive behavior support and functional behavioral assessment in schools. *Journal of Positive Behavior Interventions, 2*(3),131–143.

Horner, R. H., Sugai, G., Smolkowski, K., Eber, L., Nakasato, J., Todd, A. W., & Esperanza, J. (2009). A randomized, wait-list controlled effectiveness trial assessing school-wide positive behavior support in elementary schools. *Journal of Positive Behavior Interventions, 11*(3), 133–144.

Jennings, P. A., & Greenberg, M. T. (2009). The prosocial classroom: Teacher social and emotional competence in relation to student and classroom outcomes. *Review of Educational Research,* 79(1), 491–525.

Kallestad, J. H., & Olweus, D. (2003). Predicting teachers' and schools' implementation of the Olweus Bullying Prevention Program: A multilevel study. *Prevention & Treatment,* 6(21), 3–21.

Li, K. K., Washburn, I., DuBois, D. L., Vuchinich, S., Ji, P., Brechling, V., Day, J., Beets, M. W., Acock, A. C., Berbaum, M., Snyder, F., & Flay, B. R. (2011). Effects of the Positive Action programme on problem behaviors in elementary school students: A matched-pair randomized control trial in Chicago. *Psychology and Health,* 26(2), 187–204.

Limber, S. P. (2010). Implementation of the Olweus Bullying Prevention Program: Lessons learned from the field. In D. Espelage & S. Swearer (Eds.), *Bullying in North American schools: A social-ecological perspective on prevention and intervention* (2nd ed.) (pp. 291–306). New York: Routledge.

Limber, S. P., Olweus, D., Wang, W., Masiello, M., & Breivik, K. (2018). Evaluation of the Olweus Bullying Prevention Program: A large scale study of US students in grades 3–11. *Journal of School Psychology,* 69, 56–72.

Low, S., & Van Ryzin, M. (2014). The moderating effects of school climate on bullying prevention efforts. *School Psychology Quarterly,* 29(3), 306–319.

Low, S., Van Ryzin, M. J., Brown, E. C., Smith, B. H., & Haggerty K.P., (2014). Engagement matters: Lessons from assessing classroom implementation of steps to respect: A bullying prevention program over a one-year period. *Prevention Science,* 15(2), 165–176.

Moy, G., Polanin, J. R., McPherson, C., & Phan, T. V. (2018). International adoption of the Second Step program: Moderating variables in treatment effects. *School Psychology International,* 39(4), 333–359.

Musu-Gillette, L., Zhang, A., Wang, K., Zhang, J., Kemp, J., Diliberti, M., & Oudekerk, B. A. (2018). *Indicators of School Crime and Safety: 2017* (NCES

2018–2036/NCJ 251413). Washington, DC: National Center for Education Statistics, U.S. Department of Education, and Bureau of Justice Statistics, Office of Justice Programs, U.S. Department of Justice.

Nathanson, L., Rivers, S. E., Flynn, L. M., & Brackett, M. A. (2016). Creating emotionally intelligent schools with RULER. *Emotion Review*, 8(4), 1–6.

Netzel, D. M., & Eber, L. (2003). Shifting from reactive to proactive discipline in an urban school district: A change of focus through PBIS implementation. *Journal of Positive Behavior Interventions*, 5(2), 71–79.

Olweus, D. (1993). *Bullying at school: What we know and what we can do.* Malden, MA: Blackwell.

Olweus, D., & Limber, S. P. (2013). Summary of OBPP findings presented at IBPA. Retrieved from https://olweus.sites.clemson.edu/Summary%20of%20OBPP%20findings%20presented%20at%20IBPA.pdf.

Osher, D., Kidron, Y., Brackett, M., Dymnicki, A., Jones, S., & Weissberg, R. P. (2016). Advancing the science and practice of social and emotional learning: Looking back and moving forward. *Education Research: A Century of Discovery*, 40, 644–681.

PBIS.org. (n.d.). Positive Behavioral Interventions & Support. Retrieved from wwwpbis.org.

Polanin, J., & Espelage, D. L. (2015). Using a meta-analytic technique to assess the impact of treatment intensity measures in a multi-site cluster-randomized trial. *Journal of Behavioral Education*, 24(1), 133–151.

Reyes, M. R., Brackett, M. A., Rivers, S. E., Elbertson, N. A., & Salovey, P. (2012). The interaction effects of program training, dosage, and implementation quality on targeted student outcomes for the RULER approach to social and emotional learning. *School Psychology Review*, 41(1), 82–99.

Reynolds, A. J., Mathieson, L. C., & Topitzes, J. W. (2009). Do early childhood interventions prevent child maltreatment? A review of research. *Child Maltreatment*, 14(2), 182–206.

Ross, S. W., & Horner, R. H. (2009). Bully prevention in positive behavior support. *Journal of Applied Behavior Analysis*, 42, 747–759.

Ross, S. W., & Horner, R. H. (2014). Bully prevention in positive behavior support: Preliminary evaluation of third-, fourth-, and fifth-grade attitudes toward bullying. *Journal of Emotional and Behavioral Disorders*, 22(4), 225–236.

Ross, S. W., Horner, R. H., & Stiller, B. (2008). *Bully prevention in Positive Behavior Support: Curriculum manual developed for intervention implementation.* Eugene, OR: Educational and Community Supports, University of Oregon.

Rowe, H. L., & Trickett, E. J. (2018). Student diversity representation and reporting in universal school-based social and emotional learning programs: Implications for generalizability. *Educational Psychology Review*, 30(2), 559–583.

stopbullying.gov. (n.d.). Stop bullying on the spot. Retrieved from wwwstopbullying.gov/.

Ttofi, M. M., & Farrington, D. P. (2011). Effectiveness of school-based programs to reduce bullying: A systematic and meta-analytic review. *Journal of Experimental Criminology*, 7(1), 27–56.

U.S. Department of Health and Human Services (n.d.). Head Start Programs. Retrieved 29 August 2018, from wwwacf.hhs.gov/ohs/about/head-start.

Violence Prevention Works. (2016). Core components of the Olweus Bullying Prevention Program. Retrieved from www.violencepreventionworks.org/public/olweus_scope.page.

6

THE FRIENDLY SCHOOLS INITIATIVE

Evidence-based bullying prevention in Australian schools

Amy Barnes, Natasha Pearce, Erin Erceg, Kevin Runions, Patricia Cardoso, Leanne Lester, Juli Coffin and Donna Cross

The context of the research

In Australia, over one-quarter of students aged 8 to 14 years report being bullied, and 9% report bullying others, every few weeks or more often (Cross et al., 2009). Further, a review of studies involving over 50,000 students indicated that approximately 20% of Australian young people experience cyberbullying each year (Spears, Keeley, Bates, & Katz, 2014), a rate higher than average according to a meta-analytic study (15.2%; Modecki, Minchin, Harbaugh, Guerra, & Runions, 2014). Many young people are therefore exposed to bullying and cyberbullying incidents, and their consequences, in Australian schools.

There is robust evidence demonstrating the harmful impact of bullying and cyberbullying on students' well-being, social integration, and school success (Gini & Pozzoli, 2013; Kowalski & Limber, 2013; Moore et al., 2017). In response to community and school concerns about these issues, Australia has been very active in applied bullying prevention intervention research, including the *Friendly Schools* and *Cyber Friendly Schools* initiatives (Cross et al., 2011; Cross et al., 2016; Cross et al., 2012; Cross et al., 2019; Cross, Shaw et al., 2018). The *Friendly Schools* programme and associated research is firmly situated in the context of key theoretical approaches, including social ecological theory and family systems theory.

Theoretical approaches to bullying prevention

Social ecological theory

Social ecological theory acknowledges that health risks are not straightforward or direct outcomes of individual behaviours, but emerge due to complex interactions between young people and the contexts in which they live (Bronfenbrenner, 1995; Espelage, 2014). Hence, bullying and cyberbullying interventions must target risk and protective factors at the individual, family, peer, online, and community levels, and be mindful of interactions between these levels (for a full review, see Cross, Barnes et al., 2015).

At the individual level, demographic attributes are associated with bullying involvement (Cross et al., 2009; Fletcher et al., 2014; Ybarra & Mitchell, 2004), as are individual attitudes and psychological mechanisms, including problem-solving skills, social information processing, empathy and moral disengagement (Runions, Shapka, Dooley, & Modecki, 2013; Runions & Bak, 2015; Steffgen, König, Pfetsch, & Melzer, 2009). At the family level, parents' attitudes towards and understandings of bullying, parenting skills, and knowledge about online environments affect the likelihood of children's bullying and cyberbullying involvement (for a review see Cross & Barnes, 2014b) (Lester et al., 2017). Among peers, friends' involvement in bullying, social norms and expectations, and the diffusion of responsibility phenomenon, are associated with bullying perpetration (Almeida, Correia, & Marinho, 2009; Lester, Cross, & Shaw, 2012; Sasson & Mesch, 2014).

Community-level factors include bullying-related regulations (Langos, 2013) and the support available to students during times of stress, such as school transition (Lester, Cross, Shaw, & Dooley, 2012). Finally, aspects of the online environment itself and the importance of technology in young people's lives affect the likelihood and nature of cyberbullying (Australian Communications and Media Authority, 2013; Runions, 2013; Runions & Bak, 2015). Interventions to prevent bullying must therefore consider and address the variety of factors that influence young people's behaviour.

Family systems theories

Family systems theories emphasize the impact of functional and behavioural family patterns on the behaviour of individuals (Fingerman & Bermann, 2000; Minuchin, 1985). Children's behaviour should be considered in the context of the family system that shaped their attitudes and beliefs, and considerable research demonstrates the impact of family functioning, parental characteristics and disciplinary styles on young people's aggressive behaviour (for a review see Cross & Barnes, 2014b). School-based efforts to address bullying and cyber-bullying are therefore more successful when they engage with parents and families (Cross, Lester, Pearce, Barnes, & Beatty, 2018; Ttofi & Farrington, 2011).

The value of youth voice

Models for enhancing participant engagement emphasize the need to involve target audiences in the process of developing, testing and implementing intervention strategies, policies, and practices (Hart, 1992; Shier, 2001). This ensures the perspectives of all stakeholders are considered, and that strategies are relevant and engaging (Hart, 1992; Shier, 2001). This process is crucial for an issue like cyberbullying, where young people themselves are more knowledgeable about online behaviour and environments than their parents and teachers (Spears & Zeederberg, 2013). Australian research has therefore actively engaged young people in the development and implementation of school-based efforts to prevent bullying, especially cyberbullying (e.g. Cross, Lester, Barnes, Cardoso, & Hadwen, 2015; Spears & Zeederberg, 2013).

Need for whole-school interventions and implementation support

These theoretical approaches indicate that multi-dimensional interventions with strategies targeting all levels and members of the school community are needed to effectively reduce bullying (Rigby & Slee, 2008; Ttofi & Farrington, 2011; Vreeman & Carroll, 2007). Interventions that target only one level, such as social skills training, do not reliably reduce bullying (da Silva et al., 2018). Schools are complex systems in which a systematic approach of significant duration is needed to reduce implementation barriers (Cross & Barnes, 2014a). Given Australian teachers report they lack confidence and competence to address cyberbullying, it is also important to provide sufficient resources and training to support school staff (Barnes et al., 2012; Cross et al., 2009).

The Australian *Friendly Schools* body of research has therefore:

- Developed and implemented evidence-based strategies targeting all levels of the school environment.
- Involved all members of the school community as co-researchers and through training and support.

- Engaged students as co-developers of intervention strategies.
- Enhanced the capacity of school leaders to assess, plan, implement, and evaluate their efforts in meeting school community needs.

Underpinning research

A landmark Australian study by Rigby and Slee (1991) addressed the incidence of bullying among students in South Australian schools. Subsequently, an Australian Federal Government Senate inquiry into school violence (Commonwealth of Australia, 1994) heralded a nationwide movement to address the issue of bullying. An early outcome of this research was the PEACE Pack, led by Professor Phillip Slee; a successful intervention framework for dealing with school bullying, currently in its fourth edition (Slee, 1996; Slee & Mohyla, 2007). The PEACE Pack demonstrated that the prevalence of school bullying can be reduced, and the importance of developing intervention resources in consultation with all stakeholders (Slee & Mohyla, 2007).

Currently, one of the most empirically researched school-based programmes in Australia is *Friendly Schools*, a universal bullying prevention and social skills development intervention. Over 19 years (1999–2018), *Friendly Schools* has been tested in 7 randomized control trials and 9 quasi-experimental studies involving more than 300 primary and secondary schools in Australia, comprising over 30,000 students, their teachers, parents and school leaders (Cross & Barnes, 2014b; Cross et al., 2018; Cross et al., 2011; Cross et al., 2003; Cross et al., 2016; Cross et al., 2012; et al., 2019; Cross, Shaw et al., 2018). This research has focused on understanding bullying, developing, and evaluating whole-school evidence-based strategies to reduce all forms of bullying, and informing national and international policy and practice.

Friendly Schools *research*

In 1999, a team of Western Australian researchers led by Professor Donna Cross responded to the need for informed action from policy-makers, educators, and families to address school bullying. At this time, other than the PEACE Pack, no empirical whole-school intervention research had been conducted to determine the most effective ways to reduce harm from bullying.

An initial *formative research project* (1999) summarised evidence-based findings from international bullying-related research, which were then validated by bullying prevention research experts from around the world (Cross, Pintabona, Hall, Hamilton, & Erceg, 2004). These validated principles were used, in collaboration with students and teachers, to develop a primary school-based intervention targeting the age group that reported the highest level of bullying in Australia: children aged 10–11 years.

The *Friendly Schools* (*FS*) intervention comprised three levels of intervention: (1) building the capacity of the whole-school community to address bullying; (2) working with families to improve understanding and self-efficacy to discuss bullying with their children; and (3) providing learning resources and teaching support for students and their teachers, which focused on building pro-social skills, non-violent conflict resolution skills, problem-solving skills and empathy, as well has enhancing understanding of how to respond to bullying, and why it is unacceptable (Cross et al., 2011; Cross et al., 2003). The FS intervention was tested in a longitudinal randomized control trial (2000–2002) involving nearly 2,000 students from 29 schools, followed from Grades 4 to 6, and their teachers and families. The intervention resulted in decreased observations of bullying and increased reporting of bullying compared to the control group (Cross et al., 2011; Cross et al., 2003). The reductions in bullying were greater than the average effects for interventions of this type (Ttofi & Farrington, 2011), with results maintained three years later (Cross et al., 2011).

Friendly Schools – *primary*

The need for further research was identified, particularly to understand and refine the best combinations of student, classroom, home, and school level activities, to target the whole-school community and to build school capacity to implement the intervention (Cross et al., 2011; Cross et al., 2003). The subsequent three-year (2002–2004) project, *Friendly Schools Friendly Families* (*FSFF*), followed three cohorts of students from each of Grades 2, 4 and 6 (nearly 4,000 students) for three years, from 20 randomly selected primary schools in Western Australia. Building on the previous study, FSFF included more capacity-building support for schools and a greater focus on family level activities (Cross et al., 2018; Cross et al., 2012). A longitudinal randomized control trial compared three conditions: (a) high dose (whole-school, capacity-building support and active parental involvement); (b) moderate dose (similar to high dose but without active parental involvement); and

(c) low dose (FSFF resources without teacher training or parent support). A significant reduction in bullying perpetration and victimization was found among students who received the high dose compared to the low dose intervention (Cross, Lester et al., 2018; Cross et al., 2012).

Friendly Schools – *secondary*

Further research refined and evaluated strategies to reduce bullying among older students. The *FS transition to secondary school project* (2005–2007) involved a three-year randomized cluster comparison trial with over 3000 students from 21 Perth metropolitan secondary schools. It aimed to help students prevent or address the high prevalence of bullying following their transition to secondary school. The FS secondary intervention was found to reduce young people's experiences of bullying victimization and perpetration, and enhance their feelings of safety, and staff and peer support (Cross, Shaw et al., 2018). The study was extended (2014–2017) using an age-cohort design, to include Grades 7 to 9. This study, *Beyond Bullying*, found that implementation of the FS curriculum was associated with decreases in bullying perpetration and victimization, as well as reductions in moral disengagement (Cross et al. 2019). These findings are particularly important in the light of a meta-analysis indicating that bullying interventions tend to lose efficacy by early adolescence (Yeager, Fong, Lee, & Espelage, 2015).

Friendly Schools – *junior primary*

In 2006, the FS Junior Primary research, as part of the *Child Aggression Prevention (CAP) Project*, followed over 2,000 pre-primary school children and their families for three years (Runions, 2014). The project aimed to promote supportive school environments and social relationships among young children, and to limit aggression and disruptive behaviours. Along with a three-module curriculum comprising 15 foci addressing emotional and social understandings, the project also provided professional development on the use of 'banking time' (Driscoll & Pianta, 2010) – a strategy for working through teacher-child conflict with disruptive students – and the good behaviour game (Barrish, Saunders, & Wolf, 1969). These elements were integrated into a year-long evaluation, which did not produce significant improvements in student behaviour. This may have been due to implementation failure. For example, although early modules were taught by most teachers, later modules addressing social interactions were implemented by only 55% of teachers.

Implementation of the good behaviour game was equally limited (46% of teachers), and only 11 of 24 teachers attempted the banking strategy, with some reporting problems finding time and space for implementation.

Friendly Schools – *indigenous*

In response to the need to address bullying among higher risk young people, the *Friendly Schools* research targeted indigenous Aboriginal communities. The *Solid Kids, Solid Schools'* (SKSS) project (2006–2009) was co-designed by Aboriginal Elders, young people and community members. The Aboriginal Steering group and local Aboriginal (Yamaji) people co-developed and pilot-tested resources including an interactive website to reduce harms from bullying (Coffin, Larson, & Cross, 2010). The project found that Australian Aboriginal students experienced bullying in different ways to non-Aboriginal children. For example, Aboriginal students described physical bullying as smashing, ripping and double banking, and verbal bullying as carrying yarns, chipping, jarring, and calling someone 'winyarn' [weak]. The SKSS therefore enhanced cultural awareness of and support for the development of knowledge and skills to address bullying specific to Aboriginal young people. It attempted to improve teacher understandings of Aboriginal children's behaviour and its management, and promoted a culturally secure whole-school approach to addressing bullying (Paki, Coffin, Cross, & Erceg, 2011). Process data suggested these resources were well accepted and used by community and classroom teachers.

Cyber Friendly Schools – *secondary*

Friendly Schools research has also addressed emerging forms of bullying. The *Australian Covert Bullying Prevalence Study* (ACBPS) (2007–2008) triangulated data from over 20,000 students to better understand bullying not easily observed by adults, including covert relational bullying and cyberbullying (Cross et al., 2009). The ACBPS demonstrated the importance of building a school culture where these forms of bullying are actively discouraged. School staff reported considerable difficulty identifying and responding to cyberbullying behaviours, despite those behaviours being increasingly prevalent (Cross et al., 2009; Barnes et al., 2012). In response to these findings, along with our other cyberbullying formative research conducted from 2007–2010, the three-year *Cyber Friendly Schools Project* (CFS) began in 2010. The CFS intervention was co-developed and pilot tested with the active involvement of school staff, parents, and Grade 10 students prior to the intervention trial. Our formative findings and previous research identified a variety of risk and protective factors at the school, classroom, family, and/or individual levels, that could be regulated or mediated to reduce cyberbullying, and which were addressed by the *CFS* (Cross et al., 2016).

CFS was one of the first randomized controlled trials to evaluate a universal intervention co-developed and co-implemented by young people. This whole-school intervention targeted and followed more than 3,000 Grade 8 students as they progressed to Grade 9. The intervention had three major components, designed to target (1) the whole-school community including staff, (2) students, and (3) parents (Cross et al., 2016). Each component included teaching and learning resources and a web-based resource for students, families, and teachers. Intervention teachers and student cyber leaders received training, resources, and implementation support (Cross, Lester, et al., 2015; Cross et al., 2016).

Reflecting research on the importance of student involvement in interventions concerning them (Hart, 1992; Shier, 2001; Shute & Slee, 2015), student leaders were recruited, trained, and supported to work with school staff in implementing the *CFS* intervention, engaging with students and parents, and acting as peer supporters (Cross, Lester, et al., 2015). The intervention was associated with small but significantly greater declines in the odds of involvement in cyber-victimization and perpetration from pre- to the first post-test, although not for the subsequent follow-up. For students already involved in cyberbullying, the intervention did not affect the frequency or extent of cyberbullying exposure or perpetration (Cross et al., 2016). Teachers reported difficulty implementing the programme in a crowded curriculum and a lack of confidence to teach cyber-related content (Cross et al., 2016).

Cyber Strong Schools – *secondary teacher capacity building*

To address limited teacher capacity, an online resource called *Cyber Strong Schools* was developed and pilot-tested to build the capacity of school staff to enhance the safety of their own online behaviour and their capacity to teach and encourage students' positive online behaviours (friendlyschools.com.au/ cyberstrong).

In addition, from 2014 to 2016 the *Cyber Savvy Project* extended the CFS research to focus on a major predictor of student cyberbullying: digital image-sharing. The project aimed to help young people make more positive decisions about the images they share online and to reduce the likelihood of these being used to humiliate and bully. This project was also led by young people as co-designers of the intervention resources. Multiple and comprehensive methods, including student summits and extensive focus groups and online surveys, were used to understand what young people do online and what they identify as the risks and benefits of image-sharing. The online intervention comprised curriculum resources for teachers, Grade 8 students, and parents. The student resources also included the 'Image Up' app, designed to help them to make safer image-sharing decisions. The process evaluation of the intervention, conducted in 12 non-government schools, found that teachers, parents, and students reported positive use of and satisfaction with the intervention.

Friendly Schools – *building capacity for action*

The five-year *Strong Schools Safe Kids* study (2010–2014) comprised a series of in-depth case studies, designed to develop and test strategies to build the capacity of staff, students, and parents to implement *FS* strategies (http://friendlyschools.com.au). This capacity-building study was used to optimize the effectiveness, relevance, and implementation of the *FS* intervention. A key output of this research was the development and testing of mechanisms that assist schools to take evidence-based action to prevent bullying and effectively implement these into real world practice. Regular feedback loops identified factors affecting implementation quality and resulted in an online management system that guides school leaders through the implementation process, collates assessment and survey data, provides timely access to supports and allows teams to plan, monitor, and review progress.

Friendly Schools – *commercialization*

The collective findings from the *Friendly Schools* primary research completed in 2004 led to significant demand from schools to access the resources and training. While this interest was initially addressed by the research team, by 2005 it became necessary to seek a commercial purveyor to respond to the demand for the training and resources in Australia and several other English-speaking countries. The commercialized Friendly Schools resources and training have had four major iterations to 2018, based on new insights emerging from the FS research conducted by the research team, and continues to be disseminated commercially. The commercialization process took over a year to develop a business case, tender for suitable purveyors and select a publisher willing to sustain the integrity of associated research and resources and training. Since 2005, two publishing houses have led the sales and dissemination of FS. The income generated by this commercialization process is used to update the resources about every five years and also to support some ongoing research. The research described in this chapter is collectively translated into policy and practice through this commercialization arm of Friendly Schools. It is recognized and promoted by education systems and sectors in Australia as a successful evidence-based bullying prevention programme. The resource comprises the following.

- *Whole school activities* to build a positive social climate, enhance school connectedness and relationships, improve school policies and practices, and build school capacity to implement bullying prevention strategies. Schools are provided with assessment tools, support materials, and training.
- *Teaching and learning activities* to improve students' social and emotional learning (SEL), develop common understandings of bullying, and learn how to respond to bullying. Activities include peer interactions, role plays, stories, skills training, and observational learning. Teachers are provided with training and support to implement the learning activities.
- *Family activities* to help schools work with parents to improve their awareness and self-efficacy to address their children's bullying involvement. These activities include parent–teacher meetings, information sessions, newsletter items, and student homework.
- *Individual activities* to provide targeted support for victimized students and those who bully others, to modify behaviour and facilitate links with local health professionals.

The transition from pure research to application

To make a difference to young people's social and emotional well-being, interventions must be implemented with quality and reach many students. Although research has demonstrated the effectiveness of bullying interventions in reducing bullying victimization and perpetration frequency (Jiménez-Barbero, Ruiz-Hernández, Llor-Zaragoza, Pérez-García, & Llor-Esteban, 2016), achieving and measuring these effects in real-world school contexts poses significant methodological and translation challenges. Wider dissemination of effective bullying interventions places greater focus on external validity factors, and implementation outcomes such as acceptability, adoption, fidelity, and sustainability become important in understanding intervention impact (Durlak & DuPre, 2008).

Further, schools are complex organizations that pose significant challenges for the delivery and evaluation of health promotion initiatives (Cross & Barnes, 2014a; Skrzypiec & Slee, 2017). Facilitators and barriers to change can vary widely even within a cluster of settings that are structurally alike (e.g. schools within the same educational system). These include individual and social factors, such as students' and teachers' background knowledge and attitudes, existing programmes, availability of resources, and leadership commitment. School-based interventions to address bullying may need flexibility to ensure relevance, appropriateness and sustainability despite individual, cultural and socio-economic differences (Cross & Barnes, 2014a). Quality implementation requires a balance between fidelity to the effective intervention and adaptation to meet local needs (Domitrovich et al., 2008).

Interviews with Australian school principals highlight the difficulties associated with implementing mental health programmes (Skrzypiec & Slee, 2017). Challenges to programme implementation include crowded curricula with multiple demands on teacher time, lack of professional development, staff confidence, and the need for effective leadership. Further, challenges to programme integrity and sustainability include the conflict schools experience in adhering to guidelines they think are unsuitable (e.g. due to cultural differences) or of limited interest to students, as well as how many lessons can be taught when teachers felt pressured to deliver other programmes as well (Skrzypiec & Slee, 2017). Teacher comfort with particular topics and their perception of student comfort with these topics might also affect the extent of content implementation (Spears, Slee, & Huntley, 2015).

Friendly Schools implementation

Friendly Schools is a strengths-based, whole-school participatory process. It provides a comprehensive range of resources to enhance the capacity of school staff to determine their needs and implement evidence-based policy and practice to reduce bullying.

The *Friendly Schools* 'Evidence for Practice' book provides evidence-based guidelines to help schools implement and sustain effective social and emotional skill building and bullying reduction strategies. Key elements for action are divided into six inter-related whole-school components: (1) building capacity; (2) school culture; (3) policy and procedures; (4) staff, student, and family competence; (5) school-family community partnerships; and (6) physical environment. A range of resources developed and tested in schools to support the implementation of the key elements is provided for each whole-school component.

A five-step process guides schools to review, plan, build capacity for and implement critical evidence-based policies and practices, linking all the stages of implementation so each builds upon the others. To allow for schools' individual needs, toolkits are provided that enable staff to examine their existing strategies for bullying prevention, identify areas for improvement, and then address these gaps. These toolkits include: surveys for students and teachers, an online whole-school action scoping tool (Map-the-Gap), and review and planning tools.

The SEL of young people is addressed both formally, through classroom pedagogy and learning strategies, and informally through whole-school culture, organization, and structural development whereby these understandings, skills, and competencies are reinforced. There are currently nine *Friendly Schools* teacher resource books, organized around the five key areas of SEL: self-awareness, self-management, social awareness, relationship skills, and social decision-making. Online tools, CDs, and professional learning are also available to support schools in implementing *Friendly Schools*.

Several methodological and practical challenges were faced translating the *Friendly Schools* research into this final product, including the following.

Ensuring a sustainable implementation process for schools

A review of the *Friendly Schools* implementation process indicated that many schools had difficulty fast-tracking the readiness and planning stage to proceed to whole-school implementation and evaluation (Cross et al. 2010). An implementation model was therefore developed into a five-stage school implementation 'road map', which encourages schools to view long-term change as the result of a series of shorter-term cycles. The road map is supported by a range of auditing and planning tools for school teams to plan, record, and monitor progress.

Ensuring readiness for change

Readiness for change is necessary for sustainable efforts to implement whole-school programmes. Disregarding this stage may result in insufficient thought, time and resources being allocated for implementation, while taking the time to assess the school community's readiness to engage in a whole-school approach allows for the identification of possible barriers and enablers to implementation.

Friendly Schools provides tools to assess school readiness in committed leadership, compatibility with current priorities and actions, knowledge of student needs and family values, the priorities and capacity of staff, and the capacity of the coordinating team. The readiness stage, outlined in the *Friendly Schools* implementation plan, details how to engage leadership support, set up a team to facilitate and manage the process, and provides strategies to build staff capacity to use evidence-based information about reducing bullying in schools.

Strategies are also provided to help teams collaborate with school community members to align the programme with the school needs and contexts. The creation and acceptance of this shared vision provides the basis for common understandings, shared agreements, and consistent action to reduce bullying.

Applying principles of capacity building

With the significant barriers to implementation discussed previously, building staff capacity to create change is an essential component of *Friendly Schools*. Schools that received greater support for FS capacity-building demonstrated higher whole-school implementation capacity, higher programme implementation levels and higher levels of parent engagement, compared to schools receiving no capacity support (Pearce, 2010). The *Friendly Schools* readiness phase therefore includes critical capacity building processes, strategies, and auditing tools to ensure leadership support and system support.

Building staff engagement and capacity to implement good practice strategies

To reduce harms from bullying, school staff must be able to teach a social and emotional curriculum, respond appropriately to bullying incidents, supervise and support students in the schoolyard, and engage and collaborate with families. Staff need to feel part of the decision-making process and be prepared for proposed changes to their work practices. *Friendly Schools* provides whole-school staff training to ensure common understandings, consistency of action and shared agreements among all school staff.

Identifying training and support needs

Implementation of the *Friendly Schools* classroom curriculum relies on teachers' capacity to support their students' SEL. Teachers' social and emotional competence and well-being strongly influence learning context and infusion of SEL into classrooms and schools (Jones, Bouffard, & Weissbourd, 2013). *Friendly Schools* therefore encourages and provides professional development to enhance teacher knowledge to support students' SEL. Teachers also need time to explore the curriculum, review current practices, and collaborate with other staff to expand and embed SEL across the curriculum.

Assessing current practice and identifying strengths

Schools require different strategies according to context and programmes they have previously implemented. It is important that staff identify what is already being done well and what needs to be improved. *Friendly Schools* provides an online screening tool and a planning tool to help school teams assess current whole-school resources, practices, and processes. The tools allow staff to broadly identify components they need to work on. Involving staff in this process of identifying school strengths builds their connection and commitment to the project. It allows them to have input and ownership over a long-term plan for action, enhancing programme sustainability.

Cyber Friendly Schools: challenges and learnings

Key challenges for the *Cyber Friendly Schools* (CFS) intervention included keeping up-to-date with rapidly developing digital technologies and social media platforms, as well as ensuring student perspectives were heard to optimize intervention relevance and appropriateness. These issues were addressed in part through the establishment of a student advisory group, which maintained contact with the researchers, provided feedback on resources and materials, and reported on the emergence of new trends in technology usage.

Given the importance of the online environment in young people's lives, we worked to ensure the research design was relevant and appropriate to the project and target audience. Online surveys were used to collect data; school, student, and parent materials were made available online; and 'in-person' activities made extensive use of technology and multimedia.

Although the *CFS* results were promising, they were attenuated by poor teacher confidence to teach about cyber behaviours and hence their implementation of the classroom programme. Teachers also reported difficulty finding time in a crowded curriculum to teach the classroom intervention. Unlike other types of health behaviour, such as smoking, cyberbullying has no traditional home/time in the school curriculum. Despite a high level of interest from schools, on average only three of the nine recommended classroom activities in Grades 8 and 9 were implemented by teachers. Consequently, teachers may have missed teaching key components that contributed to student outcomes. Teacher implementation may have been enhanced by helping schools find space in their curriculum, helping to build teachers' cyber teaching self-efficacy and understanding about the core teaching components in each module, or by design features that enabled more rapid awareness of key activities.

The impact and legacy of the research

Since 1999, the *Friendly Schools* body of research has contributed to improvements in the health and well-being and other developmental outcomes for Australian children and adolescents. The programme has been continuously refined and empirically tested through 16 major research projects (including 7 randomized control trials) involving over 30,000 students, their teachers, parents, and school leaders in 300 schools. This programme has been evaluated more rigorously, across more age groups and sub-groups of higher-risk students, and over a longer duration than any other bullying prevention programme in Australia.

Over 3000 Australian schools have been recorded by its commercial publishers to have implemented *Friendly Schools* since 2005. It is also being used in schools in the USA, Canada, UK, Singapore, South Africa and New Zealand. More than 70 peer review publications have been published from *Friendly Schools* data, detailing findings including its effectiveness in consistently reducing student bullying. Additionally, *Friendly Schools* has significantly influenced Australian national and state policy, as well as several international countries' school policies and practices, e.g. Finland and New Zealand.

The *Friendly Schools* research has moved through translational research phases from intervention development to efficacy to effectiveness trials with educators, students, and families – a process integral to the relevance and impact of this research. Schools, educators and families have been instrumental in determining the research questions and each longitudinal project addressed a particular area of need (e.g. cyberbullying; Cross et al., 2016), or vulnerable group of young people (e.g. Aboriginal children; Coffin et al., 2010). The engagement of school and system educators and other cross-sectoral stakeholders (e.g. health, police) through project advisory boards helped to ensure the research answered relevant policy and practice questions with actionable outcomes for school implementation.

Partnerships between the researchers and end-users (state and regional education systems, school leaders and teachers) were facilitated through advisory boards that met regularly during the projects, with clear contribution and review protocols in place. For example, at the conceptualization and subsequent conduct of every FS research project, an advisory board of relevant and interested government and NGO organizations and consumers (e.g. students, teachers, and parents) was established to enable the effective translation of the research into relevant and meaningful outcomes. Students have been integral to the development of best practices, particularly in addressing cyberbullying, and student consultation summits and student advisory team mechanisms have enabled their input into identifying challenges and effective responses (Cross, Brown, Epstein, & Shaw, 2010).

Given findings that teachers struggled to implement the full *Cyber Friendly Schools* project, a follow-up study developed and tested online resources to build school staff capacity to teach positive cyber behaviours and online safety. These *Cyber Strong* resources were found to be particularly helpful for teachers who worked in rural and remote areas and could not easily access professional learning. A second follow-up study, *Cyber Savvy*, is exploring student behaviours, attitudes, and perceptions in relation to the sharing of digital images, including those that are sexually explicit, to inform research to prevent harms from image sharing. These findings will inform future cyberbullying research and be integrated into the commercially distributed *Friendly Schools* resources.

The increasing prevalence of cyberbullying and engagement with online environments among young children means that future research will extend the CFS research into primary schools. Enhancing understanding of safe and appropriate online behaviour among young children and their parents may help to protect children from harm as they enter adolescence and use advanced digital technologies more often and with less supervision.

Lessons learnt

Since 1999, the *Friendly Schools* research team has undertaken numerous large longitudinal research projects that have contributed to the *Friendly*

Schools intervention, with current research continuing to inform this resource. During this time, much has been learned to better understand intervention development, implementation, translation, and dissemination of school-based bullying prevention research.

The challenges facing researchers and teachers in implementing evidence-based programmes to address bullying are quite evident. Such challenges include the evaluation of programmes in the 'messy' real world of schools and classrooms, issues faced when implementing programmes with integrity and to meet local needs, and promoting evidence-based programmes when increasingly 'quick fixes' are demanded by legislators and politicians.

Many educators feel overwhelmed by the continuous introduction of new programmes and feel they have too few resources to educate and train their staff in these new initiatives. The need for immediate and urgent decisions may also force school staff into a reactive stance, preventing proactive planning. This is no less the case with bullying prevention and intervention: many schools struggle just to detect and respond appropriately to bullying incidents. This leads to an emphasis on punitive responses that can, at least, be implemented immediately. Thus, it will be important to highlight how new interventions complement and support already estab-lished initiatives, and provide easily accessible resources (online forums, websites etc.), and training. The business of schools and classrooms means there are multiple threats to programme implementation and programme integrity that researchers must be sensitive to and that school personnel need to consider when delivering a programme.

The heart of the *Friendly Schools* approach is the establishment of scaffolds to help schools make time for proactive planning and policy review, to more effectively prevent bullying incidents from arising. A stage-based approach to implementation is required, with particular support in the planning phase, and with greater focus on building capacity for change, to facilitate long-term commitment by staff and the sustainability of the intervention.

Schools may also lean toward ready-to-go curriculum responses that can be easily implemented by teachers and which put the onus for learning and change solely on students. In some cases, teaching anti-bullying curricula may help to reduce bullying in schools, but our work and other research indicates that for sustained change a whole-school approach is essential. A framework like *Friendly Schools* guides schools to identify areas in which their school's approach to bullying prevention is lacking, and address these gaps. A crucial component of this framework is providing training and support for school staff and family to ensure they understand bullying and are committed to addressing it.

At the same time, whole-school approaches to bullying intervention must engage young people in the development and implementation of strategies and policies. Children and adolescents can provide invaluable insights into online environments and behaviour that may be key to the prevention of bullying-related harm. Engaging young people as co-researchers and youth leaders, as in the *CFS* intervention, can invigorate school efforts to address cyberbullying, and help to ensure staff and school commitment to bullying prevention. Engaging with students through the *CFS* and other projects, as well as with their parents, has also shown that cyberbullying and inappropriate online behaviours are occurring amongst younger and younger students. It will be important, therefore, to explore young children's online behaviours and age-appropriate ways to maximize their safety in these environments.

Lessons have also been learned in relation to the evaluation of bullying and cyberbullying interventions. If curriculum implementation was the only active component of school-based bullying prevention, its impact would be clear within the first year of implementation. This would enable the full effects to be observed within the typical research project duration. However, we have found that whole-school interventions take much longer to realize their full potential. School policy review and planning, staff professional development, and integration of new policies into practice, take considerable effort and time, possibly years, to be fully in effect.

Lastly, we must be realistic about the high rates of teacher attrition and the realities of staff and administration turnover. These realities mean that intervention effects are often evaluated too soon to capture the real benefits made by such interventions. This may be the reason, for example, for the small effect sizes observed in the *CFS* study (Cross, Lester, et al., 2015; Cross et al., 2009). It is important to ensure interventions can be sustained over time, and are flexible enough to adapt to school changes, with appropriately timed evaluations and follow-ups to detect and measure intervention impact and outcomes.

Conclusion

Bullying and cyberbullying victimization continues to be a significant threat to the well-being of Australian children and young people. There is now a considerable body of research, including the *Friendly Schools* research described in this chapter, which demonstrates that evidence-based strategies can reduce bullying and cyberbullying. These strategies are most effectively implemented as part of a whole-school approach. The unique challenges of the school environment means that research translators, educators, and policy-makers must ensure school staff have sufficient support, time, and resources to plan, implement, and evaluate bullying prevention efforts. Despite evidence for the effectiveness and sustainability of the *Friendly Schools* intervention, there is scope for further research, particularly investigating ways to prevent cyber-bullying and ensure safer online behaviour among young children, and to explore the interplay between intervention fidelity, teacher education in-service and pre-service, and adaptation and the system level supports needed to ensure intervention implementation and sustainability.

References

Almeida, A., Correia, I., & Marinho, S. (2009). Moral disengagement, normative beliefs of peer group, and attitudes regarding roles in bullying. *Journal of School Violence*, 9(1), 23–36.

Australian Communications and Media Authority. (2013). *Like, post, share: Young Australians' experience of social media*. Canberra: Commonwealth of Australia.

Barnes, A., Cross, D., Lester, L., Hearn, L., Epstein, M., & Monks, H. (2012). The invisibility of covert bullying among students: Challenges for school intervention. *Australian Journal of Guidance and Counselling*, 22, 206–226. doi:10.1017/jgc.2012.27.

Barrish, H. H., Saunders, M., & Wolf, M. M. (1969). Good behavior game: Effects of individual contingencies for group consequences on disruptive behavior in a classroom 1. *Journal of Applied Behavior Analysis*, 2(2), 119–124.

Bronfenbrenner, U. (1995). Developmental ecology through space and time: A future perspective. In P. Moen, G. H. Elder, & K. Luscher (Eds.), *Examining lives in context: Perspectives on the ecology of human development* (pp. 619–647). Washington, DC: American Psychological Association.

Coffin, J., Larson, A., & Cross, D. (2010). Bullying in an Aboriginal context. *Australian Journal of Indigenous Education*, 39(1), 77–87.

Commonwealth of Australia. (1994). *Sticks and stones: A report on violence in schools*. Canberra: Australia Publishing Service.

Cross, D., & Barnes, A. (2014a). One size doesn't fit all: Rethinking implementation research for bullying prevention. In R. M. Schott & D. M. Søndergaard (Eds.), *School bullying: New theories in context* (pp. 405–417). Cambridge: Cambridge University Press.

Cross, D., & Barnes, A. (2014b). Using systems theory to understand and respond to family influences on children's bullying behavior: Friendly Schools Friendly Families Program. *Theory into Practice*, 53(4), 293–299.

Cross, D., Barnes, A., Papageorgiou, A., Hadwen, K., Hearn, L., & Lester, L. (2015). A social–ecological framework for understanding and reducing cyberbullying behaviours. *Aggression and Violent Behavior*, 23, 109–117. doi:10.1016/j.avb.2015.05.016.

Cross, D., Brown, D., Epstein, M., & Shaw, T. (2010). *Cyber Friendly Schools Project: Strengthening school and families' capacity to reduce the academic, social, and emotional harms secondary students' experience from cyber bullying (Public Education Endowment Trust, PEET)*. Perth: Child Health Promotion Research Centre, Edith Cowan University.

Cross, D., Lester, L., Barnes, A., Cardoso, P., & Hadwen, K. (2015). If it's about me, why do it without me? Genuine student engagement in school cyberbullying education. *International Journal of Emotional Education*, 7(1), 35–51.

Cross, D., Lester, L., Pearce, N., Barnes, A., & Beatty, S. (2018). A group randomized controlled trial evaluating parent involvement in whole-school actions to reduce bullying. *The Journal of Educational Research*, 111(3), 255–267.

Cross, D., Monks, H., Hall, M., Shaw, T., Pintabona, Y., Erceg, E., Hamilton, G., Roberts, C., Waters, S., & Lester, L. (2011). Three-year results of the Friendly Schools whole-of-school intervention on children's bullying behaviour. *British Educational Research Journal*, 37(1), 105–129. doi:10.1080/01411920903420024.

Cross, D., Pintabona, Y., Hall, M., Hamilton, G., & Erceg, E. (2004). Validated guidelines for school-based bullying prevention and management. *International Journal of Mental Health Promotion*, 6(3), 34–42.

Cross, D., Pintabona, Y., Hall, M., Hamilton, G., Erceg, E., & Roberts, C. (2003). The Friendly Schools Project: An empirically grounded school-based bullying prevention program. *Journal of Psychologists and Counsellors in Schools*, 13(1), 36–46.

Cross, D., Runions, K. C., Shaw, T., Wong, J. W. Y., Campbell, M., Pearce, N., Burns, S., Lester, L., Barnes, A., & Resnicow, K. (2019). Friendly Schools universal bullying prevention intervention: Effectiveness with secondary school students. *International Journal of Bullying Prevention*, 1, 45–57. doi:10.1007/s42380-018-0004-z.

Cross, D., Shaw, T., Epstein, M., Pearce, N., Barnes, A., Burns, S., Waters, S., Lester, L., & Runions, K. (2018). Impact of the Friendly Schools whole-school intervention on transition to secondary school and adolescent bullying behaviour. *European Journal of Education*, 53(4), 495–513. doi:10.1111/ejed.12307.

Cross, D., Shaw, T., Hadwen, K., Cardoso, P., Slee, P., Roberts, C., Thomas, L., & Barnes, A. (2016). Longitudinal impact of the Cyber Friendly Schools program on adolescents' cyberbullying behavior. *Aggressive Behavior*, 42, 166–180. doi:10.1002/ab.21609.

Cross, D., Shaw, T., Hearn, L., Epstein, M., Monks, H., Lester, L., & Thomas, L. (2009). *Australian covert bullying prevalence study (ACBPS)*. Western Australia: Report prepared for the Department of Education, Employment and Workplace Relations (DEEWR).

Cross, D., Waters, S., Pearce, N., Shaw, T., Hall, M., Erceg, E., Burns, S., Roberts, C., & Hamilton, G. (2012). The Friendly Schools Friendly Families programme: Three-year bullying behaviour outcomes in primary school children. *International Journal of Educational Research*, 53, 394–406.

da Silva, J. L., de Oliveira, W. A., Zequinao, M., da silva Lizzi, A. E., Pereira, B., & Silva, I. M. (2018). Results from inteventions addressing social skills to reduce school bullying: A systematic review with meta-analysis. *Trends in Psychology*, 26(1), 523–535.

Domitrovich, C. E., Bradshaw, C. P., Poduska, J. M., Hoagwood, K., Buckley, J. A., Olin, S., Romanelli, L. H., Leaf, P. J., Greenberg, M. T., & Ialongo, N. S. (2008). Maximizing the implementation quality of evidence-based preventive interventions in schools: A conceptual framework. *Advances in School Mental Health Promotion*, 1(3), 6–28.

Driscoll, K. C., & Pianta, R. C. (2010). Banking time in head start: Early efficacy of an intervention designed to promote supportive teacher–child relationships. *Early Education and Development*, 21(1), 38–64.

Durlak, J. A., & DuPre, E. P. (2008). Implementation matters: A review of research on the influence of implementation on program outcomes and the factors affecting implementation. *American Journal of Community Psychology*, 41(3–4), 327–350.

Espelage, D. L. (2014). Ecological theory: Preventing youth bullying, aggression, and victimization. *Theory into Practice*, 53(4), 257–264.

Fingerman, K. L., & Bermann, E. (2000). Applications of family systems theory to the study of adulthood. *The International Journal of Aging and Human Development*, 51(1), 5–29.

Fletcher, A., Fitzgerald-Yau, N., Jones, R., Allen, E., Viner, R. M., & Bonell, C. (2014). Brief report: Cyberbullying perpetration and its associations with socio-demographics, aggressive behaviour at school, and mental health outcomes. *Journal of Adolescence*, 37(8), 1393–1398.

Gini, G., & Pozzoli, T. (2013). Bullied children and psychosomatic problems: A meta-analysis. *Pediatrics*, 132(4), 720–729. doi:10.1542/peds.2013-0614.

Hart, R. (1992). *Children's participation: From tokenism to citizenship*. Florence: International Child Development Centre/UNICEF.

Jiménez-Barbero, J. A., Ruiz-Hernández, J. A., Llor-Zaragoza, L., Pérez-García, M., & Llor-Esteban, B. (2016). Effectiveness of anti-bullying school programs: A meta-analysis. *Children and Youth Services Review*, 61, 165–175. doi:10.1016/j.childyouth.2015.12.015.

Jones, S. M., Bouffard, S. M., & Weissbourd, R. (2013). Educators' social and emotional skills vital to learning. *Phi Delta Kappan*, 94(8), 62–65.

Kowalski, R. M., & Limber, S. P. (2013). Psychological, physical, and academic correlates of cyberbullying and traditional bullying. *Journal of Adolescent Health, 53* (1, Supplement), S13–S20. doi:10.1016/j.jadohealth.2012.09.018.

Langos, C. (2013). Which laws can apply to cyberbullying? *Bulletin (Law Society of South Australia)*, 35(10), 38–39.

Lester, L., Cross, D., & Shaw, T. (2012). Problem behaviours, traditional bullying and cyberbullying among adolescents: Longitudinal analyses. *Emotional and Behavioural Difficulties*, 17(3–4), 435–447. doi:10.1080/13632752.2012.704313.

Lester, L., Cross, D., Shaw, T., & Dooley, J. (2012). Adolescent bully-victims: Social health and the transition to secondary school. *Cambridge Journal of Education*, 42(2), 213–233.

Lester, L., Pearce, N., Waters, S., Barnes, A., Beatty, S., & Cross, D. (2017). Family involvement in a whole-school bullying intervention: Mothers' and fathers' communication and influence with children. *Journal of Child and Family Studies*, 26(10), 2716–2727.

Minuchin, P. (1985). Families and individual development: Provocations from the field of family therapy. *Child Development*, 289–302.

Modecki, K. L., Minchin, J., Harbaugh, A. G., Guerra, N. G., & Runions, K. C. (2014). Bullying prevalence across contexts: A meta-analysis measuring cyber and traditional bullying. *Journal of Adolescent Health*, 55(5), 602–611. doi:10.1016/j.jadohealth.2014.06.007.

Moore, S. E., Norman, R. E., Suetani, S., Thomas, H. J., Sly, P. D., & Scott, J. G. (2017). Consequences of bullying victimization in childhood and adolescence: A systematic review and meta-analysis. *World Journal of Psychiatry*, 7(1), 60–76.

Paki, D., Coffin, J., Cross, D., & Erceg, E. (2011). Solid Kids Solid Schools: Online student, teacher and family resources to reduce bullying in Aboriginal communities. www.solidkids.com.au.

Pearce, N. L. (2010). Critical success factors for building school capacity to engage parents in school-based bullying prevention interventions. PhD Thesis, Edith Cowan University.

Rigby, K., & Slee, P. (2008). Interventions to reduce bullying. *International Journal of Adolescent Medicine and Health*, 20, 165–184. doi:10.1515/IJAMH.2008.20.2.165.

Rigby, K., & Slee, P. T. (1991). Bullying among Australian school children: Reported behavior and attitudes toward victims. *Journal of Social Psychology*, 131(5), 615–627.

Runions, K. C. (2013). Toward a conceptual model of motive and self-control in cyber-aggression: Rage, revenge, reward, and recreation. *Journal of Youth and Adolescence*, 42(5), 751–771. doi:10.1007/s10964-013-9936-2.

Runions, K. C. (2014). Reactive aggression and peer victimization from pre-kindergarten to first grade: Accounting for hyperactivity and teacher–child conflict. *British Journal of Educational Psychology*, 84(4), 537–555.

Runions, K. C., & Bak, M. (2015). Online moral disengagement, cyberbullying, and cyber-aggression. *Cyberpsychology Behavior and Social Networking*, 18(7), 400–405. doi:10.1089/cyber.2014.0670.

Runions, K., Shapka, J. D., Dooley, J., & Modecki, K. (2013). Cyber-aggression and victimization and social information study processing: Integrating the medium and the message. *Psychology of Violence*, 3(4), 380–380. doi:10.1037/a0034503.

Sasson, H., & Mesch, G. (2014). Parental mediation, peer norms and risky online behavior among adolescents. *Computers in Human Behavior*, 33, 32–38.

Shier, H. (2001). Pathways to participation: Openings, opportunities and obligations. *Children & Society*, 15(2), 107–117.

Shute, R. H., & Slee, P. T. (2015). *Child development: Theories and critical perspectives*. New York: Routledge.

Skrzypiec, G., & Slee, P. (2017). Implementing quality wellbeing Programs in schools. In C. Cefai & P. Cooper (Eds.), *Mental health promotion in schools: Cross-cultural narratives and perspectives* (pp. 207–220). Rotterdam: Sense Publishers.

Slee, P. T. (1996). The PEACE Pack: A programme for reducing bullying in our schools. *Journal of Psychologists and Counsellors in Schools,* 6(S1), 63–70.

Slee, P. T., & Mohyla, J. (2007). The PEACE Pack: An evaluation of interventions to reduce bullying in four Australian primary schools. *Educational Research,* 49(2), 103–114.

Spears, B., Slee, P. T., & Huntley, J. (2015). *Cyberbullying, sexting, and the law.* Adelaide: University of South Australia.

Spears, B. A., Keeley, M., Bates, S., & Katz, I. (2014). *Research on youth exposure to, and management of, cyberbullying incidents in Australia. Part A: Literature review on the estimated prevalence of cyberbullying involving Australian minors (SPRC Report 9/2014).* Sydney: Social Policy Research Centre, UNSW Australia.

Spears, B. A., & Zeederberg, M. (2013). Emerging methodological strategies to address cyberbullying: Online social marketing and young people as co-researchers. In S. Bauman, D. Cross, & J. Walker (Eds.), *Principles of cyberbullying research: Definitions, measures, and methodology.* New York: Routledge.

Steffgen, G., König, A., Pfetsch, J., & Melzer, A. (2009). The role of empathy for adolescents' cyberbullying behaviour. *Kwartalnik Pedagogiczny= Pedagogical Quarterly,* 214(4), 183–198.

Ttofi, M. M., & Farrington, D. P. (2011). Effectiveness of school-based programs to reduce bullying: A systematic and meta-analytic review. *Journal of Experimental Criminology,* 7, 27–56.

Vreeman, R. C., & Carroll, A. E. (2007). A systematic review of school-based interventions to prevent bullying. *Archives of Pediatrics & Adolescent Medicine,* 161, 78–88. doi:10.1001/archpedi.161.1.78.

Ybarra, M. L., & Mitchell, K. J. (2004). Youth engaging in online harassment: Associations with caregiver–child relationships, Internet use, and personal characteristics. *Journal of Adolescence,* 27(3), 319–336.

Yeager, D. S., Fong, C. J., Lee, H. Y., & Espelage, D. L. (2015). Declines in efficacy of anti-bullying programs among older adolescents: Theory and a three-level meta-analysis. *Journal of Applied Developmental Psychology,* 37, 36–51. doi:10.1016/j.appdev.2014.11.005.

7

IJIME PREVENTION PROGRAMMES IN JAPAN

Yuichi Toda

Most intervention work on school bullying has been in Western countries, but one exception is Japan. Japanese bullying, or *ijime*, is distinctive and more class- and relationship-based than Western *bullying*. This affects which interventions are most likely to be suitable and effective. This chapter discusses *ijime*, and interventions against *ijime*. There has been intervention work in other eastern countries, for example South Korea and Hong Kong, for which the reader is referred to Kwak (2016) and Lin and Lai (2016).

The context of the research: the background of *ijime*

Among the serious problems in Japanese schools, *ijime* is the most shocking, as it represents a damaging of children's life by other children. After a short history of *ijime* in Japan, theory and models to explain *ijime* are presented in this section.

Serious problems in Japanese schools and ijime

Bullying (Japanese word, *ijime*) is not the only problem in Japanese schools. Shwalb, Nakazawa, and Shwalb (2005) describe in detail several aspects of development among Japanese children, including such problems as child abuse and neglect, and school refusal. Another issue is children's media use (including television, video games, and manga), which has both positive and negative aspects. Among these, however, bullying incidents shook all of Japanese society when it led to cases of suicide and wide media coverage. As for rampage school shootings, Japan has experienced rampage killing incidents involving knives in schools or on a public road, and the perpetrators seem to have done this to avenge themselves against schools or society. Preventing suicide and rampage killings is our last line of defence, and the prevention of bullying is the first line.

A short history of ijime in Japan

In 1986, Japanese society was shaken by the news of the suicide of a Japanese 8th grade boy who had been bullied not only by his peers but also by his three teachers. They bullied him, for example, by writing good-bye messages on a card and placing it on the boy's desk with a flower vase in the classroom, which indicated a 'mock funeral'. It was followed by his real one. When he hanged himself, he left the names of the perpetrators, so they were arrested and tried, and the school was found guilty.

In subsequent years, the amount of bullying noticed by teachers decreased and the media focus and people's interest turned to school absenteeism. However, it was only the visibility of *ijime* that had changed, and the second media focus on *ijime* occurred in 1994, when a 14-year-old boy hanged himself. It stemmed from crime rather than trouble in school, as the perpetrators had extorted more than 1 million Japanese yen from the victim while severely harming him physically, and finally they were arrested. The third wave of media focus happened in 2006–2007 in reports of sequential *ijime* suicides. Most media criticized the schools and local educational committees, which placed additional stress on schools and teachers.

In 2011–2012, the *ijime* suicide case of an 8th grade boy in Otsu city, located in the Kansai area, resulted in media attention and became a major social issue. The school and the local board of education were blamed for not dealing with the bullying incident properly and not reporting it sufficiently. Reacting to the enormous wave of social concern, the Japanese government implemented an Act requiring schools to be well-prepared to prevent and handle *ijime* incidents. In 2013, the Bullying Prevention Promotion Act (*Ijime Boushi Taisaku Suishin Hou*) was promulgated in June and entered in force in September.

In 2016, a 14-year-old girl committed suicide in Kobe, and in 2018 it was revealed that a memorandum detailing the girl's relationships and events around her suicide elicited from students just after the incident had been concealed by the principal of the junior high school and a member of the local board of education. The Act requires local Boards of Education and schools to define and announce their policy on preventing and dealing with bullying. However, not a few schools seem to have simply copied and pasted other schools' policies, and most schools might have not discussed the content with new students and their parents at the beginning of each school year. Though some municipalities are aware of the importance of following the Act and not only revising their policies but supporting schools in detecting and dealing with incidents in their early stages, the others are too far behind to follow sufficiently.

Theory and models to explain ijime

The first and most well-referenced theory of *ijime* was presented in detail by Morita and Kiyonaga (1986) in a book entitled *Ijime – Disease of the Classroom*. Their Four Layer Structure model distinguishes the bully, victim, onlooker, and bystander, which is similar to the participant role model of Salmivalli et al. (1996).

Nakai (1997) describes the process of psychological control used to make victims helpless. He described three steps of such a process of victimization: isolation, helplessness, and invisibility. This process describes *ijime* well. A summary of this theory follows. Isolation begins with targeting, to let others know who is marked out to be attacked, followed by spreading propaganda to justify the victimization; pupils are extremely sensitive to salient differences in behaviour or appearance. In the second step, the victim is forced to learn helplessness through violence from which they are not protected, punishment for telling adults about it, and punishment for psychological resistance. Through this process, victims come to look as if they are obeying voluntarily, and the perpetrators gain a sense of superiority in maintaining their dominance. The completion of this process makes the victim simply surrender to threats. The last step is invisibility. The victims gradually lose their own pride and dignity, and with the conspiracy of the onlookers, the *ijime* cannot then be recognized. The perpetrators control the victims psychologically, for example, depriving them of their standing to speak out against *ijime* by forcing them to participate in *ijime* toward other pupils. In addition, victims' money is wasted uselessly and/or their belongings are easily taken and damaged by the perpetrators, which harms the self-esteem of the victims. The weakened victim cannot escape from the relationship with the perpetrators.

Our Japanese practices are mostly based upon such theories and models to think about and cope with *ijime*.

Underpinning research

Among various topics of psychological research on *ijime*, some are presented here as they relate to three concerns: (1) the help-seeking of victims and maintaining their anonymity, (2) stopping the escalation of *ijime*, and (3) the worst cases and long-term influence of *ijime*. This research is considered important for constructing and evaluating *ijime* prevention/intervention practices.

Help-seeking of victims and anonymity

To prevent victimization effectively, it is important to intervene not only at the school and classroom levels but also at the individual level (Smith, Ananiadou, & Cowie, 2003). Views on victim's coping strategies have been compared between Eastern and Western countries (e.g. Kanetsuna & Smith, 2002); however, the coping strategies pupils use against *ijime* have been relatively unexamined. While there are many strategies that pupils use against bullying, one strategy would be to tell others about acts of bullying and seek help from an appropriate person (Smith & Shu, 2000).

In school settings, teachers and friends are the most common helping resources (Mizuno & Ishikuma, 2004). However, some pupils fear that telling a teacher will result in even worse bullying (Fekkes, Pijpers, & Verloove-Vanhorick, 2005). Japanese children are more likely to seek help from their friends than from teachers or counsellors (Yamaguchi, Mizuno, & Ishikuma, 2004). Therefore, the establishment of a peer support system (discussed later) appears to be one method for dealing with problems of *ijime*.

Studies in Western societies show that victims do not find it difficult to seek help from friends (Oliver & Candappa, 2007). Among Japanese pupils, Nagai (2009) points out that children who report severe peer victimization are less likely to seek help from their friends. A scale of help-seeking behaviours was developed by Tamura and Ishikuma (2001). This scale assesses two dimensions of help-seeking expectations. On the positive side, help-seeking reflects how responsible the helper is when seeking help; on the other side of help-seeking is fear and concerns over the accessibility of help-seeking. In examining the relationship between victimization and expectations of receiving help from their friends, Mizuno, Yanagida, and Toda (2018) found that early teenage Japanese boys who were victimized may expect their friends' help (responsibility expectations), but their accessibility expectations may be rather pessimistic. Girls did not show such results. Such tendencies suggest that the Q&A handout method (discussed below) would be effective, as children can report their hardships anonymously.

Kanetsuna, Smith, and Morita (2006) also suggested that because of the difficulty in finding external help as well as the fear of the ongoing *ijime* worsening, targeted victims may be much more reluctant to seek help. Some media reports have criticized teachers for not being able to detect *ijime*, but we should keep in mind how difficult it is to do so if not only the perpetrators but the victims do not report it.

Stopping the escalation of ijime

Morita et al. (2001) reported the results of cross-national research that found that fewer Japanese young teenagers answered that they would try to stop bullying than in the Netherlands and Britain. If Japanese children seem less willing to intervene in an *ijime* situation, is this a Japanese tendency? Probably we should consider the group process in Japanese schools when we think about *ijime* and its interventions.

In a school class with aggressive behaviours, imbalances of power may emerge that can give rise to *ijime*. However, without factors maintaining these power imbalances and aggression, there should be no escalation of violence. This should also hold true for *ijime* in Japan, and researchers have investigated several factors that might affect escalation. Here, studies of justifications of aggressive behaviour, group processes, victims' attempts to cope with it, and other factors are summarized.

Justification: Justification is necessary to avoid self-punishment when we commit or continue prohibited behaviours. Bandura (1986) theorized this process as a dysfunctional mechanism of the self-regulation process, and later a form of Moral Disengagement (e.g. Osofsky, Bandura, & Zimbardo, 2005).

With respect to *ijime*, based on questionnaire research on junior high school students, Inoue, Toda, and Nakamatsu (1986) elicited three reasoning factors used to justify bullying: sanctions, heterogeneity exclusion, and enjoyment. Using the same items, Onishi, Kurokawa, and Yoshida (2009) found two factors, where heterogeneity exclusion and enjoyment combined as one factor. Hara (2002) also looked at justifications for bullying among Japanese 12–14-year-old schoolchildren. Children with different types of involvement in bullying showed different justification strategies. In particular, bullies were more likely to blame the victims than were children assuming other roles.

Among the mechanisms of moral disengagement, 'diffusion of responsibility' brings collective harmfulness without ascribing responsibility to a single person. If the number of perpetrators grows, a process of 'diffusion of responsibility' sets in and the violence may escalate. Recently, 'collective moral disengagement' has been the new focus of investigation (Gini, Pozzoli, & Bussey, 2014), and such a viewpoint should be also worth examining in the Japanese situation.

Group processes: The increase in the number of perpetrators could be explained mainly by conformity. Some studies have looked in detail at the process of conformity.

Toda, Strohmeier, and Spiel (2008) showed a contingency between group size and frequency of victimization, in Japan and in Austria. When the aggression was not frequent, in half of the cases the number of perpetrators was one or two; on the other hand, when the aggression was frequent, in half of the cases in Austria and 80% of the cases in Japan, the perpetrators were a group. Kubota (2004) also showed that the number of assistants of bullying and the kinds of bullying affect the duration of bullying.

Attempts to cope and other factors: Though justification by perpetrators and the group nature of bullying may escalate, victims are not just watching the unfolding of a tragedy. They try to change, but often in vain. Also, certain important factors steer the process in a certain direction. Honma (2003) tried to clarify the characteristics and factors relevant to the cessation of *ijime*, suggesting that intervention with students belonging to 'bullying-maintaining groups' should involve not only individual bullies but also the bullying groups and other classroom members.

When such a group process is ongoing, intervention by just one hero/heroine would not ordinarily be effective, and furthermore, it could be dangerous by provoking perpetrators' anger and directing it against the intervenor as the next target of *ijime*.

Worst cases and long-term influence of ijime

The worst cases of *ijime* in Japan so far would be the numerous *ijime* suicides; some revenge murders of perpetrators by victims; and a few cases of the murder of victims by perpetrators. Mayama (2002) argued that '*ijime* suicide' (or suicide caused by bullying) was 'one of the most serious problems in Japanese primary and secondary schools since the late 1970s'. Though there have been many revenge rampage shootings by ex-victims of bullying in the US (Larkin, 2013), until 2017 Japanese society had not experienced any cases of rampage shooting in the schools (although there have been incidents with knives). However, there is no guarantee or reason for saying that such rampage shooting will never happen in Japan. Supporting and taking care of victims is also necessary to help prevent a very few but terrible cases of ex-victims fighting back against perpetrators, teachers, or schools.

Ishibashi, Wakabayashi, Naito, and Shikano (1999) clarified the lasting effects of past victimization experiences (being bullied by peers) and their relationship to college students' tendencies to fear others. The long-lasting effects included suffering from various physical, behavioural, social, and psychological symptoms. However, those students who regarded themselves as having become more patient from having been bullied did not have a stronger tendency to fear others. Also, Miyake (2004) suggested a relationship between pre-adolescent bullying experiences with the attachment relationships of college students. Their results suggest that experiences of being bullied can have lasting effects which continue after graduation from high school.

Mishima (2008) also investigated the long-term influence of bullying inflicted by intimate friends during the upper elementary school grades (5th and 6th grades). Among high school students, those who reported victimization tended to show subsequent school maladjustment in high school, as well as feeling more anxiety toward interpersonal relationships than other students.

Some studies have focused on the buffering effects of recuperation. Kameda and Sagara (2011) held a semi-structured interview with young adults to examine the factors that enhanced the sense of self-growth among ex-victims. They found that a supportive relationship may help victims recuperate. In addition to support from others, the victim's own initiative in coping with the negative experience appeared to be important in attaining a feeling of self-growth.

As for personal factors that buffer the negative effects of victimization, Araki (2005) investigated whether resilience contributes to victims' adjustment in young adulthood. Participants in the questionnaire research were Japanese young adults with a mean age of about 20 years. Those who had been peer-victimized during childhood had greater distress and anxiety than those who had not, although no difference was found in the levels of exposure to current interpersonal stressful events. The distress and anxiety were stronger for men than women, and the starting age of victimization made no difference in the severity of the problems. Both problem-focused and support-seeking coping as protective factors had a compensatory effect on the long-term negative outcomes of victimization by peers during childhood.

The transition from pure research to application

Japanese adaptation of European practices

As for new Japanese practices in recent decades for *ijime* prevention, most of them did not originate from Japanese research but from European research and earlier practices. However, in the process of application, various adaptations were made to fit into the Japanese context. These adaptations were partly based on research evidence, but mostly followed practical trials and selection by practitioners. Also, the applications were greatly supported by overseas researchers who gave Japanese researchers and practitioners ideas and training. In the 1990s, the introduction of the Sheffield Project (Smith & Sharp, 1994), the PEACE Pack (Slee, 1996), and other programmes may have had an impact on Japanese schools, but perhaps not enough of one, unfortunately, due to the lack of sufficient understanding and willingness on the part of the schools. Following these, some European programmes were introduced and influenced Japanese practice.

Peer support in the Japanese context

Before introducing various types of peer support (peer counselling, peer mediation, peer tutoring, etc.) from the UK or Canada, it is useful to consider one original Japanese type of peer support that started in Kanazawa, named the Q&A Handout Method. In this system, pupils may write their concerns using a pen-name or anonymously and place them in a box which will be opened by teachers responsible for this activity. The teachers read them and decide whether a given concern should be handed over to peer supporters or handled by the teachers in the light of its urgency or severity. If it is considered safe to share a given concern and useful for peer supporters, the teachers rewrite it to conceal the handwriting and any private information. The peer supporters discuss it and write their replies to the concerns reflecting their own experience and opinions under the careful supervision of the teachers. Then the replies which are judged adequate are printed in a Q&A handout to be delivered to all the members of the school (Toda, 2005). This method seeks to achieve the sharing of concerns and advice within a community. In addition, this activity is designed to show the students that sharing serious problems with those without expertise can be dangerous, and thus the importance of telling adults when they heard about serious/emergency problems.

From around the year 2000, owing to the efforts of Dr Helen Cowie and her colleagues, the Japan Peer Support Association (JPSA) was able to offer excellent training sessions and attracted increased membership, helping disseminate the practice. Members of the JPSA have published many practical guidebooks. Concurrently, Taki (2000) has proposed the 'Japanese Peer Support Program', which includes peer-relationship training for elder pupils in elementary schools and prepares occasions for them to make use of their aims and skills to support younger pupils. Although the practice has diminished in contrast to the widespread adoption of JPSA practice, the idea might have influenced other practices later on.

Influence of ViSC and KiVa

From the mid-2000s, an Austrian researcher, Dr Dagmar Strohmeier, was invited to Japan several times, and she spoke about the ViSC Program and its evaluation. In 2008, Dr Christiane Spiel was similarly invited and gave several lectures, including on Bildung Psychology and the ViSC programme, at Kyoto University and the Japanese Conference of Developmental Psychology. From the late 2000s, Dr Christina Salmivalli has also given lectures and presentations on the KiVa anti-bullying programme at an academic meeting and international conferences. Such talks were inspiring, but as the audience mostly included academics, their impact was still much smaller than that of the introduction of Peer Support practice.

Among these, the exception was the invitation of Dr Miia Sainio from Finland in 2013, who gave lectures and conveyed the basic experiences of the KiVa programme for Japanese practitioners in Osaka. She spoke in Japanese, so the practitioners learnt easily from her, which led to a small trial KiVa programme at that time (Toda, Yamashita, & Ogawa, 2014). Though KiVa has attracted interest not only from academics but also from companies and practitioners, the funding aspect brings difficulties for implementing KiVa in the Japanese schools.

The three programmes mentioned above, Peer Support, ViSC, and KiVa, were introduced in detail in a Japanese handbook on prevention education (Yamasaki, Toda, & Watanabe, 2013). The book covers a variety of programmes in North America, Europe, Australia, and several Asian countries. Though the same programmes have not been implemented in Japanese society, currently the way that bullying is tackled in Japan has gradually changed from 'after-incident coping' to 'prevention'.

The Student Summit and Smartphone Summit

From around 2010, a new practice emerged in Japan, named the Smartphone Summit. This aims to prevent not only cyberbullying but other problems related to smartphone usage (Takeuchi, Abe, Miyake, & Toda, 2017). The Smartphone Summit is a child-centred cross-age programme growing out of the Student Summit of representatives from all the junior high schools in a city.

The programme originated in the Neyagawa Junior High School Student Summit, a conference organized by voluntary student council members from junior high schools in Neyagawa City, Osaka. Its central aim was to discuss and resolve various problems related to the lives of their peers in the city. For example, for tackling cyberbullying, the students wrote scenarios and performed dramas which included cyberbullying cases for their peers/ teachers/parents. Their bullying prevention project dramatically reduced the number of reported cases of bullying in the city (Takeuchi & Abe, 2015). This striking evidence of success led to the extension of the practice and its replication in other areas of Japan. The nature of this child-centred practice led to the participating students naming the practice a 'Summit', reflecting the fact that representative students from each school gather to discuss their problems and collaborate to create solutions. The name Smartphone Summit was coined by a couple of students, who believed that smartphone-related problems were central to the issues of their school community.

The Smartphone Summit, mainly implemented in the western part of Japan from 2014, recruits students who are willing to contribute from many schools in an area, such as cities and prefectures. The participants share and discuss problems of the Internet and smartphones prevalent in their schools and communities, and devise approaches to address them. Specifically, the Smartphone Summit consists of several meetings. In the first meeting, participants create a relaxed and friendly atmosphere through games designed to break the ice and then actively share opinions and ideas on Internet/smartphone issues. In subsequent meetings, participants consider the background of the problems, discuss solutions to them, and clarify concrete ideas to propose to their classmates. This practice is designed to provide participants with opportunities to better understand the problems of the Internet and smartphones and to build the confidence to improve themselves and their communities. This approach follows a cascade model of dissemination. The programme is designed to change its participants' behaviour as well as to empower the participants to widen their impact by changing the behaviour of same-age and younger peers in their school and beyond. Following the activities of the Summit, participants are encouraged to implement their own school team's grassroots activities in their school community.

The Smartphone Summit has three characteristic frameworks: the cascade for dissemination, inter-school activity, and inter-generational collaboration.

The use of a cascade model is similar to the Viennese Social Competence (ViSC) programme in Austria (Atria & Spiel, 2007; and Chapter 4), but there is a difference. The implementation model of the ViSC programme consists of a cascaded train-the-trainer model in which the programme developers (researchers) train ViSC coaches (e.g. school psychologists, teacher trainers), who in turn train teachers, who then train their students (Strohmeier, Hoffmann, Schiller, Stefanek, & Spiel, 2012). The Smartphone Summit, however, implemented a cascade whereby children's ideas are conveyed to other children.

The second aspect, the inter-school activity, follows the direction of the KiVa programme in Finland (see Chapter 3), which has biannual KiVa conference days where teachers from different schools exchange their experiences and ideas for improving the programme in each school (Salmivalli, Kärnä, & Poskiparta, 2010). As for the Smartphone Summit, all or at least several of the schools in a city are invited to participate in the programme.

The third aspect is inter-generational collaboration. The Smartphone Summit includes participants of various ages. High school students and junior high school students aged 12–18 work with each other, while university students facilitate their group discussions. These university students are supervised by a university faculty advisor. The idea of such inter-generational collaboration grew out of peer support practice, but in this instance not only students and teachers but also other professionals who support children (the media, police, corporations, etc.) come together and talk freely. For example, as media report about the practice, not only parents but also local politicians learn how children are facing their challenges.

Online support

Miyakawa, Takeuchi, Aoyama, and Toda (2013) reported a non-school-based approach using a Bulletin Board System (BBS) on the Internet. The first online support using BBS on the Internet in Japan appeared in the early 1990s, and the numbers gradually increased during the 2000s. Today, there are many different kinds of online support sites for victims of *ijime*, as well as for those affected by other school and family problems, run by either the local governments or the private sector (Miyakawa et al., 2013). Mr Miyakawa himself administers one such online support site where anyone can freely write and read others' queries and advice. One of the great advantages of such online support through BBS on the Internet is that children can ask for support anonymously so that they need not worry about retaliation from perpetrators or becoming a new target of *ijime* themselves. However, generally the only support they can receive from these online support sites is advice on what to do but not actual intervention, and so it may be more useful if such online supports can be connected thoughtfully with actual interventions at school.

The impact and legacy of the research

The impact of applied practices

As already mentioned, Japanese researchers and practitioners, learning from and inspired by European research and practice, have added certain modifications and tried new ways to handle *ijime*. Though the evidence of the impact is not sufficient, some have sought to depict the impact in a unique way.

Peer support

The greatest impact of the introduction of peer support has been the establishment and growth of the Japan Peer Support Association. Though evidence regarding the impact of the practice is scarce, its programmes were introduced by practitioners to practitioners through the workshops held by the Association. Rather than academic evidence, the experience of the workshop appears to have convinced the participants that the programme might work for children. Also, positive coverage by the media would have helped disseminate the practice. Now most Japanese practitioners know the term 'peer support', though at the beginning it was sometimes misunderstood as 'pure support' or listeners asked for it to be explained in Japanese words. However, there seem to have been difficulties in maintaining the quality of the practice when transmitting it among practitioners. For this reason, the Association tried to establish a system of qualifications to certify applicable practices for children.

Numerous studies have been conducted to determine the impact of the practice. Toda and Miyamae (2009) reviewed such research in Japanese contexts and concluded that there is a lack of strong evidence of positive effects. Nevertheless, since then, the practice has spread widely and in some instances has been implemented on a city-wide scale; however, the results have not yet been published in academic journals. I hope such results will appear soon. However, the results may not be sufficiently positive. Nagai and Arai (2013) investigated the effect of peer support training on help-seeking directed towards peers among junior high school students. After peer support training, the participants showed higher scores on their help-seeking related to academic-career concerns. However, there seemed to be no difference in their help-seeking related to psychological/social concerns.

Children's initiative

Kanetsuna and Toda (2017) reported on a project conducted at a junior high school in Hyogo Prefecture during 2007 and 2008, funded by the local board of education. The project had three essential principles: a whole-school (inter-class-based) approach whereby students in every class of every grade participated in the project; a student-led approach in which, apart from the training sessions of teachers and parents, actual activities within the school were mostly conducted by the student committee; and a multi-purpose approach whose core aim was to tackle *ijime*, but which also aimed at career education for students.

The project started by building a project team within the school whose members included teachers, parents, students, and local representatives. The team then set a goal for the project, which was to raise awareness within the school and change attitudes towards the problem of *ijime* among teachers, parents, and students. In order to achieve this goal, teachers took a series of training sessions conducted by university professors. Parents were given a series of newsletters which explained what *ijime* is, how they can detect whether their children might be involved in any *ijime* situation, and how they should deal with it either by themselves or with teachers. A committee of students was elected on a representative basis, ideally one or two students per class, though in reality it was often elected by an up-or-down vote for students chosen by class teachers; this committee led various activities within the school. They first collected opinions on *ijime* from the students in order to understand their general perceptions of *ijime*. They then made a slogan for prevention activities and designed a stop *ijime* sign. Finally, as a culmination of two years of the anti-*ijime* project, they produced video footage for anti-*ijime* awareness-raising with English and Japanese subtitles, so that it can be distributed all over the world (www.youtube.com/watch?v=ZW92_9SYb-0).

One of the characteristics of this project was the support it received from a number of professionals from different fields, including academic researchers, both foreign and domestic, as well as experts of film production and theatre arts. These professionals not only gave advice to the students and supported their activities but also provided some excitement through their involvement in the project and helped give the project a positive attitude towards anti-*ijime* work. This part of the project was exactly what 'project-oriented' means, as this particular school had a problem of low self-esteem and low levels of motivation among students. Yet by meeting and working with those professionals, students gained self-esteem and started to be actively involved in anti-*ijime* work.

The effect of the project on the number of reported *ijime* cases, however, varied depending on the grades and classes, as well as the energy and effort the different groups of students put into it; those who were not members of the committee involved in anti-*ijime* activities were considered merely passively as a target whose attitudes towards *ijime* and actions against it were to be changed. Thus, an effect of the project was to split the student body between those who approved of the activities of the committee and those who did not. However, one of the positive outcomes of the project was that after it ended, attitudes towards the activities of the student committee became much more positive; many more students hoped to become members of the committee and get involved in anti-*ijime* actions within the school.

Student and Smartphone Summits and prospective evaluation

As for the original Neyegawa Junior High School Student Summit, Takeuchi (2011) reported that the drama performed by the members of Student Summit vividly expressed severe peer-relationship difficulties and made a strong impact on both teachers and students. This drama was recorded and edited for DVD and distributed to all primary and junior high schools around the region for use in anti-*ijime* activities. Takeuchi (2012) reported that, according to the statistics by the local government, there was a reduction in recognized *ijime* incidents in 2011 of about 25% in the region from 2007. Although their activities, such as a play they put on, were not the only reason for this reduction, a student-led horizontal-inter-school-based approach to handling *ijime* and net-*ijime* can still be considered to work very effectively. Another strong point of this inter-school-based approach is that even if one school falls into a serious situation and cannot recover by itself, other schools can work with it to deter or stop *ijime* or at least improve the situation.

Turning to the Smartphone Summit, Miyake, Takeuchi, and Toda (2018) investigated the variety of perspectives of junior high school students who had participated in the Smartphone Summit for appropriate usage of the Internet and smartphones in Okayama, a western Japanese city. This summit was an educational project designed to empower junior high school students to advocate appropriate usage of the Internet and smartphones among older, same-age, and younger peers within school communities and society as a whole. The participants were 26 students (7th and 8th grade) from 18 junior high schools in Okayama. In the project, the participants discussed the pros and cons of the Internet and smartphones and presented their ideas concerning possible activities to encourage their classmates to use the Internet and smartphones in appropriate ways with the help of various adult experts. A questionnaire was administered to measure the participants' evaluation of their own and their classmates' current smartphone usage as well as anticipated future smartphone usage.

The results showed that the participants evaluated their own usage as more appropriate than that of their classmates and expected that future usage would be better for both themselves and their classmates than at present. Furthermore, the participants expected their classmates' usage to change more significantly than their own because their classmates' current usage seemed to them less appropriate, thereby leaving greater room for improvement. From the analysis of the patterns of participants' impact expectations toward their peers, it was found that there were three types of perspectives: moderate, relatively lower, and relatively higher evaluations, though most of them looked very positive at the summit.

Lessons learnt

New trials and future direction

Ijime prevention/intervention is a struggle against obstacles that requires us to meet challenges; these are discussed next. At the end of this chapter, the 'Ijime Immunity Program' and future directions of *ijime* prevention will be presented.

Obstacles

Among several obstacles to proper evaluation of interventions, finding control groups and maintaining funds are the most difficult to overcome. Most of the trials of preventive programmes lack sufficient funding and participants to conduct randomized control trials. This problem may be not restricted to Japan, but compared to the situation in Europe and the United States, the Japanese situation is rather worse. However, even when funded, Japanese researchers often hesitate to contact schools to collaborate with them in implementing new programmes, knowing that Japanese teachers are overworked (e.g. OECD, 2014). This would be a fundamental problem of Japanese schools facing any implementation trials.

Challenges

To overcome the challenge of such obstacles, the author suggests an 'umbrella' form of evaluation. This is not to ask schools to implement the same programme or to conduct evaluations with the same scales and in the same timing and grades. Instead, the dataset should contain such information as programme names, evaluation scales, grades, and timing, which would constitute multi-practice, multi-scale evaluation. If some schools implement the same programme and the same scales, then the effects can be compared by grades and/or the timing of the implementation. If the scales and grades are the same, then different programmes are to be compared. This approach has a merit of not forcing schools to choose programmes and timings, but it requires a huge effort of data collection to allow adequate comparisons between practices. However, if it is feasible for all schools to share the same scales, then the dataset can be much smaller while still allowing cross-programme evaluation.

If the results show that different programmes are effective in different aspects as measured by each scale, then a combination of the programmes may make sense. Such cross-programme collaboration may prepare schools to provide future curricula with an inclusive prevention education.

Ijime Immunity Program

Learning from European challenges, Toda (2018) has proposed the 'Ijime Immunity Program'. The programme has only three sessions: FIND, STOP, and FOLLOW UP. The reason for using 'immunity' rather than 'prevention' is that we cannot prevent all aggression, including that which sets off *ijime*, so instead we should aim for children to overcome their experiences as victims/perpetrators. We hope that the immunity arising from such experiences may stop escalations of *ijime*. All the sessions are planned out in a skeleton fashion, meaning they only have goals and hints and can adopt previously proposed materials to handle *ijime*. All the sessions would be conducted as open-ended sessions that could be repeated for different classes or grades. The types of *ijime* may differ by the school system, and new types of *ijime* may appear due to new digital devices.

Of the three sessions, Session A is intended to find the first buds of *ijime*. *Ijime* is not easily detected at its earliest stage, which is why it is necessary to discuss it among children with such questions as 'How does *ijime* differ from jokes?' and 'How do fighting and *ijime* differ?' Without adults teaching children the definitions of *ijime*, children may define and detect *ijime* by themselves, and through such discussions they may realize that it is possible for them to commit *ijime* without thinking that it is *ijime*, as their definitions differ from child to child.

Session B is intended to stop the escalation of *ijime* not only by oneself but with others. 'Not only by oneself' is important here. First, it takes courage to stop it by oneself. Second, it is dangerous for someone who is not popular in the class to try to stop it, as that person can be selected as the next target of *ijime*. Collective objection would be necessary to effectively stop *ijime* as a group process. Most European anti-bullying programmes involve sincere and active discussions of how to prevent bullying, through which children might express their true attitudes against bullying. In addition to the teacher's sincerity, this attitude prevents possible bullies from acting badly when the teacher is not watching.

The last session, Session C, is intended to follow up on the bullies and victims after intervention. This should be a practice of restorative justice to prevent revenge by the victims and surreptitious escalations of bullying. However, it may be difficult to actualize the restorative policy as a lesson in class. We need ideas and trials to create relevant lessons.

Future directions

Nakai (1997) suggests that *ijime* perpetrators look arrogant and confident, but in the bottom of their hearts they fear majority opinion; perpetrators might think that their behaviours are supported by their classmates despite not having the backing of their teachers (Toda, 1997). Taking this into account, the important point would be to teach children not 'what to do' but 'how to do'. Any practice led by the teachers without the children's sincere participation may lead *ijime* perpetrators to believe that they can commit *ijime* in accordance with their classmates' will behind the teachers' back. If the perpetrators realize that their classmates are truly against bullying, they would be reluctant to commit *ijime*, as it may be of no assistance to them in gaining popularity among their classmates.

For this reason, anti-*ijime* practice should be sincere and cool for children. In June 2018, eight high school students in Arizona visited Japan to attend the Kansai-Arizona Smartphone Summit and hold discussions with Japanese high school students. They facilitated several sessions and obtained media coverage. Further inter-school and international collaboration should invite children to act 'cool' and speak out strongly against *ijime*. Starting in 2016 at a tri-national symposium (Japan, China, and South Korea) at a conference of the Japanese Psychology Society, Japanese and South Korean researchers have also been collaborating on games and apps to prevent cyberbullying. Such international relationships would appeal to children and might be taken up by younger researchers so that further mutual exchanges and collaborations may emerge that may be connected to a much wider framework of collaboration led by such bodies as UNESCO and World Kids Online.

References

Araki, T. (2005). Resilience in a personal history of peer victimization: What factors contribute to victims' adjustment in young adulthood? *Japanese Journal of Personality*, 14, 54–68 (in Japanese).

Atria, M., & Spiel, C. (2007). Viennese Social Competence (ViSC) training for students: Program and evaluation. In J. E. Zins, M. J. Elias, & C. A. Maher (Eds.), *Bullying, victimization, and peer harassment: A handbook of prevention and intervention* (pp. 179–197). New York: Haworth Press.

Bandura, A. (1986). *Social foundations of thought and action: A social cognitive theory*. Englewood Cliffs, NJ: Prentice-Hall.

Fekkes, M., Pijpers, F. I. M., & Verloove-Vanhorick, S. P. (2005). Bullying: Who does what, when and where? Involvement of children, teachers and parents in bullying behavior. *Health Education Research: Theory & Practice*, 20(1), 81–91. doi:10.1093/her/cyg100.

Gini, G., Pozzoli, T., & Bussey, K. (2014). Collective moral disengagement: Initial validation of a scale for adolescents. *European Journal of Developmental Psychology*, 11, 386–395. doi:10.1080/17405629.2013.851024.

Hara, H. (2002). Justifications for bullying among Japanese schoolchildren. *Asian Journal of Social Psychology*, 5, 197–204.

Honma, T. (2003). Cessation of bullying and intervention with bullies: Junior High School students. *Japanese Journal of Educational Psychology*, 51, 390–400 (in Japanese).

Inoue, K., Toda, Y., & Nakamatsu, M. (1986). Roles in bullying situation. *Bulletin of the Faculty of Education, University of Tokyo*, 26, 89–106 (in Japanese).

Ishibashi, S., Wakabayashi, S., Naito, T., & Shikano, T. (1999). An investigation of the lasting effects of peer victimization in college students: Relationship to anthropophagic tendencies. *Bulletin of Christian Culture Studies, Kinjo Gakuin University*, 3, 11–19 (in Japanese).

Kameda, H., & Sagara, J. (2011). Effect of past bullied experiences and factors that help develop feelings of self-growth: Examination of the development process involving past bullied experiences and the current awareness of self-growth. *Japanese Journal of Counseling Science*, 44, 277–287 (in Japanese).

Kanetsuna, T., & Smith, P. K. (2002). Pupil insights into bullying, and coping with bullying: A binational study in Japan and England. *Journal of School Violence*, 1, 5–29.

Kanetsuna, T., Smith, P. K., & Morita, Y. (2006). Coping with bullying at school: Children's recommended strategies and attitudes to school-based interventions in England and Japan. *Aggressive Behavior*, 32, 570–580.

Kanetsuna, T., & Toda, Y. (2017). Applying multiple indices to monitor bullying longitudinally: A case of a Japanese junior high school. *Psychological Test and Assessment Modeling*, 59, 135–156.

Kubota, M. (2004). Can the coping behaviors of bullied children provide effective alternatives to bullying?: Attempts to modify the stigmatic labels given by gangs of bullies. *Journal of Educational Sociology*, 74, 249–268 (in Japanese).

Kwak, K., & Lee, S. (2016). The Korean research tradition on wang-ta. In P. K. Smith, K. Kwak, & Y. Toda (Eds.), *School bullying in different cultures: Eastern and western perspectives* (pp. 93–112). Cambridge: Cambridge University Press.

Larkin, R. W. (2013). Legitimated adolescent violence: Lessons from Columbine. In N. Böckler, T. Seeger, P. Sitzer, & W. Heitmeyer (Eds.), *School shootings: International research, case studies, and concepts for prevention* (pp.159–176). New York: Springer Science + Business Media.

Lin, S.-F., & Lai, C. L. (2016). Bullying in Hong Kong schools. In P. K. Smith, K. Kwak, & Y. Toda (Eds.), *School bullying in different cultures: Eastern and western perspectives* (pp. 133–150). Cambridge: Cambridge University Press.

Mayama, H. (2002). Discourse analysis as conceptual study: Toward the dismantling of ijime suicide. *Journal of Educational Sociology*, 70, 145–163 (in Japanese).

Mishima, K. (2008). Long-term influence of 'bullying' received from intimate friends during upper elementary school grades: Focusing on retrospect of high school students. *Japanese Journal of Experimental Social Psychology*, 47, 91–104 (in Japanese).

Miyakawa, M., Takeuchi, K., Aoyama, I., & Toda, Y. (2013). Problems and support practice in the Internet. *Studies on Education and Society*, 23, 41–52 (in Japanese).

Miyake, K. (2004). Adult attachment and victimization of bullying. *Journal of Kyushu University of Health and Welfare*, 5, 1–10 (in Japanese).

Miyake, M., Takeuchi, K., & Toda, Y. (2018). Variations of perspectives of junior high school students who have participated in Smartphone Summit for appropriate usage of the Internet and smartphones. *Pastoral Care in Education*, 36, 141–153. https://doi:10.1080/02643944.2018.1464592.

Mizuno, H., & Ishikuma, T. (2004). An overview of studies on social support for children: Some implications for research and practice in school psychology in Japan. *Japanese Journal of Counseling Science*, 37, 280–290 (in Japanese).

Mizuno, H., Yanagida, T., & Toda, Y. (2018). How help-seeking expectations are associated with relational and physical victimization among Japanese adolescents. *Psychology*, 9, 1412–1425.

Morita, Y., & Kiyonaga, K. (1986). *Ijime: Kyousitsu no Yamai* [Ijime: The disease of the classroom]. Tokyo: Kaneko Shobo (in Japanese).

Morita, Y., Soeda, H., Soeda, K., & Taki, M. (1998). Japan. In P.K. Smith, Y. Morita, J. Junger-Tas, D. Olweus, R. Catalano, & P. Slee (Eds.), *The nature of school bullying: A cross-national perspective* (pp.309–323). London and New York: Routledge.

Morita, Y., Soeda, H., Taki, M., Hoshino, K., Takemura, K., Matsu'ura, Y., Hata, M. Yonezato, S., Takekawa, I., & Soeda, K. (2001). *Cross-national studies on bullying*. Tokyo: Kaneko Shobo (in Japanese).

Nagai, S. (2009). Help-seeking intentions of elementary school students: Relationship with satisfaction with school life, experience of concerns and depression. *Japanese Journal of School Psychology*, 9, 17–24 (in Japanese).

Nagai, S., & Arai, K. (2013). The effect of peer support training on help-seeking with peers among junior high school students. *Japanese Journal of School Psychology*, 13, 65–76 (in Japanese). doi:10.24583/jjspedit.13.1_65.

Nakai, H. (1997). *Ariadone kara no Ito* [Ariadne's thread]. Tokyo: Misuzu Shobo (in Japanese).

OECD. (2014). *Talis 2013 Results: An international perspective on teaching and learning*. OECD Publishing. http://dx.doi:10.1787/9789264196261-en.

Oliver, C. & Candappa, M. (2007). Bullying and the politics of 'telling'. *Oxford Review of Education*, 33, 71–86.

Onishi, A., Kurokawa, M., & Yoshida, T. (2009). Influences of students' teacher recognition on abuse. *Japanese Journal of Educational Psychology*, 57, 324–335 (in Japanese).

Osofsky, M. J., Bandura, A., & Zimbardo, P. G. (2005). The role of moral disengagement in the execution process. *Law and Human Behavior*, 29, 371–393.

Salmivalli, C., Kärnä, A., & Poskiparta, E. (2010). Development, evaluation, and diffusion of a national anti-bullying program, KiVa. In B. Doll, W. Pfohl, & J. Yoon (Eds.), *Handbook of youth prevention science* (pp. 238–252). New York: Routledge.

Salmivalli, C., Lagerspetz, K., Björkqvist, K., Österman, K., & Kaukiainen, A. (1996). Bullying as a group process: Participant roles and their relations to social status within the group. *Aggressive Behavior*, 22, 1–15.

Shwalb, D., Nakazawa, J., & Shwalb, B. (Eds.) (2005). *Applied developmental psychology: Theory, practice, and research from Japan.* Greenwich, CT: Information Age.

Slee, P.T. (1996). The P.E.A.C.E. Pack: A programme for reducing bullying in our schools. *Australian Journal of Guidance and Counselling,* 6, 63–69.

Smith, P.K., & Sharp, S. (Eds.) (1994). *School bullying: Insights and perspectives.* London: Routledge.

Smith, P. K., & Shu, S. (2000). What good schools can do about bullying: Findings from a survey in English schools after a decade of research and action. *Childhood,* 7, 193–212. doi:10.1177/0907568200007002005.

Smith, P. K., Ananiadou, K., & Cowie, H. (2003). Interventions to reduce school bullying. *Canadian Journal of Psychiatry,* 48(9), 591–599.

Strohmeier, D., Hoffmann, C., SchillerE. M., Stefanek, E., & Spiel, C. 2012. ViSC social competence program. *New Directions for Youth Development,* 133, 71–84. doi:10.1002/yd.20008.

Takeuchi, K. (2012). Study of countermeasures to mobile phones and internet problems by peer support scheme: Efforts of cyberbullying eradication by junior-high school students summit. *Proceedings of the 54 Annual Meeting of the Japanese Association of Educational Psychology,* 54, 247 (in Japanese).

Takeuchi, K. (2011). Children's own initiative to change their school: A glimmer of hope after a tragic incident. In R. H. Shute, P. T. Slee, R. Murray-Harvey, & K. L. Dix (Eds.), *Mental health and wellbeing: Educational perspectives* (pp. 347–350). Adelaide, South Australia: Shannon Research Press.

Takeuchi, K., & Abe, K. (2015). 'Smartphone Summit' by children for sharing rules and strategies to tackle Internet-related delinquency. *Japanese Journal of Morality Development,* 9, 76–83.

Takeuchi, K., Abe, K., Miyake, M., & Toda, Y. (2017). Smartphone Summit: Children's initiative to prevent cyberbullying and related problems. In M. Campbell & S. Bauman (Eds.), *Reducing cyberbullying in schools: International evidence-based best practices* (pp. 213–223). Sydney, Australia: Academic Press (Elsevier).

Taki, M. (Ed.) (2000). *Peer Support de Hajimeru Gakkou Dukuri: tyuugakkou- hen* [Change School by Japanese Peer Support Program for Junior High Schools]. Tokyo: Kaneko Shobo (in Japanese).

Tamura, S., & Ishikuma, T. (2001) Help-seeking preferences and burnout: Junior high school teachers in Japan. *Japanese Journal of Educational Psychology,* 49, 438–448 (in Japanese). doi:10.5926/jjep1953.54.1_75.

Toda, Y. (1997). Bully and/or bullied experiences and attitudes toward bullying of students in Faculty of Education. *Annual report of University Educational Centre for Practical Studies and Teaching* (pp. 19–28). Faculty of Education, Tottori University (in Japanese).

Toda, Y. (2005). Bullying and peer support systems in Japan: Intervention research. In D. Shwalb, J. Nakazawa, & B. Shwalb (Eds.), *Applied Developmental Psychology: Theory, Practice, and Research from Japan* (pp. 301–319). Greenwich, CT: Information Age.

Toda, Y. (2018). How to support bullies and victims of bullying/cyberbullying. In H. Mizuno, S. Iechika, & T. Ishikuma (Eds.), *Effective support utilizing 'Team School'.* Kyoto: Nakanishiya Shuppan (in Japanese).

Toda, Y., & Miyamae, Y. (2009). Categorization of models for evaluating peer support practice in Japan. *Japanese Annals of Peer Support*, 6, 1–9 (in Japanese).

Toda, Y., Strohmeier, D., & Spiel, C. (2008). Process model of bullying. In T. Katoh & H. Taniguchi (Eds.), *Darkside of Interpersonal Relationships* (pp.117–131). Kyoto: Kitaohji-Shobo (in Japanese).

Toda, Y., Yamashita, Y., & Ogawa, T. (2014). Tackling ijime learning from Finland. *Burakukaihou*, 698, 31–40.

Yamaguchi, T., Mizuno, H., & Ishikuma, T. (2004). Relationship between perceived problems and help-seeking preferences in junior high students. *Japanese Journal of Counseling Science*, 34, 241–249 (in Japanese).

Yamasaki, K., Toda, Y., & Watanabe, Y. (Eds.). (2013). *Sekai no Gakkou Yobou Kyouiku: Sinshin no Kenko to Tekio wo Mamoru Kakkoku no Trikumi* [Prevention education at schools in the world: The actions of each country for children's health and adjustment]. Tokyo: Kaneko-shobo (in Japanese).

8

PEER SUPPORT AND THE PUPIL'S VOICE

The *NoTrap!* programme in Italy

Valentina Zambuto, Benedetta E. Palladino, Annalaura Nocentini and Ersilia Menesini

The context of the research

NoTrap! is an Italian online and school-based universal intervention programme against bullying and cyberbullying. It is designed for adolescents attending grades 7 to 10. The programme is school-based, and it lasts four months. There are three main phases, each one conceived to address specific mechanisms responsible for bullying and cyberbullying. In brief, the first phase consists of two awareness meetings targeted at the students and faculty. The second phase is aimed at training the peer educators, the students who volunteer to assume this role (four or five per class). Finally, in the third phase two workshops are held by the peer educators with their classmates. In this phase the peer educators also provide a peer support service on the online community of the *NoTrap!* website (www.notrap.it). The programme is theory-driven, based on scientific psychological literature. For a detailed description of how each phase of the programme was conceived, with the purpose of addressing specific mechanisms responsible for bullying and cyberbullying, see Menesini, Zambuto, and Palladino (2017).

Here, we will illustrate the general theoretical framework of the programme for the first time, that is, 'peer education as part of a systemic approach'. Following this systemic perspective, in a classroom with bullying problems, negative dynamics are influenced by the interactions between many elements acting at different levels. At the class level, research has highlighted the influence that class norms have on individual behaviour concerning bullying. Pozzoli, Gini, and Vieno (2012), for instance, investigated the relationship between peer and classroom injunctive and descriptive norms. Injunctive norms are perceptions of which behaviours are typically approved or disapproved of, and the descriptive norms are coded as the frequency with which a certain behaviour is present in the group. The results of this study have shown that victim-oriented injunctive norms are positively associated with individual defending behaviour. Descriptive norms are also relevant, as the more defending behaviour there is within the class, the more likely it is that each student will put it into practice. Therefore, injunctive and descriptive norms could influence the likeliness of the individual to assume either a pro-bully or pro-victim attitude, and whether or not he/she will be an active or passive bystander.

From a systemic perspective, teachers can also play a significant role in class norms, and therefore in bullying. For instance, when the teacher does not intervene in a bullying incident, he/she legitimizes this behaviour, which can subsequently increase students' moral disengagement, and in turn the level of bullying (Campaert, Nocentini, & Menesini, 2017). Finally, students and teachers' attitudes and behaviour may be influenced by the school's anti-bullying policy (Gower, Cousin, & Borowsky, 2017; Hall, 2017), namely the general values, policy, and behaviour promoted at school level.

Following the systemic perspective, the *NoTrap!* programme aims to involve the whole school at different levels, with actions targeted at students, teachers, and to the anti-bullying policy of the school in question. Concerning the students, *NoTrap!* intervenes directly on victims and bystanders, and indirectly on bullies. The awareness meeting targeted to the entire class, and the two workshops carried out by peer educators, are focused on empowering victims and bystanders. Specifically, the awareness meeting stimulates students' reflection about how bystanders impact bullying. This paves the way for the following workshops. For instance, in the first workshop, students work in depth on victim and bystander emotions. The workshop aims at developing empathy for the victim. In the second workshop, students learn several strategies to cope with bullying from the point of view of the victim and the bystander. Empowering victims and bystanders means reducing the power of bullies.

The teacher's meeting is focused on increasing knowledge of bullying, cyberbullying, and how teachers may intervene when bullying occurs. At the end of this meeting, teachers should be able to recognize bullying dynamics in their classes. Furthermore, they should become aware of the impact that their approach to bullying could have on their students' attitudes. Finally, teachers are invited to integrate the school policy with a protocol to handle bullying emergencies.

In the systemic approach, the *NoTrap!* programme adopted a peer-led model. With this expression we refer to all the interventions in which various members of a larger group are formed to become agents of change in their reference group (Cowie & Wallace, 2001). We know that adolescents are more likely to modify their behaviours and attitudes if they receive positive messages from peers (Wye & AILVL Hepatitis C Peer Education & Prevention Program, 2006). Besides, when used within a class, peer-led models gain advantage from an already established means of sharing information and advice.

Differently from other peer-led interventions, *NoTrap!* includes actions carried out from experts and activities led by peer educators. Therefore, in the *NoTrap!* programme, peer education can be considered as a link to facilitate experts' actions, and also a means of promoting change within the group. *NoTrap!*'s peer educators, after specific training, act in the area of proximal development with their classmates. They are members of the class, so they are more capable than experts to activate a process of change. But it is important to underline that in our programme, we do not intend to give a professional role to peer educators. On the contrary, thanks to peer education, we aim to promote a process of support and reciprocal influence that are typical of classmates' interactions.

In conclusion, *NoTrap!* is the exemplification of a systemic intervention in which peer education is a joining link between experts' actions and the change in class-group dynamics. This does not mean that peer education is not important. On the contrary, it has to be well implemented, because the success of the whole programme will depend on the peer educators' work.

Underpinning research

The *NoTrap!* programme was developed within a translational approach that benefits from the integration of theoretical research and applied interventions. Translational research is best understood as a way of thinking or an alternate paradigm that seeks to blend rather than dichotomize basic and applied research towards the common goal of improving the human condition (Guerra et al., 2011). This approach implies a circular process between experimental studies, programme evaluation, and understanding models of explanation.

Concerning the theoretical research that underpins the application, most studies have highlighted that social and individual factors can explain bullying problems (Smith, 2014; Swearer & Hymel, 2015). From a developmental point of view, a promising approach is the *individual by context approach*, which implies that social contexts can either attenuate or exacerbate (i.e. moderate) the effect of individual characteristics of bullying behaviour (Juvonen & Graham, 2014). The focus on moderators can help to understand precisely which factors determine the process and how to influence them through intervention.

Traditionally, individual and social predictors of bullying have been investigated separately from each other. Several individual-level predictors of bullying have received attention (Cook, Williams, Guerra, Kim, & Sadek, 2010). An example is gender differences. Specifically, we know that males are more involved in bullying than girls (Olweus, 1993; Smith, López-Castro, Robinson, & Görzig, 2019). Furthermore, gender differences can influence the developmental trajectory of bullying. In this regard Pepler, Jiang, Craig, and Connolly (2008) found four trajectories of bullying between the ages of 10 and 17, that are high bullying, where adolescents are consistently involved in high levels of bullying from ages 10 to 17; the desisting group, who start with moderate levels of bullying in early adolescence but decrease to almost no bullying by the end of high school; the moderate group which reported consistently moderate levels of bullying over time with an increase through childhood and early adolescence up until age 14–15; and the no-bullying group which comprised adolescents who almost never reported bullying. We know that girls are underrepresented in the high and moderate bullying trajectory groups (Barker, Arseneault, Brendgen et al., 2008; Pepler et al., 2008).

Another important individual-level predictor is trait aggression. Bullies are frequently described with a profile of aggressive and externalizing problems, such as conduct problems and proactive aggression (Menesini, Modena, & Tani, 2009; Olweus, 1978; Solberg & Olweus, 2003; White & Loeber, 2008).

In the definition of bullying we can find another important individual-level predictor, social status. Social dominance is a relational variable that places individuals in a hierarchy according with their access to resources (Pellegrini, 2002). Bullying is viewed as an agonistic strategy used to obtain and maintain social dominance (Pellegrini & Long, 2002); in line with this view, bullying seems to increase during the initial stages of group formation.

Finally, moral disengagement has received attention from scholars because it can constitute an individual predictor of bullying. Specifically, a person may perceive a transgression in terms of moral responsibility, which is usually expressed through feelings of shame and guilt, or in terms of moral disengagement. With the expression of moral disengagement, we refer to a cognitive process able to deactivate moral control and personal sanctions, and to justify personal negative behaviour (Bandura, 1991, 2002). Several studies have shown that moral disengagement is a highly significant predictor of bullying behaviour (Almeida, Correia, & Marinho, 2010; Gini, 2006; Gini, Pozzoli, & Hymel, 2014; Hymel, Rocke-Henderson, & Bonanno, 2005; Obermann, 2011; Pornari & Wood, 2010). In addition to cognitive reasoning and justifications, several studies have also focused on emotional reactions as possible indicators of moral motivation and of personal sense of responsibility or disengagement (Malti, Gasser, & Buchmann, 2009; Olthof, 2012; Tangney, Stuewing, & Mashek, 2007). Specifically, given the association between reprehensible behaviour and lack of guilt and shame, morally disengaged emotions may deactivate personal sanctions and feelings of guilt, thus legitimize negative behaviour (Menesini and Camodeca, 2008; Menesini, Sanchez, Fonzi et al. 2003; Perren & Gutzwiller-Helfenfinger, 2012).

On the other hand, there are classroom-level predictors of bullying. The presence of bullying varies from classroom to classroom (Salmivalli & Voeten, 2004; Salmivalli, Voeten, & Poskiparta, 2011), and this variation can depend on *group norms*. Group norms have been defined as the acceptable and expected behaviour of the members of a social group (Henry, Guerra, Huesmann et al. 2000); individuals usually ascribe significance to group norms and use them to guide their own behaviour. One important classroom norm is the way in which bystanders who witness bullying respond. They can reinforce bullies or victims directly or indirectly, and this varying behaviour can influence the occurrence of bullying in a classroom (Salmivalli et al., 2011). It is important to underline that a given social norm does not direct behaviour unless the situation causes it to be made salient (Henry et al., 2000). In regards to bullying, the concept of norm salience is defined by virtue of higher peer rejection and lower peer popularity for bullies, as well as frequency of contingent negative or positive feedback for bullying by teachers and peers (Menesini, Palladino, & Nocentini, 2015). Dijkstra and colleagues (2008) showed that bullying behaviour was socially especially accepted in classrooms where popular students engaged in high levels of bullying, suggesting that popularity causes behaviour to become normative in the classroom.

In a classroom in which bullying is more normative, pro-bullies or passive bystanders occur more frequently. Many studies have tried to explain passive behaviour on the basis of the so-called 'bystander effect', a model developed by Latané and Darley in 1970. According to these studies, failure to help the victim in school or online depends on the failure of one of the five phases of this model: (1) noticing that something is going on; (2) interpreting the situation as an emergency; (3) feeling a certain degree of responsibility; (4) knowing the coping strategies in order to intervene; (5) implementing the action. The classroom norms surrounding bullying can influence at least the first, second, and third phases of this model. When bullying is the norm, it is difficult for bystanders to notice and interpret an accident as an emergency. They may reformulate what happens as a joke, therefore failing to perceive the gravity of the situation. This in turn decreases the degree of perceived responsibility.

Classroom and individual social norms may also be influenced by teachers' reactions to bullying incidents. Students develop an understanding of moral matters from their direct experience of harm and unfairness, from the observation of harm and unfairness caused to others, and from other people's communication when highlighting the experience of harm (Smetana, 2011; Turiel, 2006). Students are likely to observe teachers' behavioural reactions to bullying and victimization and to make sense of it through what they see, which can contribute to their understanding of the moral matter of bullying.

Within this interactional framework, we will present some studies carried out by our research group in the last few years. Specifically, we will focus on studies that show how the relation between individual vulnerability and bullying is moderated by class norms, peer behaviour, and teacher interventions.

A first example is a study by Nocentini, Menesini and Salmivalli (2013), which examined the effects of individual and classroom-level predictors on the development of bullying behaviour over three years in a sample of Italian adolescents. Results of a multilevel growth model showed that both baseline level and developmental trajectories of bullying varied significantly across individuals as well as across classrooms. At the individual level, gender, aggression, and competition for social dominance were related with baseline level bullying. Specifically, competition for social dominance was more strongly related to bullying behaviour in males. Competition for social dominance and class change were additionally associated with increases in bullying over time. This means that although trait aggression represents a dispositional risk of bullying, it is competition for social dominance that contributes to the escalation of bullying. Thus, especially in adolescence, it may be more effective to focus on dominance rather than on general aggression.

At the classroom level, pro-bullying behaviour was associated with higher baseline level bullying, whereas anti-bullying behaviour decreases bullying over time. Finally, a cross-level interaction underlined that the pro-bullying behaviour moderates the predictive role of trait aggression on the initial level of bullying. This means that the more the bully's behaviour is reinforced by bystanders' verbal or nonverbal socially rewarding cues, the more frequently bullying occurs in a classroom – on the other hand, the more classmates tend to defend the victimized peers (anti-bullying behaviour), the less frequently bullying takes place in the school classroom. These findings have relevant implications for designing intervention programmes; for instance, the focus should not be placed solely on changing bullies' attitudes, motivations, and behaviour, but on the whole class, because individual risk and social-contextual risk interact with each other. Besides, the interventions should take into account that an intervention aiming to change pro-bullying behaviour may have stronger effects on decreasing bullying in the short term, whereas promoting anti-bullying behaviour, such as empathic and prosocial behaviour toward the victim, might have even stronger effects in the long term.

In a subsequent study we explored the role of moral disengagement and group norms measures, and their interaction, in predicting student reports of bullying (Menesini, Palladino, & Nocentini, 2015). The study focused on emotions of moral disengagement, assuming that these emotions become a general pattern of emotional reaction in bullies after their negative actions, and that, as such, they may become a precedent for subsequent bullying. The results showed that students who were more morally/emotionally disengaged had higher levels of bullying. Furthermore, the association between moral emotions and bullying was contingent on the normative approval of class-mates. Students in classrooms where peers directly or indirectly encouraged bullies were more likely to show higher levels of bullying. This study also has implications for intervention policies; specifically, that interventions should focus on the context and specifically on group norms so as to moderate the association between morally disengaging emotions and the level of bullying in class.

In a more recent study (Campart, Nocentini, & Menesini, 2017), we shifted our attention to the teachers' role. Specifically, we examined the relation between teachers' responses to incidents of bullying and victimiza-tion, moral disengagement, and bullying behaviour. We found that students who perceived higher levels of disciplinary sanctions or who perceived higher levels of victim support in incidents of bullying reported lower levels of bullying, through an indirect negative effect on moral disengagement.

Furthermore, students who reported higher levels of non-intervention in incidents of bullying reported higher levels of bullying, through an indirect and positive effect of moral disengagement. At a practical level, this study suggests that teachers should be a principal target of bullying intervention programmes, because they may have a far-reaching effect on students' social and moral behaviour and cognition, and thus on bullying.

The transition from pure research to application

The translational approach implies a circular process among experimental studies, programme evaluation, and understanding models of explanation. The history of *NoTrap!* development is an example of how pure and applied research can influence each other, resulting in a progressive improvement of the efficacy of the programme.

The pilot version of *NoTrap!* was carried out in the school year 2008/2009. The original name of the programme was chosen by students, and it means 'Let's not fall into the trap' (in Italian 'Noncadiamointrappola'). The trap was a metaphor for risks of online world. The pilot and the first versions (school year 2009/2010) were, in fact, focused only on the risks of ICTs. The instrument to counter ICTs risks was offered by the opportunities brought about by new technologies (e.g. the possibility to target a large audience, to be in contact with people even if they are far, to find new information). For this reason, we used ICTs to promote online social support and to enhance positive behaviour online. The programme was an evolution of a face-to-face peer support model (Menesini, Codecasa, Benelli, & Cowie, 2003), with the difference that now the peer support was offered in the forum of the programme's website. The website was created with help of students in the pilot version, and it has been used by trained peer educators in its first version. The limits of this version were two: firstly, the lack of attention to face-to-face bullying; and secondly the low engagement of students who did not participate in the peer educators' training. These limits led to a decrease only of cyberbullying, and only for male peer educators (Menesini, Nocentini, & Palladino, 2012).

We then carried out a new trial (Noncadiamointrappola 2nd version) in the school year 2010/2011, in which we modified certain aspects of the programme in order to improve its efficacy. Specifically, starting from the limits of the first version, we decided to put equal attention into both bullying and cyberbullying. We also added the face-to-face workshop led by peer educators with their classmates in order to involve the whole class in the programme. We tried to involve teachers as well, giving them the task of organizing activities for the class together with peer educators. The activities were defined separately for each school and class, according to the curricular programme. Classroom activities were designed to create a product to be used in other versions or classes.

In order to decide the contents of the peer educators' training, we consulted the international literature. For instance, awareness of the social nature of bullying and cyberbullying (Bastiaensens, Vandebosch, Poels et al., 2015; Salmivalli, Lagerspetz, Björkqvist et al., 1996) led us to dedicate attention to all the participants in the dynamics of bullying, with a special focus on the victim and bystanders' point of view. We also know that the teaching of coping strategies makes defending behaviours more likely to occur (Pozzoli & Gini, 2013). The peer educators' training dealt with coping strategies that victim and bystanders could use in response to bullying and cyberbullying. There was an improvement in results in this second version, but not enough. We found a significant decrease in bullying, victimization, and cyber-victimization in the experimental group as compared with the control group (Menesini et al., 2012). Moreover, in peer educators we found a significant increase of adaptive coping strategies and a significant decrease in maladaptive coping strategies. These changes mediated the change in behavioural variables. Although the second version had worked in decreasing behavioural outcomes, the programme had not had the same effect on the whole class: peer educators continued to benefit more from the programme.

The third and current version was used for the first time in the school year 2011/2012. Starting from an in depth analysis of the literature, from our findings from pure research studies, and from feedback of the previous versions, we reinforced certain components of the programme and modified others. Our findings suggested that an efficacious programme must work on both the individual and class level. At the individual level it is important to promote the moral engagement of any bystanders. According to the Latané and Darley model, the first goal of the programme is to help students notice any incidents and correctly identify them as emergencies. In order to obtain this, the programme starts with an 'awareness meeting' targeted to the whole class. This step lays the foundation for the following activities. In the awareness meeting experts explain what bullying and cyberbullying are, and the consequences for victims. Also, experts underline the responsibility of bystanders within these dynamics. Next, students are invited to reflect on the most functional coping strategies to help victims. Awareness is a first step, but we know that it is not sufficient. It is important to implement practical activities in order to obtain behavioural changes. Practical activities are also important in order for the programme to work at class level. Working at the class level means trying to change the class norms regarding bullying. Class norms can impact individual pupils' moral emotions, and then their behaviour.

But how can we change class norms? The findings of Menesini and colleagues (2015) suggested that it is important to change the norm saliency of bullying in class in order to subtract power from bullies. In the *NoTrap!* programme, the adoption of a peer-led approach has the advantage of giving more visibility and popularity to students with prosocial behaviour. This in turn can change the norm saliency of bullying in the classroom.

Furthermore, the findings of Nocentini and colleagues (2013) suggested that in order to have more stable effects, we must focus on the promotion of prosocial behaviour toward the victim, rather than on changing pro-bullying behaviours. Thus, in the third version, all the activities maintain the double perspective of the victim and bystanders. We decided to systematically work to improve empathy toward the victim. We know that empathy predicts bystanders' intervention (Cappadocia, Pepler, Cummings, & Craig, 2012). We then introduced a specific module on victim emotions within the peer educators' training and in the first workshop led by peer educators with classmates. Finally, the literature and the results from the second version led us to broaden the work on functional coping strategies for the whole class. The second workshop led by peer educators is, in fact, focused on this topic.

One of the most important innovations of the third version was the standardization of the activities carried out by peer educators. This approach was needed to address the standard of evidence required for an evidence-based programme (Flay, Biglan, Boruch et al., 2005). The new activities were based on cooperative learning, even though it was led by peer educators. This decision is due to the awareness that cooperative group work is one of the most effective components of anti-bullying programmes (Ttofi & Farrington, 2011).

In the following years of implementation, we maintained the same programme structure, with only minor changes. One of the most important innovations of these versions was the major attention, with a systemic approach, to the teachers. The findings of Campaert and colleagues (2017) led us to place more responsibility on teachers in the later phases of the programme. Since the school year 2014/2015, teachers have been given the task of supervising the workshops led by peer educators in class, thus playing a scaffolding role in the project. Furthermore, we improved upon the teacher lessons in the *NoTrap!* programme. Starting from the 2015/2016 school year (third version) we dedicated more time to this phase of the programme. We also reformulated the contents of the course, with a specific section dedicated to the most functional ways for teachers to intervene when a bullying incident occurs.

The impact and legacy of the research

The third version of the programme can be considered very efficacious. Ever since the 2011/2012 version of *NoTrap!* (3rd revision), the research on the programme has been oriented to addressing the standard of evidence endorsed by the Society of Prevention Research (Flay et al., 2005; Gottfredson, Cook, Gardner et al., 2015). In the past seven years we have carried out several research designs in order to demonstrate the efficacy, the effectiveness, and growth of the programme.

The first step was to evaluate whether the programme works. The efficacy of *NoTrap!* has been demonstrated in two independent quasi-experimental trials carried out in school years 2011/2012 and 2012/2013 (Palladino, Nocentini, & Menesini, 2016). The study satisfies all the criteria needed in order to define an intervention as efficacious: we tested the *NoTrap!* programme in two rigorous independent trials with defined samples from defined population (1 & 2); we used psychometrically sound measures and data collection procedures (3); we analysed data with rigorous statistical approaches (4); we have obtained consistent positive effects without iatrogenic effects (5); and, finally, we reported one significant long-term follow-up (6). Specifically, results of these trials showed that, in contrast to the control group, in *NoTrap!* schools there is a significant decrease of bullying, victimization, cyberbullying, and cyber-victimization. These changes remain stable even six months after the end of the programme (Palladino et al., 2016). The efficacy has been confirmed in all of the following versions of the programme, with significant and strong effects. In addition to effects in bullying, victimization, cyberbullying, and cyber-victimization, in the most recent studies we also found a significant increase in defending behaviour (Zambuto, 2018). Thus, the programme seems to have an impact on the students who are directly involved (bullies and victims), and on the bystanders.

We then moved forward with our research in the direction of evidence-based interventions. Specifically, in the subsequent versions of the programme, we focused on the second level of standard of evidence: the effectiveness of the programme. According to the Society of Prevention Research (Flay et al., 2005;

Gottfredson et al., 2015), in order to demonstrate that an intervention is effective, it has to have been delivered under real-world conditions. An effective programme has to provide a description of:

'- what works', that means the causal mechanism (mediators) through which the intervention is expected to influence the outcome;
'- for whom' and 'under what circumstances' (moderators) the intervention is expected to be more or less effective.

The awareness of mediators and moderators allow us to understand '*how*' a programme works. This awareness can drive us to modify, delete, or add components to the programme (Eisner & Malti, 2012).

Relatively to 'what works', results of a study (Palladino, 2013) showed that in the experimental group the programme predicted an increase over time in support seeking, in both informational and instrumental aspects (distal advice) and in the more emotional sense of getting help from people (close support). This increase is a mediational mechanism that explains how the programme is able to decrease cyber-victimization. Reduction of cyber-victimization, in turn, is a mediational mechanism that predicts the decrease of internalizing symptoms.

Other mediation mechanisms could be explored in future studies. For instance, it is not yet clear what the causal mechanism is that makes the programme able to reduce bullying and victimization. It is possible that mediation variables could be found at class level. For instance, the increase of bystanders' defending behaviour fosters the decrease of bullying dynamics in the class.

Concerning 'under what circumstances' and 'for whom', Zambuto (2018) explored the moderation role of the peer educators' recruitment strategy (volunteering vs classmates nomination) on the efficacy of the programme. Some scholars assert that '*work with peers*' may have iatrogenic effects and increase victimization (Ttofi & Farrington, 2011). On the other hand, many authors have come to diametrically opposing conclusions (Birnbaum, Crohn, Maticka-Tyndale, & Barnett, 2010; Cowie, Naylor, Talamelli, Chauhan, & Smith, 2002; Lee, Kim, & Kim; 2015; Naylor & Cowie, 1999; Palladino et al., 2016; Zambuto et al., 2019). The different positions could be explained with what Smith, Salmivalli, and Cowie (2012) affirmed: '*working with peers*' may include a wide variety of approaches, each one potentially associated with a different level of effectiveness. Following this consideration, we tried to explore whether the way in which peer educators are recruited and the role played in the programme (peer educators vs all the other students) can impact the effectiveness of *NoTrap!*

The results showed that the programme was effective only in the 'voluntary recruitment condition', in which there was a decrease of bullying and victimization, and a concurrent increase of defending behaviour. In this condition the programme is effective for the whole class (peer educators and their classmates). On the contrary, when peer educators have been chosen by classmates, the role played in the programme moderates its efficacy. In this condition, only the peer educators increase level of defending behaviour, without any effects on the rest of the class.

These results are very promising, and we are going to replicate a similar design research in future studies.

The last step of standard of evidence is the 'scaling up level'. According to Gottfredson et al. (2015), this describes deliberate efforts to increase the impact of evidence-based interventions. In the last *NoTrap!* version (school year 2017/ 2018) we began addressing the 'scaling up level'. For the first time, the programme was implemented in 64 secondary schools, with the involvement of almost 5,000 students throughout Tuscany. This has been possible thanks to collaboration with the Tuscany Region Council, that supported our work with a public grant. The high number of schools involved required a previous investment in 'new *NoTrap!* trainers' and in manuals and courses to prepare them. We also tried to assess the fidelity of implementation with specific monitoring tools for trainers, teachers, and students. The future analysis of the results will provide us with information about the efficacy of the programme on a wider scale. While we take the first steps in scaling up the intervention, we continue to explore its effectiveness as well. This is because many research questions have yet to be answered. For instance, an interesting research question is related to the motivation that supports peer educators in undertaking their role. Do they intend to help others, or to reach a higher social status within their class? Zambuto (2018) compared two recruitment strategies, but did not consider a possible third recruitment method: teacher nomination. Future studies could investigate the characteristics and effectiveness of peer educators chosen by teachers.

Other mediation and moderation mechanisms could be further explored. First of all, the role of defending behaviour at class level. We could argue that this is the reason why the programme was not effective in the 'nominated recruitment condition'. In addition, the way classmates perceive peer educators could have a moderating effect on the success of the programme. Interviews and focus groups could be conducted with classmates in order to understand how they perceive students who voluntarily became peer educators vs the ones that are nominated for this role.

Finally, the *NoTrap!* programme can be considered within the larger class of interventions based on youth engagement and involvement. It aimed to create opportunities to facilitate the expression of students' voices and involvement in relation to bullying and cyberbullying problems. This is one of the reasons that it has shown a high level of efficacy and effectiveness in relation to the outcomes. Within this approach *NoTrap!* programme can be developed further providing more opportunities to actively involve peer educators and students in the programme.

Lessons learned

Within a translational approach, the *NoTrap!* programme development and evaluation can be viewed as a bridge between basic and the applied research; it could be a step ahead in the way for a sustainable cooperation between researchers, policy-makers, and practitioners in the framework of evidence-based interventions (Spiel, Salmivalli, & Smith, 2011; Spiel, Wagner, & Strohmeier, 2012; Spiel & Strohmeier, 2011, 2012).

Evidence-based policies and practice can be defined as an approach that helps people in making well-informed decisions about policies, programmes, and projects by placing the best available evidence from research at the core of policy development and implementation (Nutley, Walter, & Davies, 2007). Standards for research leading to evidence-based practice have been defined (Flay et al., 2005; Gottfredson et al., 2015) to assist practitioners, policy-makers, and administrators in determining which interventions are efficacious, effective, and ready for dissemination. In evaluating the efficacy of the *NoTrap!* programme, we strictly followed standards that intended to build a shared ground for research and practice that could be an opportunity for the development of both research and practice (Eisner & Malti, 2012). We tried to respond to the increased request for an evidence-based framework that can inform interventions and policies against bullying (Eisner & Malti, 2012; Ttofi & Farrington, 2010). This method is time-consuming and requires considerable commitment and resources. The *NoTrap!* programme has been in development since 2008, with different versions and trial replications (Menesini, Nocentini, & Palladino, 2012; Palladino et al., 2012; Palladino, Nocentini, Menesini, 2016; Zambuto, 2018).

It has been widely recognized that randomized control trials (RCTs) are the 'gold standard' in terms of demonstrating convincingly whether a specific treatment has any effect on an outcome (Farrington & Welsh, 2005). While it would be expected that all prevention programmes would opt to utilize randomized experiments, because of the empirical advantages of this design, several difficulties did not allow us to use a randomized trial design. Added time, costs, and cooperation necessary to enable a proper randomized experiment decrease the feasibility of a RCT; participants' refusal to participate as a control group is a common difficulty (Weisburd, Lum, & Petrosino, 2001) that we also encountered. The methods we used (matched control design) can be considered at least acceptable (Flay et al., 2005), considering that we checked for possible effects of the sampling method in all the analyses performed. Obviously, it would be desirable to replicate our findings in a new study that uses RCTs.

Another methodological question is related to the fact that the role of evaluator and of programme provider are carried out by the same individuals. The independence between the two roles is not required specifically by the standards of evidence (Flay et al., 2005) but it is recommended for evaluations to be conducted as *independent* evaluations, in which the role of the evaluators and programme developers and deliverers are institutionally separate (Eisner & Malti, 2012). Unfortunately, this was not possible in our case, due to the additional financial costs that this would impose. This problematic point should be taken into account in future replications of the evaluation trials. While we reject the idea of possible intentional misconduct, we are aware of the potential risks for unconscious cognitive biases that could play a role in academic judgements and decision making at various stages of the research process (Eisner, 2009).

Many aspects could have been carried out better. For instance, despite our considerable efforts to involve teachers, only a few participated during meetings prepared for them in several versions. On this note, recent school policy measures in Italy may have benefit for our programme. During each school year, teachers must attend 25 obligatory hours of professional training courses. According to the new school policy measures, school principals have the facility to recognize some courses as valid. This is what happened for the *NoTrap!* course in the last school year. This promoted higher participation by teachers. Also, since 2017 a new figure has been introduced to Italian schools, that is a member of faculty responsible for prevention and intervention in cases of bullying and cyberbullying. Many teachers consider themselves unequipped for this task. Therefore, some of them took the opportunity of using our course in order to improve their awareness of the problem. This notwithstanding, it remains difficult to involve teachers on the basis of their intrinsic motivation to learn how to manage bullying and cyberbullying.

In the most recent years of implementation of *NoTrap!*, we planned to collect data from teachers as well, yet only a few of them consented to filling out our questionnaires. On one hand, this low level of school involvement can be viewed as a partial failure. On the other hand, considering all of these difficulties, a peer-led model appears to be of more relevant use with adolescents: their high involvement could be a key factor for our positive results.

The involvement of students' families has also been difficult to address (Palladino, 2013); future efforts of the *NoTrap!* programme would include this focus and try to improve teachers' and parents' involvement in the programme.

In conclusion, looking back to the last ten years of work, we can recognize two main lessons learnt. The first is the importance of communication and dissemination in the community. Dissemination books, interviews on the mass media, dissemination papers, conferences, presentations of programme results, and social network communication about the programme are highly important to communicate our work in the community. For instance, at the beginning of each school year we organize a conference at regional level in order to present the results of the previous year *NoTrap*'s implementation. In this event we invite teachers and students of the *NoTrap*'s schools, journalists, policy-makers, and community in general. We also have a Facebook page of *NoTrap!*, in which we post all the news about the programme, and photos of the several activities in the schools. A second important lesson is the need for a systematic approach and a persistent attitude of our professional and research team. Being systematic and perseverant allowed us to keep on improving the programme when it was not sufficiently efficacious, and developing it further, including and evaluating promising components. Some of the initial failures pushed us to reconsider what we had done previously. This became an incentive to our studies. We were motivated to analyse more deeply the programme's components in order to understand how to improve the results. This attitude has been always relevant for us and helped us to raise new issues and research questions during programme implementation

Perseverance has been essential not only as an incentive for research but also to raise funds from local communities. Italian universities do not have many financial resources, and the possibility of having grants from bank and community institutions has been highly relevant for us and for schools as well. It helped to disseminate and make our team familiar with schools and teachers and to establish a positive cycle of translational research of mutual benefit for schools, students, communities, and for research as well.

Gradually, we received more and more requests for the *NoTrap!* programme from schools. In order to respond to this, in 2016 we founded a spin-off dedicated to transferring knowledge and programme licences in the communities. The spin-off is called 'EbiCo', which means 'Evidence Based Interventions Cooperative'. In this way we had the opportunity to spread the expertise that we had acquired in the previous years with the practical work in schools. Thanks to EbiCo we became also part of the community services network.

The increasing presence of *NoTrap!* In the community and in the schools allowed us to obtain attention from some government institutions; in fact last school year the Tuscany Regional Council financed our first scaling-up implementation trial of the programme in 70 schools of Tuscany.

In summary, there has been an increasing process of collaboration and mutual respect between the research team, schools, and community. Step by step we have seen the *NoTrap!* programme growing in efficacy and popularity and our team and the spin-off being trusted and respected as one of the most professional and scientifically prepared in the country.

References

Almeida, A., Correia, I., & Marinho, S. (2010). Moral disengagement, normative beliefs of peer group, and attitudes regarding roles in bullying. *Journal of School Violence*, 9, 23–36. doi:10.1080/15388220903185639.

Bandura, A. (1991). Social cognitive theory of self-regulation. *Organizational Behavior and Human Decision Processes*, 50, 248–287. doi:10.1016/0749-5978(91)90022-L.

Bandura, A. (2002). Selective moral disengagement in the exercise of moral agency. *Journal of Moral Education*, 31, 101–119. doi:10.1080/0305724022014322.

Barker, E. D., Arseneault, L., Brendgen, M., Fontaine, N., & Maughan, B. (2008). Joint development of bullying and victimization in adolescence: Relations to delinquency and self-harm. *Journal of American Academy Child Adolescent Psychiatry*, 47, 1030–1038.

Bastiaensens, S., Vandebosch, H., Poels, K., Van Cleemput, K., DeSmet, A., & De Bourdeaudhuij, I. (2015). 'Can I afford to help?' How affordances of communication modalities guide bystanders' helping intentions towards harassment on social network sites. *Behaviour & Information Technology*, 34, 425–435. doi:10.1080/0144929X.2014.983979.

Birnbaum, M., Crohn, K., Maticka-Tyndale, E., & Barnett, J. P. (2010). Peer-led interventions to reduce HIV risk of youth: A review. *Evaluation and Program Planning*, 33, 98–112.

Campaert, K., Nocentini, A., & Menesini, E. (2017). The efficacy of teachers' responses to incidents of bullying and victimization: The mediational role of moral disengagement for bullying. *Aggressive Behavior*, 43, 483–492. https:// doi:10.1002/ab.21706.

Cappadocia, M. C., Pepler, D. J., Cummings, J. G., & Craig, W. (2012). Individual motivations and characteristics associated with bystander intervention during bullying episodes among children and youth. *Canadian Journal of School Psychology*, 27, 201–216. doi:10.1177/0829573512450567.

Cook, C., Williams, K. R., Guerra, N. G., Kim, T., & Sadek, S. (2010). Predictors of bullying and victimization in childhood and adolescence: A meta-analytic investigation. *School Psychology Quarterly*, 27, 210–222.

Cowie, H., & Wallace, P. (2001). Peer support in action: From bystanding to standing by. *British Journal of Educational Psychology*, 71, 673–674.

Cowie, H., Naylor, P., Talamelli, L., Chauhan, P., & Smith, P. K. (2002). Knowledge, use of and attitudes towards peer support: A 2-year follow-up to the Prince's Trust survey. *Journal of Adolescence*, 25, 453–467. doi:10.1006/jado.2002.0498.

Dijkstra, J. K., Lindenberg, S., & Veenstra, R. (2008). Beyond the class norm: Bullying behavior of popular adolescents and its relation to peer acceptance and rejection. *Journal of Abnormal Child Psychology*, 36, 1289–1299. doi:10.1007/s10802-008-9251-7.

Eisner, M. (2009). No effects in independent prevention trials: Can we reject the cynical view? *Journal of Experimental Criminology*, 5, 163–183. doi:10.1007/s11292-009-9071-y.

Eisner, M., & Malti, T. (2012). The future of research on evidence-based developmental violence prevention in Europe- Introduction to the focus section. *International Journal of Conflict and Violence*, 6, 166–175.

Farrington, D. P., & Welsh, B. C. (2005). Randomized experiments in criminology: What have we learned in the last two decades? *Journal of Experimental Criminology*, 1, 9–38. doi:10.1007/s11292-004-6460-0.

Flay, B. R., Biglan, A., Boruch, R. F., Castro, F. G., Gottfredson, D., Kellam, S., & Ji, P. (2005). Standards of evidence: Criteria for efficacy, effectiveness and dissemination. *Prevention Science*, 6, 151–175. doi:10.1007/s11121-005-5553-y.

Gini, G. (2006). Social cognition and moral cognition in bullying: What's wrong? *Aggressive Behavior*, 32, 528–539. doi:10.1002/ab.20153.

Gini, G., Pozzoli, T., & Hymel, S. (2014). Moral disengagement among children and youth: A meta-analytic review of links to aggressive behavior. *Aggressive Behavior*, 40, 56–68. doi:10.1002/ab.21502.

Gottfredson, D. C., Cook, T. D., Gardner, F. E. M., Gorman-Smith, D., Howe, G. W., Sandler, I. N., & Zafft, C. M. (2015). Standards of evidence for efficacy, effectiveness, and scale up research in prevention science: Next generation. *Prevention Science*, 16, 893–926.

Gower, A. L., Cousin, M., & Borowsky, I. W. (2017). A multilevel, state wide investigation of school district anti-bullying policy quality and student bullying involvement. *Journal of School Health*, 87, 174–181.

Guerra, N., Graham, S., & Tolan, P. H., (2011). Raising healthy children: Translating child development research into practice. *Child Development*, 82, 7–16.

Hall, W. J. (2017). The effectiveness of policy interventions for school bullying: A systematic review. *Journal of the Society for Social Work and Research*, 8, 45–69. doi:10.1086/690565.

Henry, D., Guerra, N., Huesmann, R., Tolan, P., VanAcker, R., & Eron, L. (2000). Normative influences on aggression in urban elementary school classrooms. *American Journal of Community Psychology*, 28, 59–81. doi:10.1023/A:1005142429725.

Hymel, S., Rocke-Henderson, N., & Bonanno, R. A. (2005). Moral disengagement: A framework for understanding bullying among adolescents. *Journal of Social Sciences*, 8, 1–11.

Hymel, S., Schonert-Reichl, K. A., Bonanno, R. A., Vaillancourt, T., & Rocke Henderson, N. (2010). Bullying and morality: Understanding how good kids can behave badly. In S. R. Jimerson, S. M. Swearer, & D. L. Espelage (Eds.), *Handbook of bullying in schools: An international perspective* (pp. 101–118). New York: Routledge.

Juvonen, J., & Graham, S. (2014). Bullying in schools: The power of bullies and the plight of victims. *Annual Review of Psychology*, 65, 159–185.

Latané, B., & Darley, J. M. (1970). *The unresponsive bystander: Why doesn't he help?* New York: Appleton-Century Crofts. doi:10.2307/2063973.

Lee, S., Kim, C.-J., & Kim, D. H. (2015). A meta-analysis of the effect of school-based anti-bullying programs. *Journal of Child Health Care*, 19, 136–153. doi:10.1177/1367493513503581.

Malti, T., Gasser, L., & Buchmann, M. (2009). Aggressive and prosocial children's emotion attributions and moral reasoning. *Aggressive Behavior*, 35, 90–102. doi:10.1002/ab.20289.

Menesini, E., & Camodeca, M. (2008). Shame and guilt as behaviour regulators: Relationships with bullying, victimization and prosocial behaviour. *British Journal of Developmental Psychology*, 26, 183–196. doi:10.1348/026151007X205281.

Menesini, E., Codecasa, E., Benelli, B., & Cowie, H. (2003). Enhancing children's responsibility to take action against bullying: Evaluation of a befriending intervention in Italian middle schools. *Aggressive Behavior*, 29, 1–14. doi:10.1002/ab.80012.

Menesini, E., Modena, M., & Tani, F. (2009). Bullying and victimization in adolescence: Concurrent and stable roles and psychological health symptoms. *Journal of Genetic Psychology*, 170, 115–133. doi:10.3200/ GNTP.170.2.115–134.

Menesini, E., Nocentini, A., & Palladino, B. E. (2012). Empowering students against bullying and cyberbullying: Evaluation of an Italian peer-led model. *International Journal of Conflict and Violence*, 6, 314–321.

Menesini, E., Palladino, B. E., & Nocentini, A. (2015). Emotions of moral disengagement, class norms, and bullying in adolescence: A multilevel approach. *Merrill-Palmer Quarterly*, 61, 124–143.

Menesini, E., Sanchez, V., Fonzi, A., Ortega, R., Costabile, A., & Lo Feudo, G. (2003). Moral emotions and bullying: A cross-national comparison of differences between bullies, victims and outsiders. *Aggressive Behavior*, 29, 515–530. doi:10.1002/ab.10060.

Menesini, E., Zambuto, V., & Palladino, B. E. (2017). Online and school based programs to prevent cyberbullying among Italian adolescents: What works, why, and under which circumstances. In M. Campbell & S. Bauman (Eds.), *Programs to reduce cyberbullying in schools: International evidenced based programs* (pp. 135–142). London: Elsevier.

Naylor, P., & Cowie, H. (1999). The effectiveness of peer support systems in challenging school bullying: The perspectives and experiences of teachers and pupils. *Journal of Adolescence*, 22, 467–479.

Nocentini, A., Menesini, E., & Salmivalli, C. (2013). Level and change of bullying behavior during high school: A multilevel growth curve analysis. *Journal of Adolescence*, 36, 495–505. doi:10.1016/j.adolescence.2013.02.004.

Nutley, S. M., Walter, I., & Davies, H. T. O. (2007). *Using evidence: How research can inform public services*. Bristol: Policy Press.

Obermann, M. L. (2011). Moral disengagement in self-reported and peer-nominated school bullying. *Aggressive Behavior*, 37, 133–144. doi:10.1002/ab.20378.

Olthof, T. (2012). Anticipated feelings of guilt and shame as predictors of early ado- lescents' antisocial and prosocial interpersonal behavior. *European Journal of Developmental Psychology*, 9, 371–388. doi:10.1080/17405629.2012.680300.

Olweus, D. (1978). *Aggression in schools: Bullies and whipping boys*. Washington, DC: Hemisphere.

Olweus, D. (1993). *Bullying at school: What we know and what we can do*. Oxford: Blackwell.

Palladino, B. E. (2013). Evidence-based intervention against bullying and cyberbullying: Measurement of the constructs, evaluation of efficacy and mediation processes. Doctoral dissertation, University of Florence.

Palladino, B. E., Nocentini, A., & Menesini, E. (2012). Online and offline peer led models against bullying and cyberbullying. *Psicothema*, 24, 634–639.

Palladino, B. E., Nocentini, A., & Menesini, E. (2016). Evidence-based intervention against bullying and cyberbullying: Evaluation of the Noncadiamointrappola! program through two independent trials. *Aggressive Behavior*, 42, 194–206. doi:10.1002/ab.21636.

Pellegrini, A. D. (2002). Bullying, victimization, and sexual harassment during the transition to middle school. *Educational Psychologist*, 37, 151–163.

Pellegrini, A. D., & Long, J. D. (2002). A longitudinal study of bullying, dominance, and victimization during the transition from primary school through secondary school. *British Journal of Developmental Psychology*, 20, 259–280.

Pepler, D., Jiang, D., Craig, W., & Connolly, J. (2008). Developmental trajectories of bullying and associated factors. *Child Development*, 79, 325–338.

Perren, S., & Gutzwiller-Helfenfinger, E. (2012). Cyberbullying and traditional bullying in adolescence: Differential roles of moral disengagement, moral emotions, and moral values. *European Journal of Developmental Psychology*, 9, 195–209. doi:10.1080/17405629.2011.643168.

Pornari, C. C., & Wood, J. (2010). Peer and cyber aggression in secondary school students: The role of moral disengagement, hostile attribution bias, and outcome expectancies. *Aggressive Behavior*, 36, 81–94. doi:10.1002/ab.20336.

Pozzoli, T., & Gini, G. (2013). Why do bystanders of bullying help or not? A multidimensional model. *Journal of Early Adolescence*, 33, 315–340. http://doi:10.1177/0272431612440172.

Pozzoli, T., Gini, G., & Vieno, A. (2012). The role of individual correlates and class norms in defending and passive bystanding behavior in bullying: A multilevel analysis. *Child Development*, 83, 1917–1931. doi:10.1111/j.1467-8624.2012.01831.x.

Salmivalli, C., & Voeten, M. (2004). Connections between attitudes, group norms, and behaviors associated with bullying in schools. *International Journal of Behavioral Development*, 28, 246–258. doi:10.1080/01650250344000488.

Salmivalli, C., Lagerspetz, K., Björkqvist, K., Österman, K., & Kaukiainen, A. (1996). Bullying as a group process: Participant roles and their relations to social status within the group. *Aggressive Behavior*, 22, 1–15.

Salmivalli, C., Voetonen, M., & Poskiparta, E. (2011). Bystanders matter: Associations between reinforcing, defending, and the frequency of bullying behavior in classrooms. *Journal of Clinical Child & Adolescent Psychology*, 40, 668–676.

Smetana, J. G. (2011). *Adolescents, families, and social development: How teens construct their worlds*. Chichester: Wiley-Blackwell.

Smith, P. K. (2014). *Understanding school bullying: Its nature and prevention strategies*. London: Sage.

Smith, P.K., López-Castro, L., Robinson, S., & Görzig, A. (2019). Consistency of gender differences in bullying in different cross-cultural surveys. *Aggression and Violent Behavior*.

Smith, P. K., Salmivalli, C., & Cowie, H. (2012). Effectiveness of school-based programs to reduce bullying: A commentary. *Journal of Experimental Criminology*, 8, 433–441. doi:10.1007/s11292-012-9142-3.

Solberg, M. E., & Olweus, D. (2003). Prevalence estimation of school bullying with the Olweus bully/victim questionnaire. *Aggressive Behavior*, 29, 239–268.

Spiel, C., & Strohmeier, D. (2011). National strategy for violence prevention in the Austrian public school system: Development and implementation. *International Journal of Behavioral Development*, 35, 412–418. doi:10.1177/0165025411407458.

Spiel, C., & Strohmeier, D. (2012). Evidence-based practice and policy: When researchers, policy makers, and practitioners learn how to work together. *European Journal of Developmental Psychology*, 9, 150–162.

Spiel, C., Salmivalli, C., & Smith, P. K. (2011). Translational research: National strategies for violence prevention in school. *International Journal of Behavioral Development*, 35, 381–382. doi:10.1177/0165025411407556.

Spiel, C., Wagner, P., & Strohmeier, D. (2012). Violence prevention in Austrian schools: Implementation and evaluation of a national strategy. *International Journal of Conflict and Violence*, 6, 176–186.

Swearer, S.M., & Hymel, S. (2015). Understanding the psychology of bullying: Moving toward a social-ecological diathesis-stress model. *American Psychologist*, 70, 344–353.

Tangney, J. P., Stuewig, J., & Mashek, D. J. (2007). What's moral about the self-conscious emotions? In J. L. Tracy, R. W. Robins, & J. P. Tangney (Eds.), *The self-conscious emotions* (pp. 21–37). New York: Guilford Press.

Ttofi, M. M., & Farrington, D. P. (2010). School bullying: Risk factors, theories and interventions. In F. Brookman, M. Maguire, H. Pierpoint, T. Bennett (Eds), *Handbook of crime* (pp. 427–457). Cullompton, Devon: Willan.

Ttofi, M. M., & Farrington, D. P. (2011). Effectiveness of school-based programs to reduce bullying: A systematic and meta-analytic review. *Journal of Experimental Criminology*, 7, 27–56.

Turiel, E. (2006). The development of morality. In W. Damon, R. Lerner, & N. Eisenberg (Eds.), *Handbook of child psychology*, Vol. 3: *Social, emotional, and personality development* (pp. 789–857). New York: Wiley. https:// doi:10.1002/ 9780470147658.chpsy0313.

Weisburd, D., Lum, C., & Petrosino, A. (2001). Does research design affect study outcomes in criminal justice? *Annals of the American Academy of Political and Social Science*, 578, 50–70.

White, N. A., & Loeber, R. (2008). Bullying and special education as predictors of serious delinquency. *Journal of Research in Crime and Delinquency*, 45, 380–397.

Wye, S.Q., & AIVL Hepatitis C Peer Education & Prevention Program. (2006). *A framework for peer education by drug-user organizations*. Canberra: Australian Injecting & Illicit Drug Users League.

Zambuto, V. (2018). Peer led models to prevent bullying and cyberbullying: How and for whom they can be effective. Doctoral dissertation, University of Florence.

Zambuto, V., Palladino, B. E., Nocentini, A., & Menesini, E. (2019). Why do some students want to be actively involved as peer educators and other do not? Finding from *No Trap!* antibullying and cyberbullying program. *European Journal of Developmental Psychology*, 16, 373-386.

9

SPECIFIC INTERVENTIONS AGAINST CYBERBULLYING

Marilyn Campbell

Introduction

Nearly two decades after the realization that young people were using technology to bully each other, there is still a divide about the definition of this behaviour, with some researchers continuing to argue whether cyberbullying is a form of bullying or something different. Certainly in the minds of the public it is confusing as to what cyberbullying actually entails (Compton, Campbell, & Mergler, 2014). Some researchers have postulated that cyberbullying is bullying in another form through technology (Campbell, 2005). They argue that just as physical bullying is different from verbal bullying which is different from exclusion bullying, then cyberbullying is the fourth form (Wang, Iannotti, & Nansel, 2009). Other researchers have emphasized that cyberbullying is bullying but it is different from the other three forms in that it is conducted through technology and is therefore different from those acts of bullying which take place in the material world, physical, verbal, and exclusion, which are called traditional bullying (Ybarra, Boyd, Korchmaros, & Oppenheim, 2012). A third position is that cyberbullying cannot be disaggregated from cyber aggression as a sub-type, as it is too difficult to utilize the three concepts which define bullying of intent to hurt, power imbalance and usually repeated (Bauman, Underwood, & Card, 2013). If bullying by these three concepts cannot be translated into the digital world (Englander,

Donnerstein, Kowalski, Lin, & Parti, 2017) then we need another definition entirely or perhaps the word cyberbullying is not the right word.

As well as theoretical definitions of cyberbullying, we can look at what changes and what stays the same in the physical and the cyber world in terms of bullying as informed by research. One similarity is that the roles of students in traditional bullying are somewhat the same in cyberbullying. Young people who bully in the school ground also cyberbully, while those students who are victimized are often victimized both by traditional and cyberbullying (Modecki, Minchin, Harbaugh, Guerra, & Runions, 2014; Waasdorp & Bradshaw, 2015). Even bystanders to traditional and cyberbullying are usually the same students as well as those not involved (Quirk & Campbell, 2015). Another similarity is the overlap of traditional and cyberbullying where most students who are cyberbullied or are also traditionally bullied but those traditionally bullied are not necessarily cyberbullied (Thomas et al., 2017). There are also similar consequences of traditional and cyberbullying, with increasing anxiety, depression, and suicidal thoughts (Thomas et al., 2017). Although there are some studies which show that cyber victimization seems to have more negative consequences than traditional bullying (Campbell, Spears, Slee, Butler, & Kift, 2012) there are others which show that students fear traditional bullying more than cyberbullying (Corby et al., 2016). Motives for cyberbullying are also similar to motives for traditional bullying, that is, wanting to fit in with peers, assist the bully so as not to get bullied themselves and cross the line of friendly banter to hurtful actions, increase their social status and have fun (Thomas, Connor, & Scott, 2017).

The definition is an important question not just for theoretical and research reasons but also for practical implementation of prevention programmes and intervention strategies. Is it necessary to have different programmes and strategies for cyberbullying than for traditional bullying? Should cyberbullying reduction programmes be based on traditional anti-bullying programmes which have not been very successful to date (Ttofi & Farrington, 2011)? Should we have prevention and intervention strategies for different roles in cyberbullying? Therefore, how one defines cyberbullying as a unique subset of bullying due to technology (which is a subset of aggression) or as fourth subtype of bullying itself (verbal/physical/social/cyber) will determine how the programme addresses it.

Naturally, researchers who develop prevention and intervention programmes and practitioners who deliver them need a common understanding of the phenomenon. At present most bullying programmes are predicated on the understanding that traditional or bullying in the 'real' world have features in common, whereas, bullying in the 'virtual' world has some features in common with them but more features which are specific to this form of bullying. These is the ability of students to bully 24/7, increased anonymity of young people who bully (although gossip is usually anonymous in social bullying), the wider audience using technology, the rapid spread of bullying material and the permanency of the bullying online. It could be, however, that bullying programmes were designed before cyberbullying became so widespread, and thus programmes have been modified to incorporate cyberbullying into the existing programmes without necessarily a theoretical position being taken on the definition of cyberbullying. In the future, however, the nuances of definition taken by the developers of programmes for the prevention of cyberbullying and the practitioners who use the programmes could impact on the design of the programmes.

Context

History of cyberbullying

Cyberbullying came to adult attention late in the last century. The term was first used in a *New York Times* article in 1995 (Bauman, 2011) although Canadian grade teacher Bill Belsey is often credited with coining the term on his website. It was not a term young people used to describe this form of bullying (Grigg, 2010) but it is now so widely accepted by researchers, the public, and law makers with young people taught about what it means that the word is here to stay.

Prevalence

There are two issues in the prevalence of cyberbullying in young people: what is the proportion of cyberbullying to traditional bullying, and is cyberbullying increasing over time? The difficulty with answering both questions is that the measurement of cyberbullying is still plagued with inconsistencies and so there are wide variations in published studies and reports. These differences are attributed to the kind of measures used, global vs behavioural, definitions included or not, the time frames asked and the cut-off of frequency used (Huang & Cornell, 2015). Other problems are about how the data is collected (on or offline) and the way the participants are recruited (Espinoza & Juvonen, 2013).

In one of the most recent studies it was found that only 2% of students experienced cyberbullying as the only form of victimization (Thomas et al., 2017). This accords with Salmivalli and Poyhonen's (2012) study that found there were only 0.2% of students who were only cyberbullied. Hase, Goldberg, Smith, Stuck, and Campain (2015) found that almost 50% of secondary school students had been traditionally bullied in the previous month compared to 16% who had been cyberbullied; however, 93% of those traditionally bullied had also been cyberbullied. In general we can assume that most cyberbullying occurs with other forms of bullying. This has great significance for programmes of prevention and intervention of cyberbullying.

Is cyberbullying decreasing, increasing, or stable? The aforementioned problems in measurement of cyberbullying also affect the estimation of the prevalence of cyberbullying over time. Compounding this problem is that the changes in technology have also affected the prevalence of cyberbullying. Although cyberbullying was detected in the 1990s it was mainly conducted through desktop computers using email and the Internet which was not accessible to a large number of young people. However, with the advent of the mobile phone and laptops there was an increase in young people's access to cyberspace and the potential to cyberbully. With the introduction of the Smartphone and the incredible uptake of these phones especially by young people as well as the proliferation of social media sites, this accessibility leads to more potential to cyberbully. It is very difficult, however, to determine if this has translated into an increase in cyberbullying.

Taking the prevalence rates of a country with a small population, such as Australia, as a case study, we can look at studies conducted from 2004 to 2017. In 2004 it was found that 14% of secondary students were cyberbullied (Campbell, 2005), while in 2009 with a larger sample, Cross and colleagues found it was 10% for students who self-reported they were victimized 'every few weeks or more'. Another national study in 2011 with 3,119 students (ages 10 to 18 years) found 14% of cyber victimization (Campbell, Spears, Slee, Kift, & Butler, 2011; Campbell et al., 2012). In 2012 Hemphill and colleagues found 15% of students reported that they had been cyberbullied, while in the same year Cross et al. (2012) found with students aged 8–14 cyber victimization was reported by 7%. In a report to the Australian Federal government cyber victimization was found to be estimated at about 20% after examining all studies found to that time (Katz et al., 2014). In the latest 2017 national study, cyber victimization was self-reported as 6.6% for 'every few weeks or more' (Thomas et al., 2017). However, all these studies sampled different age groups, recruited differently, used different questionnaires and different time frames and cut-off points.

This difficulty with prevalence measurement needs to be overcome as it is crucial to know whether any prevention and intervention strategies for cyberbullying are working. This is also important in informing the public to confirm or counteract the view that cyberbullying is an epidemic which is increasing. Although traditional bullying has previously been linked to death by suicide (Ford, King, Priest, & Kavanagh, 2017) a lot of media link cyberbullying to death by suicide even though research has only associated cyber victimization with suicidal ideation (Kowalski, Giumetti, Schroeder, & Lattanner, 2014; Van Geel, Vedder, & Tanilon, 2014). However, suicide is usually more complicated and probably the increasing rate has more to do with increasing mental health problems in young people than cyberbullying.

Consequences

Mostly, the consequences of cyberbullying victimization for students have been found to be similar to the consequences of traditional bullying. These negative consequences include low self-esteem (Palermiti, Servidio, Bartolo, & Costabile, 2017), emotional distress (Gonzalez-Cabree, Clavete, Leon-Mejia, Perez-Sancho, & Peinado, 2017) anger and sadness (Wang, Yang, Yang, Wang, & Lei, 2017) and suicidal ideation (Schenk & Fremouw, 2012). However, some studies have shown that there are even higher levels of depression, anxiety, and social difficulties for cyber victimized students than for those traditionally bullied (Campbell, Spears, Slee, Butler, & Kift, 2012; Perren et al., 2012; Sticca & Perren, 2013). Cyberbullying victimization has also been shown to be associated with more suicidal ideation than traditional bullying (Bonanno & Hymel, 2013; Klomek, Sourander, & Gould, 2011). However, one study showed that young people thought that traditional bullying was more embarrassing as you could see your friends watching whereas online they were not visible (Corby et al., 2016). These findings have important implications for prevention programmes and intervention strategies for cyberbullying.

Evidence for programmes that reduce cyberbullying

Cyber-safety programmes

If cyberbullying is conceptualized as a social relationship problem, another way of bullying, then the thrust of cyberbullying prevention programmes would be similar to traditional bullying programmes. However, if cyber-bullying is conceptualized as a technological problem then the programmes aimed at reducing it will be very different (Topcu-Uzer & Tanrikulu, 2018). Cyber-safety programmes where students are taught the dangers of technology should therefore be shown to reduce cyberbullying if the latter conceptualization is correct.

However, programmes which are about cyber-safety have the least evidence for reducing cyberbullying. This is probably because the programmes are designed to be very broad, in protecting children from the many dangers in cyberspace such as showing how to protect themselves from paedophiles or not to watch pornography. Therefore, the programmes concentrate on showing students how to protect themselves such as not sharing their passwords or putting their social media settings to private. However, as they do not deal with not hurting others and relationship problems, these programmes usually are not researched for their effectiveness for preventing cyberbullying. Certain technological strategies can be taught about intervention or coping strategies when a young person is cyberbullied, such as deleting messages, blocking senders and having content removed from social media sites (Livingstone, Haddon, Gorzig, & Olafsson, 2011) which are helpful but only after the victimization.

Most of these cyber-safety programmes aim to keep children safe from adults, not other children. To this end, filters and blocking are advocated or even taking away the technology. In Australia there is a movement to ban mobile phones in schools so students will not have the ability to cyberbully on these devices (Education HQ news, 2018). However, we know most cyberbullying occurs outside school hours (Purdy & McGuckin, 2015) and can also be conducted on tablets and desk top computers which are not only allowed in schools but often are compulsory. Further, there is some evidence which shows banning mobile phones at school does not reduce cyberbullying (Pfetsch, Steffgen, & Konig, 2009; Steffgen, Pfetsch, Konig & Ewen, 2010).

Mishna, Cook, Saini, Wu, and MacFadden (2011) reviewed three programmes on cyber-safety, I-SAFE, Missing and Help-Assert Yourself-Humor-Avoid-Self-Talk-Own It, and found that while these programmes increased Internet safety knowledge, they did not affect risky online behaviour. An Australian programme called eSmart is promoted as a cyberbullying prevention programme even though like similar programmes it is designed for more general cyber-safety such as keeping oneself safe from predators and security settings on social media. Evaluations of the programme revealed that teachers said they were confident in advising students and knew what to do if an incident occurred. The programme had a high acceptability with 98% of principals who said they would recommend it to other schools (Foundation for Young Australians, 2013). However, there has been no research on the programme's effectiveness in reducing cyberbullying.

An unintended negative consequence of these programmes if used for reducing cyberbullying could be that if we teach children to protect themselves and they still get bullied then they could feel they have failed. This is usually referred to as bully proofing. It would seem a child might feel it was their fault if they are cyberbullied (as many do anyway) and that could also decrease reporting.

One cyber-safety programme, however, has been evaluated in terms of reducing cyberbullying. ConRed is a Spanish programme consisting of eight sessions for secondary students teaching how to use the Internet and social networking sites in a safe, positive, and beneficial manner (Casas, Del Rey, & Ortega-Ruiz, 2018). The sixth session focuses on cyberbullying. The whole programme is based on the coexistence model which underlines the importance of the quality of interpersonal relationships which have been adopted by schools in Spain for more than 20 years. ConRed was evaluated with students for eight sessions, two sessions with teachers and two with families in a quasi-experimental design with pre- and post-data with a control group (Del Rey, Casas, & Ortega, 2016). It was found that cyberbullying victimization was decreased in the experimental group more than the control group. Although the programme also reduced cyber perpetration among girls it did not do so for boys. Traditional bullying victimization was also decreased which is not surprising as the programme is grounded in relationship theory.

In summary, cyber-safety programmes, while important to be taught for their own sake and often containing some useful strategies for victim coping, do not attempt to decrease cyberbullying perpetration. These programmes appear to be the least evidence-based and least effective in reducing cyberbullying.

Traditional anti-bullying programmes

While there are many programmes which are designed to decrease traditional bullying in schools, there is only one that we know of which has been also evaluated for efficacy in reducing cyberbullying with only attention paid to traditional bullying. The ViSC programme targets traditional bullying only and has been shown to reduce this in schools (Yanagida,

Stohmeier, & Spiel, 2016; and Chapter 4). The programme is a manualized educational programme for teachers and students in lower secondary and middle school (11–15 years old) which is delivered over 12 months. In the first semester teachers are the focus of the intervention and students the focus in the second semester. The programme has also been researched for its impact on cyber perpetration and cyber victimization. In Austria in a cluster randomized control study it was found that there was an increase in both cyberbullying perpetration and victimization in the control group while there was a decrease in cyber perpetration in the intervention group and a lower increase for cyber victimization compared to the control group (Gradinger, Yanagida, Strohmeier, & Spiel, 2016).

Traditional anti-bullying programmes with a cyberbullying component

The majority of programmes which intend to prevent bullying have been devised to prevent traditional bullying and have later included cyberbullying in the programme. Three such programmes have been evaluated for their efficacy in reducing cyberbullying; Cyber-Friendly Schools, KiVa, and *No Trap!*

Cyber-Friendly Schools (see Chapter 6) is a whole-school curriculum modulized programme suitable for secondary school students aged 13–18. The programme targets students, parents, and teachers. In Western Australia 19 schools were randomized to an intervention group and 16 to a comparison group. Grade 8 students were surveyed at baseline and post-test one and two years later. Findings indicated that cyber perpetration and victimization was reduced significantly more in the intervention than in the control schools. However, the intervention did not show any differences in reduction in cyberbullying from Grade 9 to 10 (Cross et al., 2016). Unfortunately classroom teachers were only able to deliver a third of the programme in their classrooms as they felt they could not do more because of other curriculum demands.

Another anti-bullying programme is the Finnish KiVa (see Chapter 3), which also takes a whole-school approach, including manualized curriculum lessons and targeted intervention; it is designed for younger students in Years 1–9 (ages 7–15). The programme has been shown to reduce cyber victimization (Karna et al., 2011). Within the programme cyberbullying is treated as another form of bullying. After one year of intervention of KiVa in Grades 4–6 cyber victimization was reduced by 36% compared to an increase of 14% of cyber victimization in the control schools (Salmivalli, Karna, & Poskiparta, 2011). The programme's effects were significant also in reducing cyber perpetration but only with younger students, with less effect on middle school students and no effects for Grade 9 students.

A third programme is *No Trap!* (Noncadiamointrappola, 'Let's not fall into the trap!), an Italian programme which addresses all types of bullying (see Chapter 8). It is a whole-school focused programme but is delivered mostly online. The programme targets 7th to 10th Grade students. It is a peer-led programme which is delivered over a four-month period. Both teacher and student meetings are held separately, followed by peer educators' training for a day in a face-to-face format and then online training on their own. The peer educators then lead workshops under teacher supervision in regular classes. Compared to a control group, cyberbullying perpetration was reduced by 28% and cyber victimization by 25% for the students in the experimental group doing the programme (Palladino, Nocentini, & Menesini, 2016). In addition, the results were stable after 12 months with no difference for boys or girls. There was also a decrease in internalizing symptoms for students in the experimental group.

Anti-cyberbullying specific programmes

Media Heroes (Medienhelden) is a programme designed for cyberbullying prevention and intervention only. It is a manualized programme for Years 7–10 designed in Germany as a prevention programme to target cyberbullying in secondary-aged students which is delivered by teachers (Schultze-Krumbholz, Zagorscak, & Scheithauer, 2018). It is a universal intervention in which teachers are trained to implement the programme based on creating empathy, perspective-taking, and moral engagement. This is because perpetrators of cyberbullying have been shown to lack empathy for their targets (Schultz-Krumbholz, Schultze, Zagorscak, Wolfer, & Scheithauer, 2016) and think their behaviour does no harm. The programme is based on social learning and cognitive-behaviour theory and uses student-to-parent and peer-to-peer learning methods. The programme's acceptance rate by teachers was shown as excellent and rated very good by students. The programme's effectiveness was also established with cyberbullying perpetration decreasing after the ten-week programme while increasing in the control group (Schultz-Krumbholz, Zagorscak, Wolfer, & Scheithauer, 2014a, 2014b) but there was no corresponding decrease of cyber victimization (Chaux, Valasquez, Schultz-Krumbholz, & Scheithauer, 2016). This could mean that the perpetrators realized their behaviour was not acceptable and therefore reported they would not do it or if they really did stop then the other perpetrators increased their behaviour. Interestingly this programme had positive carry over effects on traditional bullying.

Social-emotional learning programmes

Many programmes have considered that if young people are taught the opposite to hurtful bullying behaviour, that is, being kind and respectful, it could reduce cyberbullying. The intention to hurt is the same for all forms of bullying with the knowledge that the perpetrator will not be hurt as there is an imbalance of power. Therefore, social-emotional learning and teaching pro-social behaviours is paramount to assisting students to find other ways to fulfil their own needs rather than bullying. While some of these social-emotional learning programmes have been evaluated few have been examined to see whether the programme reduces cyberbullying. One exception is the American programme Second Step (see Chapter 5). In a clinical trial of Second Step Middle School programme the impact on cyberbullying perpetration among other behaviours was assessed (Espelage, Low, Van Ryzin, & Polanin, 2015). It was found that there were decreases in cyberbullying perpetration over three years from when the students were 11 to 14 years old which was an indirect effect of decreases in self-reported delinquency.

What are the common critical elements in these programmes?

Unfortunately, we do not yet know what the common critical elements for effective programmes to reduce cyberbullying are. Below is a list of some of the common elements in the above evidence-based programmes

The programme's name is positive

Beginning with Media Heroes, to Cyber-Friendly Schools the names of the programmes are usually positive. KiVa means against bullying but also means someone who is kind to others. ConRed is based on cybercoexistence and ViSC means together against violence, while *No Trap!* means 'Let's not fall into the trap!'

The programme is based on theory

While there are many system theories and individual level theories there is no one single theory that encapsulates all bullying behaviour (Thomas, Connor, & Scott, 2017). However, as Barlett (2017) has noted, cyberbullying interventions which are underpinned by theory can be more successful. Most of the programmes described here are based on different theories. Media Heroes is based on the Theory of Reasoned Action (Madden, Ellen, & Ajzen, 1992), where attitudes such as empathy, injunctive norms (where students learn their peers do not expect them to cyberbully others) and behavioural control such as help-seeking behaviour are believed to influence behavioural intentions which directly influence actual behaviour. *No Trap!* is based on the social-ecological model, that bullying is group behaviour and therefore addressed the whole school and community, similar to ViSC and Cyber-Friendly Schools. ConRed is grounded in the theory of Normative Social Behaviour (Rimal, Lapinski, Cook, & Real, 2005) which is very similar to the Theory of Reasoned Action.

Involves students, teachers, and parents

We know from studies of traditional bullying programmes that the most effective ones intervene on an individual level, involve peers and include teachers and parents (Cook, Williams, Guerra, Kim, & Sadek, 2010). It would seem that those programmes which look to reduce cyberbullying would have the same wide stakeholder engagement. Cyber-Friendly Schools, KiVa, Media Heroes, *No Trap!*, ConRed all target students, teachers, and parents.

Involves young people in the design and execution of the programme

As young people have grown up with technology and are usually more proficient in its use than adults to date, it seems logical to involve them in the development of programmes and in their delivery, by co-researching with academics, being peer leaders in school, conducting cross-age peer tutoring and educating parents (Spears & Zeederberg, 2012). Many of the programmes detailed above do include young people in the design and/or delivery of the programme. As an example the Cyber-Friendly Schools programme includes 'cyber' leaders to develop and implement whole-school activities (Cross, Lester, Barnes, Cardoso, & Hadwen, 2015). *No Trap!* is entirely student led in its delivery but not in its development (Menesini, Zambuto, & Palladino, 2018).

Is flexible enough to include changing technologies

Many of these programmes have been developed over time as anti-bullying programmes for traditional bullying and have been revised to include cyberbullying. They have also been revised after research has shown what did not work (Menesini, Palladino, & Nocenti, 2016).

We do not know, however, what are the effective components of the programmes to successfully prevent and intervene in cyberbullying. This is a concern as many programmes are not fully implemented when practitioners and not researchers deliver the programme (Cross et al., 2016). Adaptations for local conditions are often made which could also affect the efficacy of the programme.

Issues with existing programmes

Age of young people?

Most anti-bullying programmes are designed for either primary (elementary) or secondary school students. However, with cyberbullying programmes most seem to target secondary school students with the assumption that they will use technological devices more and have more technological skills. But there is evidence that traditional bullying programmes do not work as well with secondary pupils as with younger children (Polanin, Espelage, & Pigott, 2012), and can even have a detrimental effect (Yeager, Fong, Lee, & Espelage, 2015). This is concerning as, except for KiVa, most cyberbullying prevention programmes are targeted at secondary school pupils and perhaps more programmes should target primary aged children as they have also been shown to cyberbully.

Classroom teachers or specialists?

In the early stages of research when evaluating a programme the researchers who designed the programme often deliver it to schools. However, this is not sustainable and therefore teachers need to be trained in the programme. Although many programmes are manualized which aids in their fidelity there are often problems with teachers cherry-picking the activities and not showing fidelity with the programme. Cyberbullying prevention programmes need to be robust enough to be delivered by different people.

Online in the classroom or interactive?

If cyberbullying is a technological problem then delivering programmes online would seem to be called for. However if bullying is a relationship problem, then interactive activities in the classroom might be more effective. Or perhaps a combination of both would be the best solution. The programmes in this chapter seem to combine both online and classroom activities. Cyber-Friendly Schools is mainly classroom orientation but does have a website which contains information, tutorials, strategies, and resources. KiVa is similar, where there are many classroom activities but also online games are provided. *NoTrap!* also provides a webpage and Facebook page as well as meeting activities. Interestingly Media Heroes is entirely class based.

Length of programme?

As most programmes are designed for schools and the length of terms is usually ten weeks then most programmes try to fit into that time frame, although some programmes are shorter or much longer. It has been shown that a longer-running cyberbullying prevention programme is more effective than a short programme (Schultz-Krumbholz et al., 2014a) with the effects of Media Heroes over a ten-week programme superior to the one-day programme. However, many schools, especially in the US, still rely on a 45-minute talk on cyberbullying to reduce the behaviour (Salazar, Roberto, Eden, & Savage, 2018).

One programme?

The curriculum in most schools is of a spiral nature. That is, a topic is not just taught once but is revisited several times with increasing complexity as the student becomes older (Bruner, 2009). Information is reinforced each year and there is a logical progression from simple ideas when children are younger which grow in more complex as the student gains in cognitive capacity. This is tied in with the length of a programme but is more extensive, making sure that the messages are revisited each year so that learning can become consolidated. Unfortunately there are no programmes yet which teach developmentally from kindergarten, yet from early childhood classes on, students use technology. One programme however, Cyber-Friendly Schools, does have a curriculum for Grade 8 and an expanded curriculum for Grade 9.

Costs of programmes?

At present as researchers are the ones who design programmes and if shown to be effective then sell the programme, many schools cannot afford to buy multiple programmes. To overcome this problem each education department could write programmes which are trialled and provide them to schools with the appropriate resources similar to History and Mathematics curricula. Those bullying programmes which are the most researched have usually been supported by the country's national government in the research and implementation, such as KiVa.

Cultural differences in programmes?

Can these programmes be successful in different cultures? We know that Olweus's successful programme for reducing traditional bullying in Norway did not have the same success in the United States (see also Chapters 2 and 5). However, ViSC is currently being used in Turkey, Romania, and Cyprus with evaluation studies being conducted (Solomontos-Kountouri, Gradinger, Yanagida, & Strohmeier, 2016).

Issues in programme implementation

There appear to be few studies to date about the implementation of anti-cyberbullying programmes. Even if programmes have been found to be effective in reducing cyberbullying they may be implemented poorly, or a less effective programme could be implemented well. Only providing information, such as mail-outs, educational presentations, or even training, have been found to be ineffective in implementing interventions (Ellis, Robinson, Ciliska, Amour, & Brouwers, 2003). Implementation is a process (Fixsen, Naoom, Blasé, Friedman, & Wallace, 2005) which has several steps:

Readiness for a programme, that is, do the staff think there is a need for an anti-cyberbullying programme? Unfortunately, most programmes for cyberbullying have only been implemented in schools if there has been a tragic event or there is an outside influence. Incidents such as a student dying by suicide, in which cyberbullying was one factor, often prompts a school to take some decisive action and search for an effective evidence-based programme. Outside influences could be researchers involving the school in a cyberbullying intervention which was successful in reducing cyberbullying and the school decides to continue the programme. Another outside influence is if the controlling body of the school, the board, or the government, mandates that an evidence-based programme for cyberbullying reduction will be implemented.

Do all the stakeholders then have 'buy-in' for the programme, is everybody involved so the programme will be sustainable? Most successful programmes have been shown to be 'whole-school' approaches. That is, the programme is not just a few teachers teaching a couple of lessons but all teachers implementing it, together with a review of policies and procedures and always involving parents. Most often, however, although there could be a champion in the school who promotes the programme, the whole school community does not fully commit for sustained periods of years which it takes to effect behaviour change.

Are staff going to be provided not only with training but also coaching and feedback until they become very confident in delivering the programme? Not only are feedback and coaching rarely given with programme implementation but also there is often no induction of new staff to make the programme faithfully implemented and sustainable.

Can the programme be fitted into the school day, is there enough time in the curriculum to teach it? Most controlling bodies for schools, either governments or boards do not support reduction of other curriculum areas' teaching hours to enable the cyberbullying programme to be taught.

Will the programme continue to be assessed at least annually? A survey on well-being and cyberbullying needs to be carried out each year with students to ascertain if the programme is actually reducing cyberbullying in that school. The programme might also need to be modified in our ever changing world, especially in relation to evolving new technologies.

Does the school have the resources to implement the programme, both the start-up costs in funding and staff and with future funding for sustainability? This last point is very important as behaviour change takes a long time and many teachers give up on new programmes after a year if there is no discernible change (Trip et al., 2015). Unfortunately the public also wants a quick solution to cyberbullying. This is often shown by calls to lawmakers to have specific laws on cyberbullying which people believe will fix the problem (Campbell & Zavrsnik, 2013).

What is needed is a long-term multi-level approach and research into the interaction of different implementation factors so that evidence-based cyberbullying programmes can be implemented successfully (Fixsen et al., 2005). That is, multi-level factors of implementation such as actively choosing the most appropriate programme, having training, coaching and feedback, and evaluation need to be researched, both to see what are the critical components of implementation and also to see how they interact with other so that best practice for implementation can be established.

Other strategies

Similar to traditional bullying, prevention approaches for cyberbullying should include awareness raising sessions of the problem in the first instance. Legal approaches and school policies also need to be considered. There are also emerging strategies which are drawn from other fields such as online social marketing for campaigns and motivational interviewing for students who persistently cyberbully.

Legal solutions

Many sectors of the community are calling for a specific law on cyberbullying which criminalizes the behaviour (Taylor, 2018; Wu, 2014). It seems the public would prefer laws and punishments as the prevention of cyberbullying is complex, difficult, and time-consuming. In Australia there are numerous parliamentary inquiries into whether such a law should be passed (Legal and Consitutional Affairs Senate References Committee, 2018) as well as the media representing families who attribute the death by suicide of their children to cyberbullying (Aikman, 2018). While Australia and the United Kingdom do not have such a law, the USA and Canada have some laws pertaining to cyberbullying (Butler, 2018). Schools are often in a difficult position, although the law is clear on their duty of care to students; investigating and applying the law is complex. In the United States the position is also much less clear because of the context of the First Amendment for the provision of freedom of speech and expression (Butler, 2018). Unfortunately, however, Dasgupta (2018) found that in states in the US which either legally required schools to adopt sanctions for cyberbullying, or provided criminal sanctions for cyberbullying, the incidence itself did not decrease with the introduction of the laws, although students' reporting of it did.

School policies

Schools are often exhorted to include cyberbullying as a form of bullying in their school policies and indeed in many countries it is mandated by educational authorities. However, if school policies are only paper implementation, that is, manuals on shelves and not fully implemented, then they are useless (Fixsen et al., 2005). In the ranking of effective components of anti-bullying programmes it was found that whole-school policies were ranked only seventh and that they seemed to be useful for a reduction in perpetration and not victimization (Ttofi & Farrington, 2011). This is probably because of the tremendous difficulties in making and implementing school policies which seem to be seen as a quick fix for cyberbullying problems (Campbell, 2018). For the creation of a school anti-bullying policy and its implementation the school should be collegial, communicating with all stakeholders and showing mutual respect (Richard, Schnedier, & Mallet, 2011). If a school does not have a positive school climate they are less likely to communicate and thus be able to articulate and develop and implement an effective policy. Unless there are strong cultures and norms in the school as well as formal procedures and policies it is unlikely that students will have respectful relationships (Powell, 2012). If any of the procedural steps are left out then the policy becomes ineffective. If the policy is not disseminated, followed, revised, evaluated then it becomes ineffective (Campbell, 2018).

Campaigns

Many cyberbullying researchers now perceive that it is a public health issue (Spears, Taddeo, Daly, Stretton, & Karklins, 2015; Zych, Baldry, & Farrington, 2017). Additionally, taking Bronfenbrenner's social-ecological model (1977), which shows the relationship between a person and their environment, to include community influence, then perhaps public health campaigns could be successful in reducing cyberbullying. Most public health campaigns which have successfully changed behaviour in Australia have been television-based such as the Grim Reaper for AIDS prevention, Slip, Slop, Slap for sun cancer prevention, and Quit for a reduction in cigarette-smoking. However, these campaigns ran for many years before behaviour change was noticed. Today, young people are more likely to be on social media than watching television. They are more likely also to be swayed by 'influencers' on social media than by high-profile people.

One such online social marketing approach was used in Australia to reduce cyberbullying (Spears, Taddeo, & Barnes, 2018). The campaign had four stages and was co-designed with young people. Cyberbullying as a negative peer issue was reframed as positive messages to peers, such as *Appreciate a Mate* and *Keep it Tame*. Although this first attempt at a public online campaign had good reach and perhaps nudged young people to conduct respectful relationships online, after three years there was no change in the representative age cohort samples of anxiety and depression (Spears et al., 2018).

Motivational Interviewing

Not all programmes or interventions are suitable for all young people (Schultze-Krumbholz et al., 2016). In fact perpetrators of bullying are not a homogeneous group (Thomas, Connor, & Scott, 2018). Thus additional strategies are needed especially for young people who persistently bully. These students usually have little desire to change their behaviour and are thus resistant to change. Taking a strategy originally developed for assisting people with drug and alcohol problems, motivational interviewing is based on the assumption that the problem behaviour fulfils a need in the person and stopping the behaviour would be seen as detrimental to that person (Rollnick & Miller, 1995). Therefore, if the young person is first listened to for their own reasons for cyberbullying and second, the reasons for change they present are selectively strengthened, could provide a strategy to resolve ambivalence and deepen their motivation to change. Recently a project in Australian has been researching whether motivational interviewing (MI) might have a role in working with youth who persistently bully others (Cross, Runions, Resnicow, Britt, & Gray, 2018).

Ways forward

Action research in schools

Although these programmes to reduce cyberbullying in young people have been mostly evidence-based, in that research has shown that under controlled conditions they work, what is needed in the next step is to research the delivery in schools under regular school conditions. Usually, the research has been carried out by the developers of the programme and schools have 'co-operated' by following all the researchers' directions. However, action research needs to be carried out to see whether the programmes are sustainable in schools without the researchers. Training of staff, cost of the programme, motivation of staff, and time constraints all need to be taken into account.

Youth voice

Youth voice is an empowering approach to cyberbullying prevention and intervention which is youth centred and designs programmes with young people (Spears & Kofoed, 2013). If programmes use youth language and behavioural examples that are meaningful for them then it would seem that young people would more readily engage in the programmes. This is especially important in secondary schools where they are becoming more independent and autonomous and finding their own identity.

Changes in society

All bullying is a complex social relationship problem which is deeply embedded in our society. Domestic violence, sexual harassment, and workplace bullying by adults are examples for young people to follow in conducting their own relationships. In some ways we need fundamental values in society to become more respectful which hopefully this generation of students will lead.

References

Aikman, A. (2018). We must make a stand against bullies, says Dolly Everett's dad. The Australian, 13 January, p. 5. Retrieved from: https://gateway.library.qut.edu.au/login?url=https://search.proquest.com/docview/1987257584?accountid=13380.

Barlett, C. P. (2017). From theory to practice: Cyberbullying theory and its application to intervention. Computers in Human Behavior, 72, 269–275. doi:10.1016/j.chb.2017.02.060.

Bauman, S. (2011). Cyberbullying: What counselors need to know. Alexandria, VA: American Counseling Association.

Bauman, S., Underwood, M., & Card, N. (2013). Definitions: Another perspective and proposal for beginning with cyberaggression. In S. Bauman, D. Cross, & J. Walker (Eds.), Principles of cyberbullying research: Definitions, measures, and methodology (pp. 44–46). New York: Routledge.

Bonanno, R. A., & Hymel, S. (2013). Cyber bullying and internalizing difficulties: Above and beyond the impact of traditional forms of bullying. Journal of Youth and Adolescence, 42, 685–697. doi:10.1007/s10964–10013–9937–9931.

Bronfenbrenner, U. (1977). Toward an experimental ecology of human development. American Psychologist, 32, 513–531. doi:10.1037/0003-066x.32.7.513.

Bruner, J. S. (2009). The process of education. Cambridge, MA: Harvard University Press.

Butler, D. (2018). Cyberbullying and the law: Parameters for effective interventions? In M. Campbell & S. Bauman (Eds.), Reducing cyberbullying in schools: International evidenced-based best practices (pp. 49–60). London: Academic Press.

Campbell, M. A. (2005). Cyber bullying: An old problem in a new guise? Australian Journal of Guidance and Counselling, 15, 68–76. doi:10.1375/ajgc.15.1.68.

Campbell, M. A. (2018). Paper tiger or effective guidelines: The use of policies and procedures to address school bullying. In H. Cowie & C. Meyers (Eds.), Bullying in schools: Intervention and prevention (pp. 169–179). London: Routledge.

Campbell, M. A., Spears, B., Slee, P., Kift, S., & Butler, D. (2011). The prevalence of cyberbullying in Australia. 5th World conference and IV Iberoamerican congress on violence in school. Investigations, interventions, evaluations and public policies, April, Mendoza, Argentina.

Campbell, M. A., Spears, B., Slee, P., Butler, D., & Kift, S. (2012). Victims' perceptions of traditional and cyberbullying, and the psychosocial correlates of their victimisation. *Emotional and Behavioural Difficulties*, 17, 389–401. doi:10.1080/13632752.2012.704316.

Campbell, M. A., & Zavrsnik, A. (2013). Should cyberbullying be criminalized? In P.K. Smith & G. Steffgen (Eds.), *Cyberbullying through the new media: Findings from an international network* (pp. 65–82). London: Psychology Press.

Casas, J. A., Del Rey, R., & Ortga-Ruiz, R. (2018). The ConRed program: Education in cybercoexistence and cyberbullying prevention by improving coexistence projects in schools. In M. Campbell & S. Bauman (Eds.), *Reducing cyberbullying in schools: International evidence-based best practice* (pp. 203–211). London: Academic Press.

Chaux, E., Velasquez, A. M., Schultze-Krumbholz, A., & Scheithauer, H. (2016). Effects of the cyberbullying prevention program media heroes (Medienhelden) on traditional bullying. *Aggressive Behavior*, 42, 157–165. doi:10.1002/ab.21637.

Compton, L., Campbell, M. A., & Mergler, A. (2014). Teacher, parent and student perceptions of the motives of cyberbullies. *Social Psychology of Education*, 17, 383–400. doi:10.1007/s11218–11014–9254-x.

Cook, C. R., Williams, K. R., Guerra, N. G., Kim, T. E., & Sadek, S. (2010). Predictors of bullying and victimization in childhood and adolescence: A meta-analytic investigation. *School Psychology Quarterly*, 25(2), 65–83.

Corby, E.-K., Campbell, M. A., Spears, B. A., Butler, D., Kift, S., & Slee, P. (2016). Students' perceptions of their own victimisation: A youth voice perspective. *Journal of School Violence*, 15, 322–342. doi:10.1080/15388220.2014.996719.

Cross, D., Lester, L., Barnes, A., Cardoso, P., & Hadwen, K. (2015). If it's about me, why do it without me? Genuine student engagement in school cyberbullying education. *International Journal of Emotional Education*, 7, 35–51.

Cross, D., Runions, K., Resnicow, K., Britt, E., & Gray, C. (2018). Motivational interviewing as a positive response to high-school bullying. *Psychology in the Schools*. doi:10.1002/pits.22120.

Cross, D., Shaw, T., Dooley, J. J., Epstein, M., Hearn, L., & Monks, H. (2012). Cyberbullying in Australia: Is school context related to cyberbullying behaviour? In Q. Li, D. Cross, & P. K. Smith (Eds.), *Cyberbullying in the global playground: Research from international perspectives* (pp. 75–98). Chichester: Wiley-Blackwell.

Cross, D., Shaw, T., Hadwen, K., Cardoso, P., Slee, P., Roberts, C., Thomas, L., & Barnes, A. (2016). Longitudinal impact of the Cyber Friendly Schools program on adolescents' cyberbullying behaviour. *Aggressive Behavior*, 42, 166–180. doi:10.1002/ab.21609.

Cross, D., Shaw, T., Hearn, L., Epstein, M., Monks, H., Lester, L., & Thomas, L. (2009). *Australian Covert Bullying Prevalence Study (ACBPS)*. Child Health Promotion

Research Centre, Edith Cowan University, Perth. Retrieved from: http://ro.ecu. edu.au/ecuworks/6795/.

Dasgupta, K. (2018). Youth response to state cyberbullying laws. *New Zealand Economic Papers*, online 1–19. doi:10.1080/00779954.2018.1467959.

Del Rey, R., Casas, J. A., & Ortega, R. (2016). Impact of the ConRed program on different cyberbullying roles. *Aggressive Behavior*, *42*, 123–135. doi:10.1002/ab.21608.

Education HQ News Team. (2018). NSW review may ban smart phones in schools. *Education Week Australia*, 21 June.

Ellis, P., Robinson, P., Ciliska, D., Amour, T., & Brouwers, M. (2003). Diffusion and dissemination of evidence-based cancer control interventions. *Evidence Report/Technology Assessment Number 79*. Rockville, MD: Agency for Healthcare Research and Quality.

Englander, E., Donnerstein, E., Kowalski, R., Lin, C., & Parti, K. (2017). Defining cyberbullying. *Pediatrics*, *140*, s148. doi:10.1542/peds.2016–1758U.

Espelage, D. L., Low, S., Van Ryzin, M. J., & Polanin, J. R. (2015). Clinical trial of Second Step Middle School Program: Impact on bullying, cyberbullying, homophobic teasing and sexual harassment perpetration. *School Psychology Review*, *44*, 464–479.

Espinoza, G., & Jovonen, J. (2013). Methods used in cyberbullying research. In S. Bauman, D. Cross, & J. Walker (Eds.), *Principles of cyberbullying research: Definitions, measures, and methodology* (pp. 112–124). New York: Routledge.

Fixsen, D. L., Naoon, S. F., Blasé, K. A., Friedman, R. M., & Wallace, F. (2005). *Implementation research: A synthesis of the literature*. Tampa, FL: University of South Florida.

Ford, R., King, T., Priest, N., & Kavanagh, A. (2017). *Bullying and mental health and suicidal behaviour among 14-to 15-year-olds in a representative sample of Australian children. Australian and New Zealand Journal of Psychiatry*, *51*, 897–908. doi:10.1177/0004867417700275 A.

Foundation for Young Australians. (2013). *Evaluation of eSmart program*. Retrieved from: https://www.kidsmatter.edu.au/health-and-community/enewsletter/cybersafety-program-works.

Gonzalez-Cabree, J., Calvete, E., Leon-Mejia, A., Perez-Sancho, C., & Peindo, J. M. (2017). Relationship between cyberbullying roles, cortisol secretion and psychological stress. *Computers in Human Behavior*, *70*, 153–160. doi:10.1016/j.chb.2016.12.054.

Gradinger, P., Yanagida, T., Strohmeier, D., & Spiel, C. (2016). Effectiveness and sustainability of the ViSC social competence program to prevent cyberbullying and cyber-victimization: Class and individual level moderators. *Aggressive Behavior*, *42*, 181–193. doi:10.1002/ab.21631.

Grigg, D. W. (2010). Cyber-aggression: Definition and concept of cyberbullying. *Australian Journal of Guidance and Counselling*, *20*, 143–156.

Hase, C. N., Goldberg, S. B., Smith, D., Stuck, A., & Campain, J. (2015). Impacts of traditional and cyberbullying on the mental health of middle school and high school students. *Psychology in the Schools*, *52*, 607–617. doi:10.1002/pits.21841.

Hemphill, S. A., Kotevski, A., Tollit, M., Smith, R., Herrenkohl, T., Toumbourou, J., & Catalano, R. (2012). Longitudinal predictors of cyber and traditional bullying perpetration in Australian secondary school students. *Journal of Adolescent Health, 51,* 59–65. doi:10.1016/j.jadohealth.2011.11.019.

Huang F. L., & Cornell, D. G. (2015). The impact of definition and question order on the prevalence of bullying victimization using student self-reports. *Psychological Assessment, 27,* 1484–1493. doi:10.1037/pas0000149.

Karna, A., Voeten, M., Little, T. D., Poskiparta, E., Alanen, E., & Salmivalli, C. (2011). Going to scale: A nonrandomized nationwide trial of the KiVa antibullying program for grades 1–9. *Journal of Consulting and Clinical Psychology, 79,* 796–805. doi:10.1037/a0025740.

Katz, I., Keeley, M., Spears, B., Taddeo, C., Swirski, T., & Bates, S. (2014). *Research on youth exposure to, and management of, cyberbullying incidents in Australia: Synthesis report* (SPRC Report 16/2014). Sydney: Social Policy Research Centre, UNSW Australia. Retrieved from: https://www.sprc.unsw.edu.au/research/projects/cyberbullying/.

Klomek, A. B., Sourander, A., & Gould, M. S. (2011). Bullying and suicide: Detection and intervention. *Psychiatric Times, 28*(2), 27–31.

Kowalski, R. M., Giumetti, A. N., Schroeder, M. R., & Lattanner, M. R. (2014). Bullying in the digital age: A critical review and meta-analysis of cyberbullying research among youth. *Psychological Bulletin, 140,* 1073–1137.

Legal and Constitutional Affairs Senate References Committee. (2018). *Adequacy of existing offences in the Commonwealth Criminal Code and of state and territory criminal laws to capture cyberbullying.* Canberra, Australia. Retrieved from: https://www.ap h.gov.au/Parliamentary_Business/Committees/Senate/Legal_and_Constitutional_ Affairs/Cyberbullying/Report.

Livingstone, S., Haddon, L., Gorzig, A., & Olafsson, K. (2011). *Risks and safety on the Internet: The perspective of European children: Full findings and policy implications from the EU Kids Online Survey of 9–16 year olds and their parents in 25 countries.* London: LSE.

Madden, T. J., Ellen, P. S., & Azjen, I. (1992). A comparison of the theory of planned behavior and the theory of reasoned action. *Personality and Social Psychology Bulletin, 18,* 3–9. doi:10.1177/0146167292181001.

Menesini, E., Palladino, B. E., & Nocentini, A. (2016). Online and school based intervention to prevent cyberbullying among adolescents. In T. Vollink, F. Dehue, & C. McCuckin (Eds.), *Cyberbullying: From theory to intervention* (pp. 56–175). New York, NY: Routledge.

Menesini, E., Zambuto, V., & Palladino, B. (2018). Online and school-based programs to prevent cyberbullying among Italian adolescents: What works, why and under which circumstances. In M. Campbell & S. Bauman (Eds.), *Reducing cyberbullying in schools: International evidenced-based best practices* (pp. 135–143). London, UK: Academic Press.

Mishna, G., Cook, C., Saini, M., Wu, M.-J., & MacFadden, R. (2009). Interventions to reduce cyber abuse of youth: A systematic review. *Research on Social Work Practice, 21,* 5–14. doi:10.1177/1049731509351988.

Modecki, K. L., Minchin, J., Harbaugh, A. G., Guerra, N. G., & Runions, K. C. (2014). Bullying prevalence across contexts: A meta-analysis measuring cyber and traditional bullying. *Journal of Adolescent Health, 55,* 602–611. doi:10.1016/j.jadohealth.2014.06.007.

Palermiti, A. L., Servidio, R., Bartolo, M. G., & Costabile, A. (2017). Cyberbullying and self-esteem: An Italian study. *Computers in Human Behavior, 69,* 136–141. doi:10.1016/j.chb.2016.12.026.

Palladino, B. E., Nocentini, A., & Menesini, E. (2016). Evidenced-based intervention against bullying and cyberbullying: Evaluation of the Noncadiamointappola! program through two independent trial. *Aggressive Behavior, 42,* 194–206. doi:10.1002/ab.21636.

Perren, S., Corcoran, L., Cowie, H., Dehue, F., Garcia, D. J., McCuckin, C., & Vollink, T. (2012). Tackling cyberbullying: Review of empirical evidence regarding successful responses by students, parents, and schools. *International Journal of Conflict and Violence, 6,* 283–292. doi:10.4119/UNIBI/ijcv.244.

Pfetsch, J., Steffgen, G., & Konig, A. (2009). *Banning solves the problem!? Effects of banning mobile phone use in schools on cyberbullying.* Poster presentation at the 14th Workshop Aggression, Berlin, Germany.

Polanin, J. R., Espelage, D. L., & Pigott, T. D. (2012). A meta-analysis of school-based bullying prevention programs' effects on bystander intervention behavior. *School Psychology Review, 41*(1), 47–65.

Powell, A. (2012). *More than ready: Bystander action to prevent violence against women in the Victorian community.* Melbourne: Victorian Health Promotion Foundation.

Purdy, N., & McGuckin, C. (2015). Cyberbullying, schools and the law: A comparative study in Northern Ireland and the Republic of Ireland. *Educational Research, 57,* 420–436. doi:10.1080/00131881.2015.1091203.

Quirk, R., & Campbell, M. A. (2015). On standby? A comparison of online and offline witnesses to bullying and their bystander behaviour. *Educational Psychology: An International Journal of Experimental Educational Psychology, 35,* 430–448. doi:10.1080/01443410.2014.893556.

Richard, J., Schneider, B., & Mallett, P. (2011). Revisiting the whole-school approach to bullying: Really looking at the whole school. *School Psychology International, 33,* 263–284.

Rimal, R. N., Lapinski, M. K., Cook, R. J., & Real, K. (2005). Moving toward a theory of normative influences: How perceived benefits and similarity moderate the impact of descriptive norms on behaviors. *Journal of Health Communication, 10,* 433–450.

Rollnick, S., & Miller, W. R. (1995). What is motivational interviewing? *Behavioural and Cognitive Psychotherapy, 23,* 325–334. doi:10.1017/S135246580001643X.

Salazar, L. R., Roberto, A. J., Eden, J., & Savage, M. (2018). A short intervention on cyberbullying for students and their parents. In M. Campbell & S. Bauman (Eds.), *Reducing cyberbullying in schools: International evidenced-based best practices* (pp. 245–254). London, UK: Academic Press.

Salmivalli, C., Karna, A., & Poskiparta, E. (2011). Counteracting bullying in Finland: The KiVa program and its effects on different forms of being bullied. *International Journal of Behavioral Development, 35*, 405–411. doi:10.1177/0165025411407457.

Salmivalli, C., & Poyhonen, V. (2012). Cyberbullying in Finland. In Q. Li, D. Cross, & P. K. Smith (Eds.), *Cyberbullying in the global playground: Research from international perspectives* (pp. 57–72). Chichester: Wiley-Blackwell.

Schenk, A. M., & Fremouw, W. J. (2012). Prevalence, psychological impact, and coping of cyberbully victims among college students. *Journal of School Violence, 11*, 21–37. doi:10.1080/15388220.2011.630310.

Schultz-Krumbholz, A., Schultz, M., Zagorscak, P., Wolfer, R., & Scheithauer, H. (2016). Feeling cybervictims' pain – The effect of empathy training on cyberbullying. *Aggressive Behavior, 42*, 147–156. doi:10.1002/ab.21613.

Schultze-Krumbholz, A., Zagorsck, P., & Scheithauer, H. (2018). A school-based cyberbullying preventive intervention approach: The Media Heroes program. In M. Campbell & S. Bauman (Eds.), *Reducing cyberbullying in schools: International evidenced-based best practices* (pp. 145–158). London: Academic Press.

Schultz-Krumbholz, A., Zagorsck, P., Wolfer, R., & Scheithauer, H. (2014a). Promotion of media competence and prevention of cyberbullying using the Medienhelden program: Results from an evaluation study. *Praxis der Kinderpsychologie und Kinderpsychiatrie, 63*, 379–394.

Schultz-Krumbholz, A., Zagorsck, P., Wolfer, R., & Scheithauer, H. (2014b). Prevention of cyberbullying and reduction of aggressive behavior using the Medienhelden program: Results of an evaluation study. *Diskurs Kindheits – und Jugendforschung, 2014(1)*, 61–79.

Solomontos-Kountouri, O., Gradinger, P., Yanagida, Y., & Strohmeier, D. (2016). The implementation and evaluation of the ViSC program in Cyprus: Challenges of cross-national dissemination and evaluation results. *European Journal of Developmental Psychology, 13*, 737–755. doi:10.1080/17405629.2015.1136618.

Spears B., & Kofoed, J. (2013). Transgressing research binaries: Youth as knowledge brokers in cyberbullying research. In P. K. Smith & G. Steffgen, G. (Eds.), *Cyberbullying through the new media: Findings from an international network* (pp. 201–221). New York: Psychology Press.

Spears, B. A., Taddeo, C. M., & Barnes, A. (2018). Online social marketing approaches to inform cyberbullying prevention and intervention: What have we learnt? In M. Campbell & S. Bauman (Eds.), *Reducing cyberbullying in schools: International evidenced-based best practices* (pp. 75–94). London: Academic Press.

Spears, B. A., Taddeo, C. M., Daly, A. L., Stretton, A., & Karklins, L. T. (2015). Cyberbullying help-seeking and mental health in young Australians: Implications for public health. *Journal of Public Health, 60*, 219–226. doi:10.1007/s00038-00014-0642-y.

Spears, B., & Zeederberg, M. (2012). Emerging methodological strategies to address cyberbullying: Online social marketing and young people as co-researchers. In S.

Bauman, D. Cross, & J. Walker (Eds.), *Principles of cyberbullying research: Definitions, measures and methodology* (pp. 166–179). New York: Routledge.

Steffgen, G., Pfetsch, J., Konig, A., & Ewen, N. (2010). Interdire pour prevenir? Les effects de li'interdiction d'utiliser le telephone mobile a l'ecole pour luttre contre le cyber-bullying: une experience au Luxembourg. In C. Blaya (ed.), *Violence a l'ecole: Recherches et interventions* (pp. 185–206). Paris: L'Harmattan.

Sticca, F., & Perren, S. (2013). Is cyberbullying worse than traditional bullying? Examining the differential roles of medium, publicity, and anonymity for the perceived severity of bullying. *Journal of Youth and Adolescence*, 42, 739–750. doi:10.1007/s10964–10012–9867–9863.

Taylor, P. (2018). Cyberbullying leads to rise in calls for help. Editorial, *The Weekend Australian*, 13–14 January.

Thomas, H. J., Connor, J. P., Lawrence, D. M., Hafekost, J. M., Zubrick, S. R., & Scott, J. G. (2017). Prevalence and correlates of bullying victimisation and perpetration in a nationally representative sample of Australian youth. *Australian and New Zealand Journal of Psychiatry*, 51, 909–920. doi:10.1177/0004867417707819.

Thomas, H. J., Connor, J. P., & Scott, J. G. (2017). Why do children and adolescents bully their peers? A critical review of key theoretical frameworks. *Social Psychiatry and Psychiatric Epidemiology*, 53, 437–451. doi:10.1007/s00127–00017–1462–1461.

Topcu-Uzer, C., & Tanrikulu, I. (2018). Technological solutions for cyberbullying. In M. Campbell & S. Bauman (Eds.), *Reducing cyberbullying in schools: International evidenced-based best practices* (pp. 33–47). London: Academic Press.

Trip, S., Bora, C., Sipos-Gug, S., Tocai, I., Gradinger, P., Yanagida, T., & Strohmeier, D. (2015). Bullying prevention in schools by targeting cognitions, emotions and behaviour: Evaluating the effectiveness of the REBE-ViSC Program. *Journal of Counseling Psychology*, 62, 732–740. doi:10.1037/cou0000084.

Ttofi, M., & Farrington, D. (2011). Effectiveness of school-based programs to reduce bullying; a systematic and meta-analytic review. *Journal of Experimental Criminology*, 7, 27–56.

Van Geel, M., Vedder, P., & Tanilon, J. (2014). Relationship between peer victimization, cyberbullying and suicide in children and adolescents: A meta-analysis. *Journal of American Medical Association Pediatrics*, 168, 435–442.

Waasdorp, T. E., & Bradshaw, C. P. (2015). The overlap between cyberbullying and traditional bullying. *Journal of Adolescent Health*, 56, 483–488. doi:10.1016/j.jadohealth.2014.12.002.

Wang, J., Iannotti, R. R., & Nansel, T. R. (2009). School bullying amongst adolescents in the United State: Physical, verbal, relational, and cyber. *Journal of Adolescent Health*, 45, 368–375.

Wang, X., Yang, L., Yang, J., Wang, P., & Lei, L. (2017). Trait anger and cyberbullying among young adults: A moderated mediation model of moral disengagement and moral identity. *Computers in Human Behavior*, 73, 519–526. doi:10.1016/j.chb.2017.03.073.

Wu, N. (2014). Does Australia need tougher cyberbullying legislation? Retrieved from: http://rightnow.org.au/opinion-3/does-australia-need-tougher-cyberbullying-legisla tion/.

Yanagida, T., Strohmeier, D., & Spiel, C. (2016). Dynamic change of aggressive behavior and victimization among adolescents: Effectiveness of the ViSC program. *Journal of Clinical Child and Adolescent Psychology*, online, 1–15. doi:10.1080/ 1574416.2016.1233498.

Ybarra, M. L., Boyd, D., Korchmaros, J. D., & Oppenheim, J. (2012). Defining and measuring cyberbullying within the larger context of bullying victimization. *Journal of Adolescent Health, 51*, 53–58. doi:10.1016/j.jadohealth.2011.12.031.

Yeager, D. S., Fong, C. J., Lee, H. Y., & Espelage, D. L. (2015). Declines in efficacy of anti-bullying programs among older adolescents: Theory and a three-level meta-analysis. *Journal of Applied Developmental Psychology, 37*, 36–51. doi:10.1016/ j.appdev.2014.11.005.

Zych, I., Baldry, A. C., & Farrington, D. P. (2017). School bullying and cyberbullying: Prevalence, characteristics, outcomes, and prevention. In V. B. Van Hasslet & M. L. Bourke (Eds.), *Handbook of behavioral criminology* (pp. 113–138). Champaign, IL: Springer.

10

CONCLUSIONS

Different levels of challenge in tackling school bullying

Peter K. Smith

After some 35 years of research on school bullying, we know a great deal more about the nature of peer harassment, the consequences for all involved but especially the victims, and much about the causative factors that make bullying more or less likely. And after some 30 years of intervention efforts, but much of this especially in the last 10–15 years, we now have learnt quite a lot about what works or does not work, and the challenges and pitfalls involved. As recent meta-analyses have shown (see Chapter 1), school bullying can be reduced; many interventions have some success. But on a broad scale, the success is moderate – reductions in prevalence rates of around 20%. There is clearly still much to learn and to put into practice in this effort. The eight main chapters of this book showcase current leading interventions, and the authors vividly illustrate not only the successes of their work, but also many of the difficulties encountered.

Much of the work in this area (by no means all) has been carried out by psychologists, who traditionally put emphasis on the individual or on small group phenomena. This could include work on individual characteristics, friendships, and family background factors. From the start a considerable amount of intervention effort was at this level; this continues to be so, but the work on the social dynamics of bullying (Salmivalli, 2010), and input from other disciplinary perspectives (Thornberg, 2011), clearly shows the importance of looking at class level factors, and school level factors. Beyond that however, what is going on in the community, and the wider region (state or national level), will have important ramifications. Given the trans-national nature of intervention work (see Chapter 7 for example), even what happens in one country may influence developments in another country. These different levels of influence are familiar from Bronfenbrenner's ecological model (Bronfenbrenner, 1989). We can envisage upward or outward influences in this model – for example passionate individuals bring about change which ripples out through their institution into wider society. We can also envisage downward or inward influences – for example legal changes relevant to school bullying have a trickle-down effect on attitudes and behaviour. These are bidirectional or multi-directional processes.

The ensuing discussion considers some of what we have learnt about school bullying interventions, from these decades of research and as illustrated in the eight main preceding chapters. First it examines interventions at different levels; and then it looks at some factors that may help or hinder the efficacy of multi-level interventions: preparation, programme, and implementation, sustainability, evaluation, and generalizability and impact.

Individual level interventions

Interventions at the individual pupil level could be targeted at victims, bullies, or at bystanders. For victims or those at risk of being victims, this might be assertiveness training or rational problem solving to improve coping strategies (e.g. Jacobs, Vollink, Dehue, & Lechner, 2014), or cognitive behavioural techniques to reduce anxiety and depression (e.g. Fite, Cooley, Poquiz, & Williford, 2018). While often given in a small group setting, these are essentially targeted at individual characteristics. For those bullying others, reactive strategies such as negative sanctions, restorative justice approaches, support group methods or Pikas approach (Rigby, 2010) or the meaningful roles approach (Ellis et al., 2016), or motivational interviewing (Cross et al., 2017; Pennell et al., in press), seek in various ways to change an individuals' motivation to bully, even though again a small group setting may often be involved. Finally, programmes to encourage bystanders to intervene pro-actively, as defenders, have had some success (Polanin, Espelage, & Pigott, 2012). In a study of 58 high schools in Maryland, Waasdorp and Bradshaw (2018) found that schools with more pupils in the defender role had pupils more likely to believe that other pupils intervened against bullying, and also felt a greater connection with school staff.

At this individual level can also be considered interventions with parents or carers. They can have an important role in working with schools, supporting anti-bullying initiatives, and liaising with schools if they have concerns about a child's behaviour. In turn, schools can involve parents, usually through information in newsletters or booklets, and/or parent–teacher meetings (Axford et al., 2015). In a randomized control trial, Healy and Sanders (2014) found reductions in aggression and victimization in 6–12-year-olds, following a family based intervention over eight sessions. Nickel et al. (2006) found positive effects from a randomized control trial of brief strategic family therapy, over 12 sessions, in reducing bullying behaviour in 15-year-old girls. Parents have a particular role in cyberbullying as regards knowing about and advising on their child's Internet use (Ang, 2015; Gómez-Ortiz, Romera, Ortega-Ruiz, & Del Rey, 2018), probably best done by concerned involvement but without being overly restrictive (Sasson & Mesch, 2014).

Finally, at this level can be considered teacher training. This might be in the context of general training on school bullying; for example Williford et al. (in press) describe the development of a workshop and manual for K–12 teachers in the USA, including basic knowledge about bullying, and intervention strategies. Macaulay, Betts, Stiller and Kellezi (2018) reviewed 20 studies internationally on teachers' perceptions of and responses to cyberbullying; many teachers recognized the importance of the problem, but fewer felt confident or skilful about addressing the issue, suggesting the need for specific training in this area.

Specific training is generally provided in an intervention programme, such as in Chapters 2, 3, 4, and 8. These chapters make it abundantly clear that teacher motivation and commitment are vitally important in programme implementation. Olweus (2004) found Perceived Staff Importance (of bullying), and Read Programme Information (by teachers) to be important predictors for success of the OBPP, and the general pupil perception of a home-room teacher's attitude to bullying was a significant predictor of levels of victimization in the KiVa project (Saarento, Kärnä, Hodges, & Salmivalli, 2013).

Individual level factors in context

Several studies have now indicated that intervention programmes may impact differently on pupils with different individual characteristics. So far this evidence has come from detailed evaluation of the impact of the KiVa programme (Chapter 3) in different countries. An analysis in Finland found that while KiVa reduced bullying rates in bullies who were less popular or of average popularity in the peer group, it did not do so with bullies who were high in perceived popularity (Garandeau et al., 2014). An analysis using KiVa data from the Netherlands, by Kaufman et al. (2018), found that decreases in victimization were least for those pupils who experienced very high levels of peer rejection, and who had high internalizing problems and poorer parent–child relationships. The 'healthy context paradox', referred to in Chapter 3, and Garandeau, Lee, and Salmivalli (2018), suggests that pupils who remain as victims, in a context where an anti-bullying intervention has had some general success, may feel especially depressed. Huitsing et al. (in press), also using data from KiVa in the Netherlands, found that pupils who remained victims in KiVa schools following intervention actually became more depressed and had lower self-esteem.

Menesini (2019) has referred to the 'individual by context' phenomenon, whereby pupils may be differentially affected by an intervention. Using data from KiVa in Italy, she found that temperamental characteristics, and also environmental sensitivity, predicted the impact of the intervention on both bullying and victimization rates.

These findings suggest the importance of interventions tailored to individuals, as well as more universal interventions for whole classes and schools. So far this work has focused on pupil variables, but it could be fruitful to examine teacher variables in a corresponding way. We know that teachers do vary on preferred ways of dealing with bullying, with gender and teaching experience being important variables (Burger et al., 2015). It would be interesting to know which teachers are more responsive to anti-bullying programmes, and implement them more effectively.

Class and school level interventions

Interventions are generally conceived of at the whole-school level. Much is likely to be implemented at the class level, for example through curricular approaches such as in KiVa (Chapter 3), and the OBPP has included a component where each class decides on rules against bullying (Olweus, 2004). The success of such interventions is correspondingly measured by changes in class and school levels of victimization or perpetration (e.g. Chapters 2, 3, 4). Curriculum approaches may be relatively non-specific to bullying, for example Social and Emotional Learning (SEL) programmes (Durlak et al., 2011; Cefai & Cavioni, 2014). Others can be very specific; see for example Chapters 5 and 6. Some programmes are being devised specifically for cyberbullying; see Chapter 9 and, for example, Calvo-Morata et al. (2018).

Other studies not connected to intervention programmes have found that school factors are significantly associated with victim risk (Chapter 1). For example, a study in Israel by Khoury-Kassabri, Benbenishty, Astor and Zeira

(2004) with students in Grades 7–11 at 162 schools, found that variance between schools accounted for between 9% and 15% of the variance in pupil victim rates. Some other relevant issues in considering such school factors are school policies, school climate, and the existence of peer support schemes.

School policies

A whole-school policy is usually a short handout or brochure, available for everyone in the school community in print and on the school website. It should define bullying, state the responsibilities of all concerned in the school if it happens, and clearly explain what actions will be taken to reduce bullying and deal with incidents when they occur.

There is only modest evidence that having a good policy translates into lower rates of school bullying or violence. In an analysis of 78 schools in England, Smith et al. (2012) related a quality score for the whole-school anti-bullying policy, to data on bullying as perceived and experienced by pupils in these schools. Most correlations were not significant, but in schools whose policies had more strategies to prevent bullying, there were fewer reports of pupils bullying others. A good school policy should encourage pupils to report bullying, so straightforward correlations to incidence rates based on pupil self-report at one time point may not be very informative. Rather, policies should be seen as providing a framework for the school's response involving the whole school community: pupils, teachers, learning mentors, school support staff, governors, and parents/carers.

School climate

School climate – how safe and happy pupils feel in school – has been suggested as a key factor in predicting levels of bullying. The climate of the school can provide a generally supportive environment for pupils in trouble, including experiencing bullying, and encourage active defending behaviour (Chapter 1). The study in Israel by Khoury-Kassabri et al. (2004) found much of the school variation in victim rates was accounted for by school climate (a composite measure of students perceptions of school rules and policies at reducing violence; teacher support; and student participation). Astor and Benenishty (2018) discuss methods of assessing and improving school climate in order to reduce violence and bullying.

The authoritative school climate theory posits that two domains of school climate are key to a safe and effective school (Cornell, Shukla, & Konold, 2015).

The first domain is of high disciplinary and academic expectations for students, referred to as the demandingness or *structure* of the school climate. In a structured school, teachers and other school staff members enforce discipline in a strict but fair manner, and they communicate high academic expectations for all students. The second domain is the responsiveness or *supportiveness* of teacher-student relationships. In a supportive school, teachers and other school staff members interact with students in a respectful, caring, and helpful manner. These dimensions have been linked to lower rates of bullying and peer victimization (Cornell et al., 2015).

Peer support schemes

One contributor to a positive school climate may be the use of peer support schemes (Cowie & Smith, 2010). Here, some pupils are trained as peer supporters, and with appropriate supervision, they run schemes designed to improve student well-being and reduce bullying. In primary schools, these are often befriending schemes at break or recess times, or playground pals leading structured games activities. In secondary schools, these are often mentoring or counselling by older students of younger ones.

As described in Chapter 1, critical views have come from the meta-analysis by Ttofi and Farrington (2011), who argued that 'it seems from our results that work with peers should not be used' (p. 44), and from the study by Flygare et al. (2011), suggesting peer mediators could have negative effects. On the other hand, a meta-analysis by Lee, Kim, and Kim (2015) found peer counselling to be associated with reductions in victimization. There are certainly some problematic issues around peer support schemes (Cowie & Smith, 2010); their effectiveness depends greatly on the type of scheme used, how it is supported, and many other factors. Some schemes have not been successful and might even be counterproductive. However, peer support schemes are developing, schools are learning from past experience, and new methods are evolving (Smith, Salmivalli, & Cowie, 2012). The KiVa project uses a version of peer support successfully (Chapter 3), and other successful results have come from the *No Trap!* interventions reported by Menesini, Nocentini, and Palladino (2012) and in Chapter 8, and in work in Japan described in Chapter 7.

Theoretical perspectives at individual, class, and school levels

Ideally, anti-bullying interventions would be grounded in well-supported theoretical perspectives. What currently exists are a range of theoretical approaches, applicable in different ways or at different levels. Thomas, Connor, and Scott (2018) summarize a number of these. At the individual level they discuss genetic, developmental psychopathology, resource control, and social-cognitive approaches; at the systems level they discuss social-ecological, family systems, and peer-group socialization perspectives. They conclude that 'Each theory adds a unique perspective; however, no single framework comprehensively explains why bullying occurs' (op. cit., Abstract).

Many interventions cite one or more theoretical approaches to support the design of their programme (for example, peer-group socialization, in KiVa). The social-ecological model is widely cited; see for example Chapters 4 and 5. In a study in Turkey, Albayrak, Yildiz and Erol (2016) cited both a behavioural-ecological model, and the Neuman Systems Model (derived from nursing science) as inspirations for a school anti-bullying programme. Thomas et al. do not explicitly mention evolutionary approaches, which may help to explain bullying behaviour (Kolbert & Crothers, 2003; Volk, Camilleri, Dane, & Marini, 2012), and which led to the suggestion of the meaningful roles intervention (Ellis et al., 2016).

Hawley and Williford (2015) have given one view of the theoretical underpinning of anti-bullying interventions. Using the Theory of Planned Behaviour, they argued that successful intervention will require changes in perceptions (of what bullying is), attitudes (about bullying behaviour and towards victims; reporting bullying and intervening), subjective norms (how do others think or expect I should behave?), and efficacy beliefs (feeling confident that actions such as reporting or defending will be successful and not result in negative consequences). All these would be necessary for changing actual behaviours. Invoking ideas from organizational science, they argue that it is necessary to target these with pupils, teachers, and other staff in or relevant to the school, if changes in the school culture (assumptions, values, and beliefs) are to match up with changes in the school climate (such as actual behavioural changes in bully and victim rates).

The work on individuals in context also points to the importance of combining universal interventions such as these, with tailored interventions for individual pupils likely to be resistant to the intervention, such as very popular bullies, and very severe victims (Thomas et al., 2018). Popular bullies might be better tackled by providing them with meaningful prosocial roles (Ellis et al., 2016), or ways of persuasion that do not threaten status or self-respect (Yeager, Dahl, & Dweck, 2018). Severely rejected victims may benefit from family therapy, training in coping strategies and assertiveness, and/or cognitive behavioural techniques (Fite et al., 2018; Healy & Sanders, 2014; Jacobs et al., 2014).

Community and society level

It might be expected that levels of violence and antisocial behaviour in the neighbourhood or community would impact on school bullying levels. Some evidence for this came from a study in the US by Schwartz and Proctor (2000). Children who had witnessed community violence were more likely to be aggressive to classmates; this link was mediated by social cognitions supporting aggression. They also found that those who had been victims of community violence were more likely to be victims at school as well; here, emotional regulation was a mediating factor. Thus, neighbourhood violence may change normative beliefs about aggression (facilitating bullying in some children), and may particularly upset those who are victims in both school and community settings, increasing their vulnerability. A study in Columbia by Chaux, Molano and Podlesky (2009), from 1,000 schools in 308 municipalities across the country, found significant associations of a neighbourhood violence measure to bullying involvement.

There are substantial country variations in rates of bullying and victimization, as shown by large-scale surveys such as HBSC, EU Kids Online, TIMSS, GSHS, and PISA; although these different surveys do not always agree highly with each other (Smith, Robinson, & Marchi, 2016). There are many problems in interpreting cross-national differences, including issues of translating the term *bullying* across languages/countries (Smith et al., 2002; Smith, Kwak, & Toda, 2016). Although the phenomenon of bullying does seem to be recognized in every country, the prevalent forms and characteristics can vary. For example, *ijime* in Japan and *wang-ta* in South Korea are the terms most similar to *bullying*, but are not identical in meaning. There is a greater emphasis on social exclusion in these countries, and this is reflected in a greater ratio of bullies to victims compared to studies in England or Western countries.

Explanations of country differences

The EU Kids Online project suggested five main factors to consider in country differences: cultural values, education system, technological infrastructure, regulatory framework, and socio-economic stratification. There is evidence for the impact of all of these (Smith, Görzig & Robinson, 2018).

Cultural values: Research in this area has often used the framework provided by Hofstede, Hofstede and Minkov (2010); they proposed six main dimensions: power distance, individualism–collectivism, masculinity–femininity, uncertainty avoidance, long-term orientation, indulgence vs restraint. A study by Smith and

Robinson (2019), mainly using HBSC data, found bullying prevalence to be higher in highly individualistic countries in the 1990s, as might be predicted theoretically, but with a shift this century to bullying prevalence being higher in more collectivist countries. The authors hypothesized that this change over the last two decades was due to greater regulatory framework initiatives in higher individualist societies.

Education system: relevant variables here include age of transitions, extent of grade retention, class groupings, school and class size, structure of school day, break times and supervision. These have been reviewed systematically by Jessel (2016). Some effects on victim and bully rates have been documented; for example Kanetsuna (2016) invoked use of home-room classes, and supervision of break times, in explaining differences between *ijime* in Japan and *bullying* in England. Grade retention, whereby pupils performing less well are held back in a grade, has been linked to bullying rates in Portugal (Pereira et al., 2004).

Technological infrastructure: this could include penetration of mobile phones, smart phones and the Internet. This is clearly very relevant for cyberbullying. Use of other media beyond the Internet may be important, such as television, movies, and especially violent video games. Calvete et al. (2010) in Spain, and Fanti et al. (2012) in Cyprus, found links from violent media exposure to both cyber bullying and cyber victimization. Hamer et al. (2014) suggested a 'Cyclic Process' model of this: adolescent victims of (mainly traditional) bullying feel anger and frustration, thus they may tend to use violent media more, as a way of coping with or finding outlets for their anger feelings, and this exposure in itself may lead to cyberbullying behaviours (through mechanisms such as desensitization, imitation, modelling of action scripts). The cyberbullying might then increase the chances of being a victim again.

Regulatory framework: this can include legal aspects, and anti-bullying initiatives, at the country level. So far as legal aspects are concerned, there is some evidence for the impact of laws against bullying or cyberbullying. In the USA, Hatzenbuehler et al. (2015) found that having some anti-bullying laws was associated with reduced rates of being both bullied and cyberbullied across 25 states. Ramirez et al. (2016) found an increase in victim rates in Iowa state after an anti-bullying law was introduced, possibly due to increased reporting, but then a decrease for offline but not online victim rates. In the USA, all states now have some legal provision against bullying. Legal provision varies widely in other countries, but is often seen as inadequate or poorly understood; see for example Samara et al. (2017) in the UK, and Hernández, López and Ramirez (2019) in Spain. Legal issues around cyberbullying are particularly salient, given the rapid development of technologies; see Chapter 9, and a review by Yang and Grinshteyn (2016).

Socio-economic stratification: relevant measures here have been examined primarily with HBSC data. In relation to bullying generally, victim prevalence rates have been linked to lower country wealth (Chaux et al., 2009; Elgar et al., 2009; Viner et al., 2012) and greater income inequality (Elgar et al., 2009, 2015; Viner et al., 2012). Using a sample of 18 countries from EU Kids Online, Görzig, Milosevic and Staksrud (2017) found that regional level cyber-victimization rates were positively linked with GDP and crime rates whilst they showed a negative relationship with life expectancy and population density.

Factors to consider in implementing anti-bullying programmes

By now, we have considerable knowledge about factors affecting the success and impact of anti-bullying programmes. Not everything is agreed! For example, there is still debate about the advisability of peer support programmes, as described above. However, much has been learnt. All of the case study chapters in this book provide useful examples and illustrations. Chapter 9 covers critical issues for cyberbullying intervention programmes. This final section thus runs the risk of some repetition, but attempts to draw together important aspects around five main headings: preparation; programme and implementation; sustainability; evaluation; and generalizability and impact.

Preparation

Even with the best of intentions, it is unlikely to be productive introducing an anti-bullying intervention into a school without some preconditions or groundwork. Chapter 2 for example indicates how scepticism of the value of this kind of work can hinder progress. Partly this will be affected by general societal attitudes to bullying, how it is featured in the media, and what regulatory frameworks are in place. More specifically, it will be helpful if school staff have, or have had, some basic training covering the nature of bullying and its consequences – the kinds of information featured in Chapter 1. Does the school have an anti-bullying policy? Is it reviewed and updated? Do parents know about it, and what the school is doing about bullying if it happens? More generally, is the school climate authoritative rather than authoritarian, or lax? Are pupils encouraged to show respect for others, and do they feel safe in the school and connected to the school's values? If they do, this will provide more fertile ground for interventions specifically on bullying.

Programme and implementation

A variety of programmes are presented in this book. However, they do share some common features. To some extent, they have a theory base. As discussed above, there are a range of theoretical perspectives on why bullying happens, and no one embracing theory; however, intervention programmes do draw on aspects of our knowledge of bullying, and on specific theoretical approaches. These are particularly apposite currently in considering the motivation of bullying children, and how to change this. It is clear that some bullying children, and in some contexts, can get advantages from their behaviour, in terms of status in the peer group. This needs to be borne in mind in intervention work; the 'meaningful roles' approach (discussed above) is one possible approach here, which is still to be properly evaluated.

One clear lesson, coming from the socio-ecological framework but evidenced in many studies and by the 'individual by context' approach, is that we need both universal and targeted intervention work. Universal work should apply to the whole school; certainly to all pupils. However, it should also involve teachers, and ancillary, staff and anyone working in the school. At a minimum, they should know about the school policy and what to do if pupil–pupil bullying occurs. However, ideally an anti-bullying policy should apply not only to pupils but be relevant for the whole school community. It could be relevant for pupil–teacher, teacher–pupil, or teacher–teacher bullying, for example.

Targeted interventions will be needed in addition to this universal work (or primary prevention). The evidence from the KiVa project especially (Chapter 3, and discussion above), shows that some popular bullying pupils, and also some badly rejected victims, may not be changed much (or even changed for the worse, in the 'healthy context paradox') by universal interventions. The whole-school work is vital of course, but other interventions, such as discussed above at the individual, family, and/or small group level, will be needed as well. We still have much to learn about which combination of targeted interventions will work best with a universal intervention. Sometimes, targeted interventions may be focused on particular at-risk groups (secondary intervention), and/or very specific individuals (tertiary prevention).

In the case of specific programmes such as the OBPP, KiVa, ViSC, and Friendly Schools, then fidelity to the programme is important (see Chapters 2, 3, 4, and 6). This relates back to preparation, as teachers who are convinced of the importance and value of the work are likely to be most committed to the time and resources needed for high-quality implementation. Ongoing evaluation of the programme – how successful it is being, and updates of it in response to this and to feedback generally – will be helpful (Chapters 3, 9). It is also important to keep parents informed and, as much as possible, 'on board' with the schools' efforts (Chapter 8).

Pupil voice: one aspect given more attention in recent years is what is often called 'pupil voice'. This has been summed up in the slogan 'Don't do it about us, without us'. It refers to involving pupils in meaningful ways in designing and implementing interventions. This has been especially voiced by Australian colleagues (Chapters 6, 9) and is evident in Cyber Friendly Schools (Chapter 6), where student cyber leaders develop activities, in Italy in *NoTrap!*, where peer educators play an important role (Chapter 8), and in Japan in activities such as the Smartphone Summit (Chapter 7).

Ybarra et al. (in press) argue that getting the perceptions of students about bullying prevention programmes 'provides opportunities to craft prevention programme content that better speaks to the experiences and concerns that youth have' (op. cit., Abstract). Treseder (1997) provided a model of child participation in research, which identifies five different kinds of participation: assigned but informed; consulted and informed; adult-initiated, shared decisions with young people; young people-initiated and directed; and young people-initiated shared decisions with adults. The last two kinds would give more power to young people themselves, than envisaged in Ybarra et al. (in press), but may be worth considering in certain contexts.

Sustainability

A common danger in intervention work is that initial enthusiasm and success may fade as the programme continues into subsequent years. In PRISM (Practical, Robust Implementation and Sustainability Model), Woodbridge et al. (2014; see also Chapter 3) provide a model, including participant and organizational perspectives and characteristics, that can affect this. In addition, as indicated in Chapters 2 and 6, staff turnover can provide a challenge, with an ongoing need to introduce new staff to the policy and intervention.

To produce long-term sustainable change, it is helpful to have national organizations that maintain awareness of the issue, provide resources, and keep pressure up on governments to support anti-bullying work. Examples are PrevNet, in Canada (Pepler & Craig, 2011), focused on knowledge mobilization, conferences, and publications; the Anti-Bullying Alliance (www.anti-bullyingalliance.org.uk) in England, which brings together over 50 national organizations and has supported the development of a portfolio of resources, and anti-bullying weeks held annually; and the National Safe Schools Framework (NSSF) in Australia (Cross, Epstein, et al., 2011), which encourages sharing of information, resources and successful practices, and encourages schools to adopt whole-school programmes.

Evaluation

Besides some formative evaluation while an intervention is ongoing, to give feedback and provide opportunities for updating, some summative evaluation is vitally important when a new programme is being developed and offered more widely. If results are positive, this can motivate all concerned to continue their efforts, and – combined ideally with some cost/benefit analyses, see below – help persuade policy-makers and politicians to support wider resourcing of the programme. If results are more mixed, neutral, or even negative, then this too is important in learning what does not work, and hopefully understanding why – knowledge that also has a continuing contribution to make.

Randomized control trials (RCTs) are seen as the strongest kind of evaluation, as they go furthest in removing alternative explanations for the findings. It was probably very important for the early development and support nationally of the KiVa programme, that an RCT evaluation was used (Chapter 3). A considerable number of RCT evaluations of different interventions have now been carried out. However an RCT design is not always practical or feasible given constraints of working in real-life situations (see Chapters 7 and 8). Randomly assigning schools to intervention or control is a somewhat unnatural procedure; and once a programme is found to be effective, there are ethical issues too in assigning control status. An RCT may thus be most valuable at the start of programme development, possibly on a relatively small scale (as in KiVa).

An evaluation design that does not include control schools is the Extended Selection Cohorts design, which has been used for example in OBPP evaluations (Chapter 2). This controls for age effects (but not history effects). It is also useful to look at the dosage-response relationship, given variation in schools and classes in the extent or duration of implementation of the programme.

Ryan and Smith (2009) provide a review of evaluation procedures for anti-bullying interventions, and make a number of important recommendations. Measures should be taken of the extent of promotion and take-up of the programme, and the fidelity with which it is followed. Besides pre- and post-test data, follow-up data is very desirable. Where possible, multiple assessment measures should be employed (for example, attitudes as well as behaviours) and multiple informants (for example self, peer, teacher). Both quantitative and qualitative measures are useful; quantitative measures are the norm for demonstrating the existence of changes, and effect sizes, but qualitative data can provide context for how the intervention and changes are perceived, and insight into process that may go beyond preconceived categories used in survey questionnaires. So far as quantitative data is concerned, they recommend multi-level statistical modelling to separate out effects of individuals, classes, and schools.

Cost/benefit factors: another aspect of evaluation, poorly used so far, is a cost/benefit analysis of the intervention. There are clearly costs to any programme, including researcher time (for introduction and evaluation), trainer time (for training the teachers and others involved), teacher time (for implementation), and cost of any resources such as books, videos, etc. These costs can be calculated relatively easily. What benefits can justify these costs? Here a principal source of evidence is the long-term effects of (especially) experiences of being a victim (Chapter 1). Successful programmes can reduce mental health costs and have benefits for educational achievement and later productivity.

A few studies have started to examine the cost-effectiveness of anti-bullying programmes. Persson and Svensson (2013), and Beckman and Svensson (2015), examined the cost-effectiveness of two Swedish anti-bullying programmes, one called Friends, and the OBPP. They primarily assessed this in terms of what tax increases people would be prepared to accept, in order to implement such a programme in their local schools. They assumed standard levels of victimization (around 10%) and of programme effectiveness (around 20%). They then calculated a 'willingness to pay' metric, and found that acceptable tax increases considerably exceeded the cost of an anti-bullying programme. They also compared the costs favourably with actual costs of court settlements brought by individuals against schools or education authorities for being bullied in school; and for actual compensation costs for injuries. Subsequently, Persson et al. (2018) examined the cost-effectiveness of KiVa, assessing benefits in terms of victim-free school years and quality adjusted life years (a measure of later health status). The cost-effectiveness compared favourably with those for OBPP calculated earlier.

Cost calculations might also examine damage done to victims and costs to society in relation to areas such as mental health, education, and earnings.

Drydakis (2013) has provided some estimated costs of school bullying in relation to later employment prospects and wages. The Highmark Foundation (n. d.) has examined costs in relation to early dropping out of school, employment opportunity, involvement with the justice system, and reliance on public assistance; supporting the cost-effectiveness of the OBPP in the US context.

Overall, these studies point to the cost-effectiveness of anti-bullying programmes, but are at an early stage of what could be an important and growing field of enquiry.

Generalisability and impact

This book is part of a series, designed to show how research on human behaviour can have a real practical impact. The research on school bullying, in my opinion, provides a paradigm example of this, in a rewarding sense. The evidence is that anti-bullying interventions do, by and large, result in positive changes – reductions in victim prevalence rates, reductions in bullying prevalence rates, increases in defender behaviour, and positive changes in attitudes. The findings are sometimes patchy, and the effect sizes are often moderate rather than large, but the outcomes are clearly worthwhile in terms of human happiness, and may well be cost effective in purely financial terms.

How generalizable is this research programme? One aspect concerns how narrowly we should focus on bullying, or more broadly on school safety, violence, harassment, gang violence, weapons in schools, and similar issues. Astor and Benbenishty (2019) argue strongly for a broader focus of this nature. This may partly be a matter of practicalities, political concern, and funding available, in particular countries and at particular times. We know these sets of problems are to some extent inter-related. Nevertheless, there is near-universal agreement that school bullying, and notably pupil–pupil bullying, is one aspect of school life that is undesirable, violates ideas of human rights, and needs to be tackled, whether on its own or as part of some broader initiative.

Another issue is the extent to which an intervention developed in one country or context, can be translated effectively into a different one. We do know that bullying takes different forms in different countries, especially when comparing Eastern countries, especially Japan and South Korea, with Western countries in North America, Europe, and Australasia (Smith, Kwak, & Toda, 2016). Within Western countries, differences appear less obvious. The OBPP, KiVa and ViSC programmes have been used in other countries (Chapters 2, 3, 4), with some success, although not always at the same level as in the country of origin (Chapter 5). In these cases the programme has usually been adapted in minor ways. A programme may also serve as an inspiration in broader ways, and lead to rather different developments embedded in that new cultural context, as for example described in Chapter 7 regarding the influence of some Western intervention ideas in Japan.

Considering overall feasibility and impact of anti-bullying interventions, one must come back to the socio-ecological model and spheres of influence with multiple pathways. Most interventions have focused on individuals, classes, and schools. This is where training and implementation, as well as assessment, has very largely taken place. However, changes at these levels are bound up with, and interact reciprocally with, changes at the societal level. Research into school bullying and its consequences, plus actual events such as suicides (for example in Norway, or Japan), or school shootings (such as in the USA), have fed, via wide publicity in the mass media, into changed perceptions and attitudes about the topic. This kind of process is described for example in Japan, at the start of Chapter 7, and I have described it (Smith, 2016) in the case of the UK.

Societal attitudes and pressure on politicians can lead to political decisions that impact on funding and resources for anti-bullying work. In many countries over the past two decades, there have been signs of increasing awareness of school bullying and the importance of measures to deal with it, and also some modest decreases in rates of victimization (Rigby & Smith, 2011). However, it is possible for things to slip back. Funding for intervention programmes and for research may get tighter again, as is described for example at the end of Chapter 5. In England, Adrienne Katz, Director of the UK-based consultancy Youthworks, has written that:

> It is distressing to think that things have gone backwards to such an extent. During the years of the national Anti-Bullying programme when we had Regional Advisers training local authorities and schools for 6 years, we did get a level of knowledge and expertise into schools across England with good outcomes for young people. But this ended in 2008 and with the subsequent cuts ... it seems that a large number of schools have simply pushed bullying onto the back burner. (Personal communication, 7 February 2019; and Youthworks, 2018)

At times, researchers can take an opportunity to maximize or revitalize impact, by use of the media and by cultivating links with relevant decision-makers (see also the six steps for policy impact described in Chapter 4).

These can push things in a positive direction. Societies change, but often gradually. Thinking of the EU Kids Online model, described above, cultural values, education systems, and socio-economic stratification, which are probably important influences on bullying, change rather slowly. Technological infrastructure changes more quickly, certainly in the case of ICT and the explosion of smart phone ownership and social networking in young people, at the time of writing the subject of vigorous discussion. Regulatory frameworks, whether of ICT use, or more generally legal requirements, policies and resources and expectations about bullying, are perhaps the most amenable to change, of these five factors. Together, increases in regulatory frameworks and associated resources, together with universal interventions at school level and targeted interventions at individual, family, or small group level, hold promise for substantive change. Research on school bullying will continue to have a vital role in improving and evaluating programmes, and maximizing their effectiveness and the impact they have in society and for the well-being of pupils at school.

References

Albayrak, S., Yildiz, A., & Erol, S. (2016). Assessing the effect of school bullying prevention programs on reducing bullying. *Children and Youth Services Review*, 63, 1–9.

Ang, R. P. (2015). Adolescent cyberbullying: A review of characteristics, prevention and intervention strategies. *Aggression and Violent Behavior*, 25, 35–42.

Astor, R. A., & Benbenishty, R. (2018). *Mapping and monitoring bullying and violence: Building a safe school climate*. New York: Oxford University Press.

Astor, R. A., & Benbenishty, R. (2019). *Bullying, school violence, and climate in evolving contexts: Culture, organization, and time*. Oxford: Oxford University Press.

Axford, N., Farrington, D. P., Clarkson, S., Bjornstad, G. J., Wrigley, Z., & Hutchings, J. (2015). Involving parents in school-based programmes to prevent and reduce bullying: What effect does it have? *Journal of Children's Services*, 10, 242–251.

Beckman, L., & Svensson, M. (2015). The cost-effectiveness of the Olweus Bullying Prevention Program: Results from a modeling study. *Journal of Adolescence*, 45, 127–139.

Bowes, L., Arsenault, L., Maughan, B., Taylor, A., Caspi, A., & Moffitt, T. E. (2009). School, neighborhood, and family factors are associated with children's bullying involvement: A nationally representative longitudinal study. *Journal of the American Academy of Child and Adolescent Psychiatry*, 48, 545–553.

Bronfenbrenner, U. (1989). Ecological systems theory. *Annals of Child Development*, 6, 187–249.

Burger, C., Strohmeier, D., Spröber, N., Bauman, S., & Rigby, K. (2015). How teachers respond to school bullying: An examination of self-reported intervention strategy use, moderator effects, and concurrent use of multiple strategies. *Teaching and Teacher Education*, 51, 191–202.

Calvete, E., Orue, I., Estévez, A., Villardón, L., & Padilla, P. (2010). Cyberbullying in adolescents: Modalities and aggressors' profile. *Computers in Human Behavior*, 26, 1128–1135.

Calvo-Morata, A., Rotaru, D. C., Alonso-Fernández, C., Freire-Morán, N., Martínez-Ortiz, I., & Fernández-Manjón, B. (2018). Validation of a cyberbullying serious game using game analytics. *IEEE Transactions on Learning Technologies*, 1–3. doi:10.1109/TLT.2018.2879354.

Cefai, C., & Cavioni, V. (2014). *Social and emotional education: Integrating theory and research into practice*. New York: Springer.

Chaux, E., Molano, A., & Podlesky, P. (2009). Socio-economic, socio-political and socio-emotional variables explaining school bullying: A country-wide multilevel analysis. *Aggressive Behavior*, 35, 520–529.

Cornell, D., Shukla, K., & Konold, T. (2015). Peer victimization and authoritative school climate: A multilevel approach. *Journal of Educational Psychology*, 107, 1186–1201.

Cowie, H., & Smith, P. K. (2010). Peer support as a means of improving school safety and reducing bullying and violence. In B. Doll, W. Pfohl, & J. Yoon (Eds.), *Handbook of youth prevention science* (pp. 177–193). New York: Routledge.

Cross, D., Epstein, M., Hearn, L., Slee, P., Shaw, T., & Monks, H. (2011). National Safe Schools Framework: Policy and practice to reduce bullying in Australian schools. *International Journal of Behavioral Development*, 35, 398–404.

Cross, D., Runions, K. C., Resnicow, K. A., Britt, E. F., & Gray, C. (2017). Motivational interviewing as a positive response to high-school bullying. *Psychology in the Schools*, 55, 464–475.

Drydakis, N. (2013). Bullying at school and labour market outcomes. *International Journal of Manpower*, 35, 1185–1211.

Durlak, J. A., Weissberg, R. P., Dymnicki, A. B., Taylor, R. D., & Schellinger, K. B. (2011). The impact of enhancing students' social and emotional learning: A meta-analysis of school-based universal interventions. *Child Development*, 82, 405–432.

Elgar, F. J., Craig, W., Boyce, W., Morgan, A., & Vella-Zarb, R. (2009). Income inequality and school bullying: Multilevel study of adolescents in 37 countries. *Journal of Adolescent Health*, 45, 351–359.

Elgar, F. J., McKinnon, B., Walsh, S. D., Freeman, J., Donnelly, P. D., de Matos, M. G., Gariepy, G., Aleman-Diaz, A. Y., Pickett, W., Molcho, M., & Currie, C. (2015). Structural determinants of youth bullying and fighting in 79 countries. *Journal of Adolescent Health*, 57, 643–650.

Ellis, B. J., Volk, A. A., Gonzalez, J-M., & Embry, D. D. (2016). The meaningful roles intervention: An evolutionary approach to reducing bullying and increasing prosocial behavior. *Journal of Research on Adolescence*, 22, 622–637.

Fanti, K. A., Demetriou, A. G., & Hawa, V. V. (2012). A longitudinal study of cyberbullying: Examining risk and protective factors. *European Journal of Developmental Psychology*, 9, 168–181.

Fite, P. J., Cooley, J. L., Poquiz, J., & Williford, A. (2018). Pilot evaluation of a targeted intervention for peer-victimized youth. *Journal of Clinical Psychology*, 2018, 1–20. https://doi:10.1002/jclp.22697.

Flygare, E., Frånberg, G-M., Gill, P., Johansson, B., Lindberg, O., Osbeck, C., & Söderström, Å. (2011). *Evaluation of anti-Bullying methods.* Report 353, National Agency for Education, Stockholm. www.skolverket.se.

Garandeau, C. F., Lee, I. A., & Salmivalli, C. (2014). Differential effects of the KiVa anti-bullying program on popular and unpopular bullies. *Journal of Applied Developmental Psychology*, 35, 44–50.

Garandeau, C. F., Lee, I. A., & Salmivalli, C. (2018). Decreases in the proportion of bullying victims in the classroom: Effects on the adjustment of remaining victims. *International Journal of Behavioral Development*, 42(1), 64–72.

Gómez-Ortiz, O., Romera, E. M., Ortega-Ruiz, R., & Del Rey, R. (2018). Parenting practices as risk or preventive factors for adolescent involvement in cyberbullying: Contribution of children and parent gender. *International Journal of Environmental Research and Public Health*, 15. doi:10.3390/ijerph15122664.

Görzig, A., Milosevic, T., & Staksrud, E. (2017). Cyberbullying victimisation in context: The role of social inequalities in countries and regions. *Journal of Cross-Cultural Psychology*, 48(8), 1198–1215.

Hamer, A. den, Konijn, E. A., & Keijer, M. G. (2014). Cyberbullying behavior and adolescents' use of medias with antisocial content: A cyclic process model. *Cyberpsychology, Behavior, and Social Networking*, 17, 74–81.

Hatzenbuehler, M. L., Schwab-Reese, L., Ranapurwala, S. I., Hertz, M. F., & Ramirez, M. R. (2015). Associations between antibullying policies and bullying in 25 states. *JAMA Pediatrics*, 169(10), e152411.

Hawley, P. H., & Williford, A. (2015). Articulating the theory of bullying intervention programs: Views from social psychology, social work, and organizational science. *Journal of Applied Developmental Psychology*, 37, 3–15.

Healy, K. L., & Sanders, M. R. (2014). Randomized controlled trial of a family intervention for children bullied by peers. *Behavior Therapy*, 45, 760–777.

Hernández, F. J. R., López, A. D., & Ramírez, F. C. (2019). Bullying y cyberbullying: la respuesta de las comunidades autónomas. *Revista Electrónica Interuniversitaria de Formación del Profesorado*, 22, 145–147. doi:10.6018/reifop.22.1.332311.

Highmark Foundation. (n.d.). *The cost benefit of bullying prevention.* Pittsburgh, PA: Highmark Foundation. https://www.highmarkfoundation.org/pdf/publications/HMK_Bullying%20Report_final.pdf.

Hofstede, G., Hofstede, G. J., & Minkov, M. (2010). *Cultures and organizations: Software of the mind.* New York: McGraw-Hill.

Huitsing, G., Lodder, G. M. A., Oldenburg, B., Schacter, H. L., Salmivalli, C., Juvonen, J., & Veenstra, R. (in press). The Healthy Context paradox: Victims' adjustment during an anti-bullying intervention. *Journal of Child and Family Studies.* doi:10.1007/s10826–018–1194–1.

Jacobs, N. C. L., Vollink, T., Dehue, F., & Lechner, L. (2014). Online Pestkoppen-stoppen: Systematic and theory-based development of a web-based tailored intervention for adolescent cyberbully victims to combat and prevent cyberbullying. *BMC Public Health*, 14, 396.

Jessel, J. (2016). Educational systems: A basis for some comparative perspective. In P. K. Smith, K. Kwak, & Y. Toda (Eds.), *School bullying in different cultures: Eastern and western perspectives* (pp. 229–258). Cambridge: Cambridge University Press.

Kanetsuna, T. (2016). Comparisons between English *bullying* and Japanese *ijime*. In P. K. Smith, K. Kwak, & Y. Toda (Eds.), *School bullying in different cultures: Eastern and western perspective* (pp. 153–169). Cambridge: Cambridge University Press.

Kaufman, T. F. L., Kretschmer, T., Huitsing, G., & Veenstra, R. (2018). Why does a universal anti-bullying program not help all children? Explaining persistent victimization during an intervention. *Prevention Science*, 19, 822–832.

Khoury-Kassabri, M., Benbenishty, R., Astor, R. A., & Zeira, A. (2004). The contributions of community, family, and school variables to student victmization. *American Journal of Community Psychology*, 34, 187–204.

Kolbert, J. B., & Crothers, L. M. (2003). Bullying and evolutionary psychology: The dominance hierarchy among students and implications for school personnel. *Journal of School Violence*, 2, 73–91.

Lee, S., Kim, C., & Kim, D. H. (2015). A meta-analysis of the effect of school-based anti-bullying programs. *Journal of Child Health Care*, 19, 136–153.

Macaulay, P. J. R., Betts, L. R., Stiller, J., & Kellezi, B. (2018). Perceptions and responses towards cyberbullying: A sysyematic review of teachers in the education system. *Aggression and Violent Behavior*, 43, 1–12.

Menesini, E. (2019). Translating knowledge into interventions: An 'individual by context' approach to bullying. *European Journal of Developmental Psychology*.

Menesini, E., Nocentini, A., & Palladino, B. E. (2012). Empowering students against bullying and cyberbullying: Evaluation of an Italian peer-led model. *International Journal of Conflict and Violence*, 6, 314–321.

Nickel, M., Luley, J., Krawczyk, J., Nickel, C., Widermann, C., Lahmann, C., Muehlbacher, M., Forthuber, P., Kettler, C., Leiberich, P., Tritt, K., Mitterlehner, F., Kaplan, P., Gil, F. P., Rother, W., & Loew, T. (2006). Bullying girls – Changes after brief strategic family therapy: A randomized, prospective, controlled trial with one-year follow-up. *Psychotherapy and Psychosomatics*, 75, 47–55.

Olweus, D. (2004). The Olweus Bullying Prevention Program: Design and implementation issues and a new national initiative in Norway. In P. K. Smith, D. Pepler, & K. Rigby (Eds.), *Bullying in schools: How successful can interventions be?* (pp. 13–36). Cambridge: Cambridge University Press.

Pennell, D., Campbell, M., Tangen, D., Runions, K., Brooks, J., & Cross, D. (in press). Facilitators and barriers to the implementation of motivational interviewing (MI) for bullying perpetration in school settings. *Scandinavian Journal of Psychology*.

Pepler, D., & Craig, W. (2011). Promoting relationships and eliminating violence in Canada. *International Journal of Behavioral Development*, 35, 389–397.

Pereira, B., Mendonça, D., Neto, C., Valente, L., & Smith, P. K. (2004). Bullying in Portuguese schools. *School Psychology International*, 25, 241–254.

Persson, M., & Svensson, M. (2013). The willingness to pay to reduce school bullying. *Economics of Education Review*, 35, 1–11.

Persson, M., Wennberg, L., Beckman, L., Salmivalli, C., & Svensson, M. (2018). The cost-effectiveness of the Kiva anti-bullying program: Results from a decision-analytic model. *Prevention Science*, 19, 728–737.

Polanin, J. R., Espelage, D. L., & Pigott, T. D. (2012). A meta-analysis of school-based bullying prevention programs' effects on bystander intervention behavior. *School Psychology Review*, 41, 47–65.

Ramirez, M., Ten Eyck, P., Peek-Asa, C., Onwuachi-Willig, A., & Cavanaugh, J. E. (2016). Evaluation of Iowa's anti-bullying law. *Injury Epidemiology*, 3(1), 15.

Rigby, K. (2010). *Bullying interventions in schools: Six basic approaches.* Camberwell, Victoria: ACER.

Rigby, K., & Smith, P. K. (2011). Is school bullying really on the rise? *Social Psychology of Education*, 14, 441–455.

Ryan, W., & Smith, J. D. (2009). Antibullying programs in schools: How effective are evaluation practices? *Prevention Science*, 10, 248–259.

Saarento, S., Kärnä, A., Hodges, E. V. E., & Salmivalli, C. (2013). Student-, classroom-, and school-level risk factors for victimization. *Journal of School Psychology*, 51, 421–434.

Salmivalli, C. (2010). Bullying and the peer group: A review. *Aggression and Violent Behavior*, 15, 112–120.

Samara, M., Burbidge, V., El Asam, A., Foody, M., Smith, P. K., & Morsi, H. (2017). Bullying and cyberbullying: Their legal status and use in psychological assessment. *International Journal of Environmental Research and Public Health*, 14. doi:10.3390/ijerph14121449.

Sasson, H., & Mesch, G. S. (2014). Parental mediation, peer norms and risky online behaviors among adolescents. *Computers in Human Behavior*, 33, 32–38.

Schwartz, D., & Proctor, L. J. (2000). Community violence exposure and children's social adjustment in the peer group: The mediating roles of emotion regulation and social cognition. *Journal of Consulting and Clinical Psychology*, 68, 670–683.

Smith, P. K. (2016). Research and practice in the study of school bullying. In K. Durkin, & R. Schaffer (Eds.), *Blackwell handbook of developmental psychology in action* (pp. 290–310). Oxford: Blackwell.

Smith, P. K., & Robinson, S., (2019). How does individualism-collectivism relate to bullying victimization? *International Journal of Bullying Prevention*, 1, 3–13.

Smith, P. K., Cowie, H., Olafsson, R., & Liefooghe, A. (2002). Definitions of bullying: A comparison of terms used, and age and sex differences, in a 14-country international comparison. *Child Development*, 73, 1119–1133.

Smith, P. K., GörzigA., & Robinson, S. (2018). Issues of cross-cultural variations in cyber-bullying across Europe and beyond. *Media@LSE Working Paper Series*, WP 49, pp. 1–28.

Smith, P. K., Kwak, K., & Toda, Y. (2016). Reflections on bullying in eastern and western perspectives. In P. K. Smith, K. Kwak, & Y. Toda (Eds.), *School bullying in different cultures: Eastern and western perspectives* (pp. 399–419). Cambridge: Cambridge University Press.

Smith, P. K., Robinson, S., & Marchi, B. (2016). Cross-national data on victims of bullying: What is really being measured? *International Journal of Developmental Science*, 10, 9–19.

Smith, P. K., Salmivalli, C., & Cowie, H. (2012). Effectiveness of school-based programs to reduce bullying: A commentary. *Journal of Experimental Criminology*, 8, 433–441.

Thomas, H. J., Connor, J. P., & Scott, J. G. (2018). Why do children and adolescents bully their peers? A critical review of key theoretical frameworks. *Social Psychiatry and Psychiatric Epidemiology*, 53, 437–451.

Thornberg, R. (2011). 'She's weird!' – The social construction of bullying in school: A review of qualitative research. *Children, & Society*, 25, 258–267.

Treseder, P. (1997). *Empowering children and young people*. London: Save the Children.

Viner, R. M., Ozer, E. M., Denny, S., Marmot, M., Resnick, M., Fatusi, A., & Currie, C. (2012). Adolescence and the social determinants of health. *The Lancet*, 379(9826), 1641–1652.

Volk, A. A., Camilleri, J. A., Dane, A. V., & Marini, Z. A. (2012). Is adolescent bullying an evolutionary adaptation? *Aggressive Behavior*, 38, 222–238.

Waasdorp, T. E., & Bradshaw, C. P. (2018). Examining variation in adolescent bystanders' responses to bullying. *School Psychology Review*, 47, 18–33.

Williford, A., Fite, P. J., DePaolis, K. J., Cooley, J. L., Hawley, P. H., & Isen, D. (in press). A comprehensive training initiative for educators to develop and implement effective anti-bullying policies in K-12 schools. *Journal of Applied School Psychology*, doi:10.1080/15377903.2018.1528489.

Woodbridge, M. W., Sumi, W. C., Yu, J., Rouspil, K., Javitz, H. S., Seeley, J. R., & Walker, H. M. (2014). Implementation and sustainability of an evidence-based program: Lessons learned from the PRISM applied to First Steps to Success. *Journal of Emotional and Behavioral Disorders*, 22, 95–106.

Yang, Y. T., & Grinshteyn, E. (2016). Safer cyberspace through legal intervention: A comparative review of cyberbullying legislation. *World Medical and Health Policy*, 8(4), 458–477.

Ybarra, M. L., Espelage, D. L., Valido, A., Hong, J. S., & Prescott, T. L. (in press). Perceptions of middle school youth about school bullying. *Journal of Adolescence*. doi:10.1016/j.adolescence.2018.10.008.

Yeager, D. S., Dahl, R. E., & Dweck, C. S. (2018). Why interventions to influence adolescent behavior often fail but could succeed. *Perspectives on Psychological Science*, 13, 101–122.

Youthworks. (2018). Make a Noise programme: Evaluation, 12 month report. https://youthworksconsulting.co.uk/.

INDEX

.